TRAVELOGUE

TRAVELOGUE

FORTY YEARS
FILMING THE WORLD

A Life

DOUG JONES

Travelogue:
Forty Years Filming the World
Copyright © 2016 by Doug Jones

International Travel Films Publishing
3710 Lowry Road
Los Angeles, California 90027
www.InternationalTravelFilms.com

All rights reserved. No part of this publication may be reproduced, stored in a retrieval system, or transmitted, in any form or by any means, electronic, mechanical, photocopying, recording, or otherwise, without the prior written permission of the author except by a reviewer who may quote passages in a review.

ISBN-13: 978-0-9979632-0-5
LCCN: 2016913491

Cover photographs courtesy of the Cunard Line and Amtrak

First Edition

Printed in the United States of America

This book is dedicated to my parents,
Harold and Maxine Jones,
whose unending love, encouragement,
and support made my life
and this book possible.

And to John Sanger, my one great love.

CONTENTS

Introduction xi

Prologue – Looking Forward and Reflecting Back 1
Chapter 1 – A Boy From Kansas City 3
Chapter 2 – New York City and the 1964 World's Fair. 11
Chapter 3 – The Travelogue Business 21
Chapter 4 – Trans World Airlines to London 27
Chapter 5 – Twenty-Four Hours to the Other Side of the World 31
Chapter 6 – The Clock was Ticking 37
Chapter 7 – College Days and Glee Club Grief 41
Chapter 8 – My First Camera—the Super 8 45
Chapter 9 – Filming Belgium. 49
Chapter 10 – My Big Break in the Travelogue Business 59
Chapter 11 – Graduation and the Dreaded Draft. 69
Chapter 12 – Paris and the Parisians. 73
Chapter 13 – The Indianapolis Years 79
Chapter 14 – Filming New York City, Hawaii, and Venice. 89
Chapter 15 – Royal London. 99
Chapter 16 – Off to Egypt. 105
Chapter 17 – Moving East - Indianapolis to New York 113
Chapter 18 – Filming the National Parks. 119
Chapter 19 – San Francisco – the City at the End of the Rainbow. 125
Chapter 20 – The World Cruise of the Queen Elizabeth 2 129
Chapter 21 – The Plague 145
Chapter 22 – Unlucky in Love. 151
Chapter 23 – Out of the Frying Pan and into the Fire 163
Chapter 24 – Sailing Down Under on the QE2 169
Chapter 25 – Filming the Great Cities of Europe. 177
Chapter 26 – North to Alaska 187
Chapter 27 – Learning to Fly. 195
Chapter 28 – The Canadian Transcontinental Train Ride. 207
Chapter 29 – New Technology that Would Change the World. 215
Chapter 30 – Another Relationship, Two Films, Three Flops 225
Chapter 31 – Flying the Cessna 310. 237
Chapter 32 – Living in the Wild in the Hollywood Hills 251

Chapter 33 – Shooting Stock Footage on Three Continents 257
Chapter 34 – Finding Happiness 269
Chapter 35 – Mother Russia 279
Chapter 36 – The Other Shoe Drops 291
Chapter 37 – Sailing Down to Rio 301
Chapter 38 – Marriage and a Few Bumps Along the Way 313
Chapter 39 – The Unexpected Turns of Life 329

Epilogue 339

Postscript 343

Travelogue Makers and Presenters of Another Time 347

Acknowledgments 367

A NOTE REGARDING VIDEO CLIPS

eBook edition:
If you are reading the eBook edition there
are video links at the end of most chapters.
To view the videos, simply click on the links.

Print edition:
If you are reading the print edition go to:
Youtube.com/IntTravelFilms/videos
Scroll through the clips to find the chapter or section
you are reading and click on the start arrow to view.

INTRODUCTION

If you have opened this book based on the title, you probably have an interest in travel.

For most people the urge to travel is instinctive. Whether it is to see what is on the other side of the road, or the other side of the world, people have been setting out on journeys, short and epic, since the beginning of time.

I've had a fortunate life. For forty years I traveled the world filming travelogues, a nearly extinct form of informative entertainment that reached its heyday not in the early part of the 20th century as most people assume, but later; the 1960s through the 1990s.

I would shoot feature-length motion picture films, usually during the summer, in the farthest reaches of the globe. Then from September to April I would travel across the United States and Canada showing the films and narrating them live in auditoriums and theaters on travelogue lecture series to audiences who came to learn about places they wanted to visit, relive journeys they had taken, or see places they would never go.

From my first film on Belgium to my last shoot in Istanbul, my travels took me to sixty-eight countries. I traveled on ocean liners, aboard trains, in coaches, cars, and of course on lots and lots of airplanes, small and large.

I gave six thousand live lecture travelogue presentations in the smallest towns of America (Tribune, Kansas) to the biggest auditoriums in the nation (Constitution Hall in Washington D.C. for the National Geographic Society).

To get to my travelogue lecture dates, I flew my own plane, a twin engine Cessna 310. I made over fifty coast-to-coast solo flights showing my films. I spoke to nearly four million people and worked in every state in the country and most provinces of Canada.

Burton Holmes, the father of the travelogue and, in fact, the man who coined the word *travelogue* at the turn of the 20th century, wrote in 1953, five years before his death, "The only things I own which are still worth what they have cost me are my travel memories, the mind-pictures of places which I have been hoarding like a happy miser for more than half a century."

Like Holmes, I too value the memories of a lifetime of travel and the experience of sharing that with other people. In many respects my life has been a continuous vacation. I got paid to see the world and tell others about it. Who could want more than that? This book is my effort to remember those experiences, personal and professional, good and bad, and recount the amazing journeys that took me to "far away places with strange sounding names."

Burton Holmes: Born in Chicago 1870, died in Hollywood 1958.
The father of the Travelogue.

PROLOGUE

LOOKING FORWARD AND REFLECTING BACK

February 11, 2004. The Bahia Mar Hotel, Fort Lauderdale, Florida. The alarm went off at 3:00 a.m. I rolled over and silenced the clock. I had not been sleeping much. I had to be out of bed and ready to film at 5:00 a.m. The *Queen Mary 2*, Cunard's new flagship, was arriving in America to board passengers for a twenty-four day journey to Rio de Janeiro. I would be onboard. It was the start of another film, my eighteenth feature-length travelogue, *Sailing Down to Rio on the Queen Mary 2*.

3:00 a.m. is never my best time. I have always been a night owl, more likely to be going to bed at that hour than getting up. But the ship was arriving and scheduled to berth before dawn. I quickly showered, dressed and went flying out of the hotel with my camera and tripod. I was carrying a new Panasonic digital camera. It was my first experience using digital technology. I had always shot 16mm film before.

I made my way down the deserted beach heading to the jetty to catch the predawn arrival of the *Queen Mary 2*. She had just been launched in Southampton, christened by the Queen herself and she was, on that day at least, the largest ship in the world; 150,000 tons, an amazing accomplishment of engineering and design.

She was the fourth Queen to be launched by Cunard. The original *Queen Mary* was launched in 1934, the *Queen Elizabeth* in 1938, and the *Queen Elizabeth 2*—the *QE2*—was launched in 1969. The *Queen Mary 2* was replacing the *QE2* on the transatlantic route but before she went into transatlantic service, Cunard sent the new ship to Fort Lauderdale to pick up twenty-six hundred passengers and set sail for Rio de Janeiro for

Carnaval. The ship was duplicating an historic journey that had been made by the *Normandie*, the flagship of the French Line, in 1938.

For me, it was the beginning of another film shoot and another journey. I had spent over four hundred days on the *QE2* over many years sailing around the world and making different films aboard the ship. I love ocean liners and I was ready to get to work. It was February and pitch black, the sun would not come up for hours. I found a spot atop the rocks on the north side of the channel entrance. I set up the tripod, mounted the camera, and checked the digital settings on my new equipment and I waited.

Then at about 4:00 a.m., in the very far distance, I could see a light. Over the course of the next hour I watched the ship approach. Finally she was there, approaching the port, getting larger with each passing moment. She was bigger than any ship I had ever seen, majestic and grand beyond words. But there was no time to watch. I had to get busy. The camera was running. I had to work fast. The ship would pass by and continue on to her berth in a matter of minutes. I did not have time to contemplate the wonder of the moment. I had to work quickly and get the shots. There would be time for reflection later. For now, quick work, snap decisions on framing, camera movement, and following the motion of the ship were at the front of my mind.

In a few minutes she was gone and turning into her berth. I would board her later in the afternoon. I had the opening shots that I needed to start the film. I returned to the hotel and went back to bed for a couple of hours. Then I got up, packed, and headed to the pier to board the *Queen Mary 2*. It was routine. I had done similar work many times before, but this moment was special.

Just one year before I had been clinging to life at the University of Pittsburgh Medical Center. I was near death. In my lonely hospital room I would think about my life and how I had hoped to sail on the great new Cunarder. I didn't think it would ever happen. But it did. I recovered, and I went on to make another film and set out on another great journey.

Life can be amazing.

CHAPTER ONE

A BOY FROM KANSAS CITY

According to my mother, I was in a hurry. My father rushed her to Bethany Hospital in Kansas City, Kansas on the morning of June 25, 1948, and within an hour of their arrival I was born. Being in a hurry is a trait I have never lost. I have always believed you have only so much time on this planet and you'd better make the most of every moment.

I was born to Harold and Maxine Jones, a young couple, who already had a four-year-old daughter, my sister Roxanna. We lived on the outskirts of Kansas City, Kansas near a town called Muncie. My father, who had come from a farm in western Kansas, tended a large garden on our acre and a half of land; we ate what we grew and sold the rest. My mother was a homemaker in a time when homemaking was a full time job and she worked very hard at managing our home and our lives. My father was a blue-collar union worker. But his job had an amazing benefit that would make my life rich beyond words.

My father was an aircraft engine inspector for Trans World Airlines at the overhaul base in Kansas City.

When he went to work for TWA, it was the luxury airline of the stars. Howard Hughes, who owned TWA, made it into a thriving company by commissioning Lockheed Martin to build the Constellation. The elegant "Connie" was like a graceful loon when it taxied up to the gates of the Municipal Airport in Kansas City.

Its unique tri-rudder design had a story associated with Kansas City. Supposedly, Hughes told Lockheed that the Constellation had to fit in the TWA Kansas City hangar. The resulting short, wide, three-rudder design allowed for just that. The hangar is still there, operated by Signature Flight

Service for general aviation, as is Hughes' angled glass-walled office in the upper northwest corner. My father would tell stories of Howard Hughes wandering through the hangar talking to the men working on his planes.

We often forget that modern airline travel did not really get underway until the 1950s. For half a century, from the Wright brothers' flight at Kitty Hawk until the end of World War II—almost half the history of aviation—airplanes had, other than an occasional crop duster, one purpose: to kill people. The magic of aviation was co-opted by war and the military. But after the Second World War, America was ready to travel and the airplane trip was the ultimate luxury experience.

In those days, airplanes were rarely full. Air travel was expensive. In 1960, a round-trip ticket from Los Angeles to New York was over $400. A half a century later, we often pay less than people did in the 1950s and 1960s for airplane tickets. A perk of working for an airline was free travel as a "non-rev" (non-revenue passenger) if there were empty seats onboard, and in those days there were always empty seats.

My parents were interested in improving themselves and seeing their children have a better life. Unlike many of the other workers at the Kansas City overhaul base who rarely, if ever, got on a plane, my parents used their vacations to fly the routes of the TWA system—and what a system it was. TWA Flight #1 started in Kansas City, went directly to New York, then on to Paris, Rome, Tel Aviv, Riyadh, Bombay, and Bangkok before ending in Hong Kong where it turned around and went back the other way to Kansas City. As a college student I went to Hong Kong on that flight—the long way around: twenty-six hours and eight stops to the farthest corners of the world.

My earliest travel memories are less pleasant. In 1954, as a six-year-old, we went to visit relatives in Dodge City, Kansas. In 1954, flying meant unpressurized DC-3s. The lumbering DC3, with its radial engines, stopped in Topeka, Wichita, and Great Bend before landing in Dodge City. Being unpressurized, the DC3s flew low—and that meant under the weather, not above. The flight was chaotic; a roller coaster ride of harrowing take-offs, turbulence, and rough landings. I kept throwing up through it all, as a six-year-old would be prone to do. My Dad sat next to me holding a bag and each time I heaved he would ask me if I was all right and I nodded that everything was *just* fine. It was not, but that early memory of travel speaks of a youthful determination to let nothing stand in the way of my setting out to see the world.

It was my experience—and the same experience of thousands of air travelers—that motivated Howard Hughes to build the Constellation. It would be pressurized and that would allow the planes to fly above the weather. Before pressurization, planes were limited to an altitude of about 12,000 feet and that often put the planes dead in the center of the worst weather. The new turbo-charged engines the Constellation would use allowed the planes to fly higher and get "on top" of the weather, making the ride more comfortable and less stomach churning. Prior to pressurization, air travelers had to be adventurous because while air travel was fast, it was often uncomfortable.

The trip that I remember better was when we went to visit a colorful uncle in Santa Barbara who was on his fourth marriage (and soon into his fourth divorce). It was 1957. We were flying on a TWA Constellation non-stop from Kansas City to Los Angeles. The company forewarned non-revs that we were to be dressed in our best clothes. Coats and ties, dresses and hats, were required. That was how all the passengers dressed. Flying in a cross-country four engine Constellation was the air equivalent of boarding the *Queen Mary*. It was luxury in the air. Non-revs were seated in first class if there were seats available and there usually were.

So at the age of nine, dressed in a blue plaid suit, with my sister in her best dress and my parents in their nicest clothes, we went to the Municipal Airport in Kansas City on a dark evening in June of 1957. The flight left Kansas City at 9:00 p.m. I remember sitting by the gate door that night waiting for the Constellation to arrive. This was long before the Jetway; the planes came right up to the door and you boarded on rolling staircases. You could hear the plane before you saw it, the low deep-throated churning of those four Wright radial engines, spinning three-bladed propellers. Then out of dark it appeared, tall and lanky on the tripod landing gear (DC3s were tail draggers, the Connie had a nose gear and stood tall and regal). The plane pulled right up to the gate and one by one the four engines spun down, the stairway was rolled out, people from New York got off, and it was now time to board the Kansas City passengers bound for L.A. My mother held my sister's hand, my father held my hand, and as a family we climbed the stairs with the TWA logo and entered a world of leather seats, deep plush carpets, stewardesses in stylish uniforms, and the Captain greeting us and welcoming us aboard. It was a world I immediately never wanted to leave.

Maxine and Harold Jones. They were married in Kansas City in 1941.

I'm probably about two, holding onto a sycamore tree that would, in time, grow to a massive height.

My sister Roxanna and me sitting on the front porch of our Kansas City home around 1952.

Can you say "precocious"? Age 4, 1952. The television set that brought *The Ed Sullivan Show*—and a bigger world—into my life.

Looking back on that trip and the ones that were to follow, I have obvious nostalgia. The one word you would not use in describing air travel today is "glamorous." Back then it was. But in truth, had it not been for my father's job, it was something I would never have experienced. It was a luxury that would have been out of our reach. Air travel is easy to criticize today with all its hassles, but one positive change is its shift from an activity of the rich to an activity for everyone. And that's a good thing. Everyone should have the chance to see the world.

The flight to California was wonderful. Hot meals came out of the onboard galley. Real silverware, cloth napkins, and service on a level we were not accustomed to. We arrived in Los Angeles late at night. My jovial Uncle Allen was there to pick us up with wife number four. My parents were skeptical of her, as well they should have been. She had a lover named Henry living under the same roof at the same time she was married to my Uncle Allen. Even we—hicks from Kansas—could figure this out.

After several days in this house of strange "goings-on" we left Santa Barbara in my uncle's new 1957 Ford, which we had borrowed to drive to Disneyland, which had just recently opened. We drove onto the 101 in Santa Barbara about 3:00 p.m., which put us in the center of Los Angeles on the Hollywood Freeway at five o'clock. My father was a wreck, my mother in a near panic; we had never seen traffic like this—lane after lane of bumper-to-bumper traffic flying along. But we made it to Anaheim and Disneyland and spent the next two days in the "Happiest Place on Earth" in its second year of operation. Our family was together. We were experiencing all the joy great travel can bring.

The next day we boarded a TWA flight at LAX and took off out over the Pacific Ocean before the plane turned back and circled above L.A. I remember looking out of the window and thinking, "I'll be back." And I returned many times, ultimately making Los Angeles my home.

We made several more trips to California as a family. But in 1963, when I was fifteen, I was allowed to go visit Allen and his last wife Marie on my own. By then the great Constellations had been retired and the new fleet of Boeing 707 fan-jets had arrived. TWA pilots were especially careful landing the Boeing 707s in Kansas City because there was no room for error. Kansas City had one of the shortest runways for commercial aviation in the country and there was no space to expand the runways because the airport had been built on a bend of the Missouri River where the Kansas

River joins. There wasn't enough runway to do a go-around if the landing went bad. I don't recall a major accident ever happening at the Kansas City Municipal Airport, but in the 1970s, commercial air traffic was moved twenty miles north to Mid-Continent International Airport.

But in 1963 they were still landing and taking off the 707s at the downtown airport at the junction of the two great rivers of the plains. When they would start the engines at the gate and begin the taxi the roar was deafening. The early engines were screamers. The sound was something you never forgot.

For a fifteen-year-old kid, going to California alone was a thrill. I wore a gray flannel suit. I was put in first class. I had a gin and tonic—why the stewardess ever thought I was old enough to drink will remain a mystery lost in time—but there I was, a cocktail in hand, suit and tie, gazing out first at the Great Plains, then the Rockies as we headed to L.A.

I changed planes at LAX and took a United Airlines flight to Santa Barbara. As the plane came in for landing, I looked out at the ocean and the lush green hills that rose into the Santa Maria Mountains. It was, and still is, one of the most beautiful places on earth.

My aunt and uncle met me at the airport. They were driving a white 1960 Cadillac Sedan de Ville. The car was huge, one of the biggest cars ever built by General Motors (though toned down from the 1959 model; the giant fins of that year being replaced by shorter, stubbier fins).

Coming from a family that had little, this was luxury I liked. We drove up into the hills to their home in Hope Ranch. It was impressive. My uncle was a milkman. He found himself in this miraculous situation due to a friendship with a fellow Mason who was Marie's late husband. Allen delivered her milk (and I suspect he delivered more than a bottle of milk to that house). Ruth, Allen's fourth wife was on her way out the door, divorce in hand, to marry Henry, her on-site lover. Mel, Marie's former husband, had died of a heart attack, and there was my Uncle Allen, milk bottles in hand, ready to marry and move into this grand estate in Hope Ranch. You would have had to know him to appreciate the unlikeness of it all. He had eternal charm, a never-ending smile, and after struggling his whole life he found himself living in the lap of luxury. Such was the luck of one Santa Barbara milkman.

The purpose of my trip was to see the Santa Barbara Fiesta. It was nice, but I have little lasting memory of the day beyond the colorful skirts of the senoritas swirling to the sounds of mariachi music. But as my week drew to a close, Allen and Marie decided to take me directly to LAX by way of a two-day trip to Hollywood. Well, that certainly perked up my attention. Off we went in that giant white Cadillac down the 101 to Tinseltown. We went to Grauman's Chinese Theatre and put our feet and hands in the cement impression left by the stars. We visited the Hollywood Wax Museum, the Griffith Park Observatory, and drove out Sunset Boulevard with a star map open looking for the homes of celebrities. After a long and exhausting day we checked into the Ambassador Hotel on Wilshire Boulevard.

The following day we had lunch at the Brown Derby across the street and late that night we went to the Coconut Grove, which was located in the Ambassador Hotel. Freddy Martin and his Orchestra were playing and Dianne Carroll was the headliner. The dance floor was crowded with Hollywood's beautiful people. We were seated in a tall leather booth. I looked out and surveyed the surroundings and thought, "I like this. There is a big world out there."

Many years before I began to travel, when I was only six or seven, there would be drawing lessons in elementary school. Everyone else drew pictures of horses or barns, or dogs or cars. But I was drawing pictures of nightclub marquees, flashing neon signs, the bright lights of Broadway. I can still remember giving the teacher a brightly colored drawing of my imagining of the Copacabana in New York. This was no doubt from endless Sunday nights perched in front of the Montgomery Ward black and white TV watching *The Ed Sullivan Show*. If there was ever an eye into the bigger world for me, it was *The Ed Sullivan Show*.

At a very early age, I dreamed of a big life. Sitting at the Coconut Grove in Los Angeles at fifteen, I wanted to make those dreams come true. For a boy from my background this seemed like a daunting task, but through sheer luck, determination, and chutzpah that seemed wired into my DNA, it would all come to pass.

To this day, I still drive an old Cadillac. My friends think I'm nuts, but it's a small token statement of my appreciation to my Aunt Marie and Uncle Allen for showing me there was a big world out there just waiting for me.

CHAPTER TWO

NEW YORK CITY AND THE 1964 WORLD'S FAIR

The next big trip was to New York City for the 1964 World's Fair. After countless nights of watching *The Ed Sullivan Show* glamorizing New York, my expectations could not have been higher. I was excited beyond words about the trip. I had studied the city by going to the library and reading travel books. I knew about as much as I could know about New York for a sixteen-year-old from the center of the country.

My parents and I took a TWA Boeing 707 out of the Municipal Airport in Kansas City on a warm June day in 1964 headed for John F. Kennedy International Airport. It had recently been given that name following the Kennedy assassination in 1963. My sister was in college and did not come along so it was only the three of us.

Just walking off the plane was a shock. People were loud, pushy, they had broad accents, and they were anything but polite. It was the crazy whirlpool of nuttiness that was New York in the 1960s. We got in a cab and headed to the Dixie Hotel on 42nd Street. The hotel still exists, seedy as ever, though it was renamed The Carter during the Jimmy Carter administration. It was in the heart of Times Square on 42nd Street with all the porn shops and twenty-four hour movie theaters of the "Deuce," as 42nd Street was then known. The cab drove and drove and drove. I was certain we were not supposed to cross the Triborough Bridge, the George Washington Bridge and the Lincoln Tunnel to get to the Dixie Hotel from JFK. We were rubes. The hack could see this and literally took us for a ride. I did not mention this to my father who, I felt, would be embarrassed. He paid the outrageous fare and gave what he felt was a reasonable tip and was sad that the cabbie did not say, "Thank you." Oh brother, did we have a lot to learn!

In 1964, New York was a gray and dingy place. Arriving in Manhattan today it's hard to realize how downtrodden most American cities were in the 1960s. White flight, rising crime, a rush to the suburbs—it had taken a terrible toll on almost all large American cities. New York was hit particularly hard. The New York I was first exposed to in the 1960s was seedy and dangerous.

I was shocked. I had a glamorous vision of the city and it was not living up to the mind pictures I had in my head from watching *The Ed Sullivan Show*. Still, I did not let the porn shops and street hustlers deter me. I went straight to the concierge desk at the Dixie Hotel and announced that I wanted reservations for my family at the Copacabana. And so after our first day at the fair, we returned to the city on the #7 train, got into our best clothes, and off we went in a cab to the Copa on 61st Street off Fifth Avenue.

My childhood drawing of the marquee of the Copacabana was sadly misjudged. There was no neon sign, no blinking lights. Instead there was a stylish green canopy with the name *Copacabana* discretely printed on the side. There was a doorman to open the cab; it was elegant. This was my first exposure to Manhattan's Upper East Side.

Inside it was magical. Brightly painted metal palm trees, linen tablecloths, round backed aluminum chairs with velvet cushions, and a full orchestra playing while couples danced the Foxtrot and the Cha-cha-cha. As I recall, dinner and the show was $7.00 apiece. I had already been to the Coconut Grove in Los Angeles and now the Copacabana in New York. My parents didn't know what to make of it all but they were having fun, so why not?

Bobby Vinton was the headliner. He had just released "Blue Velvet" and he was a big star. He was preceded by the warm up act, a young unknown comedienne named Totie Fields. She was short, overweight, Jewish, and played on those traits for laughs. She went on to become a big star in her own right (I saw her headline at the Latin Quarter a few years later). Sadly, she lost a leg, but continued to work with the "amputee" aspect added to her shtick, but ultimately she died of cancer at a young age. She was a favorite on *The Ed Sullivan Show* and was a very funny woman of her time, one of the first great comediennes.

At age fourteen playing banjo at the Kansas City *Firemen's Ball*. 1962.

At fifteen on a hula float in Kansas City. I had not gotten the memo about bare feet in Hawaii (boat shoes and white socks!). 1963.

After dinner the show began, first with the Copa Girls, an eight-member chorus line of young, skimpily clad, beautiful women who danced two numbers. And then from off stage the announcer said "Jules Podell proudly presents... Bobby Vinton!" At the time I had no idea who Jules Podell was. I would learn later he was the front man for Frank Costello and the mob that owned and ran the Copa. We were sitting at a ringside table and were oblivious to the mob people who sat farther from the stage.

Over the next few years I went back to the Copa several times. I saw Sammy Davis Jr., Paul Anka, Julius LaRosa, and Jerry Vale and feel lucky that I did this. If I had not I would have missed a whole genre of American entertainment because it was all gone in only a few short years.

Oh, the World's Fair—it was a little like the Fiesta in Santa Barbara. It was nice but it didn't hold a candle to Bobby Vinton and Totie Fields at the Copacabana.

Meanwhile, back in Kansas City, I was about to graduate from Washington High School and enter the University of Missouri-Kansas City, where I majored in radio and television broadcasting.

I put myself through school and paid for my TWA overseas trips by working as a banjo player. I was "The Wizard of the Strings," the boy-wonder banjo player of Kansas City. I played tenor (four string) banjo, an instrument of Dixieland jazz. Somehow I missed the popular music of my day. I had no passion for Rock and Roll or the Beatles. But I was a master at playing everything from "Toot Toot Tootsie Goodbye" to "I'm Looking Over a Four-leaf Clover." I had an act and I would go out on the summer fair circuit, playing on rickety stages. I had an agent named Johnny Coon (who named his son Rack). He had no compunction about lying to get a booking.

Each winter, fair representatives from throughout the Midwest would gather at The Muelbach Hotel in Kansas City to see and buy the acts they would feature at their summer fairs. The agents had one basic job, to get them as drunk as they could and sell them every act they had on their roster. The county fair entertainment coordinator (often a local farmer or hardware store owner) would leave Kansas City with a hangover and return to their homes far away wondering just what they had bought.

Months would pass and then the summer fair circuit would get underway. I traveled with magicians, jugglers, balloon artists, the whole gamut of variety entertainment. We would be waiting by the grandstand,

My straw hat (which I still have), my fair circuit suitcase (no ego evident there), and my cane. I have no idea why I had a cane. Early 1960s.

★ STARS ★ For Inaugural Ball

DEE NICHOLSON
HULA DANCER

JEFF WILLIAMS
FAMOUS HUMORIST

DOUG JONES
"WIZARD OF THE STRINGS"

One of my first gigs working under the moniker "The Wizard of the Strings." The standards for "stardom" were low. But I was working the Dee Nicholson, Hula Dancer, and Jeff Williams, "Famous Humorist." 1965.

which was usually in front of a dirt racetrack of some sort, and the emcee would announce… "So you've seen him on *The Johnny Carson Show*, *The Ed Sullivan Show* and *The Steve Allen Show*… The Wizard of the Strings… Doug Jones!" The farmer who had booked me and the other acts in a drunken stupor at The Muelbach Hotel months before would be sitting in the stands, nudging his wife to remind her of how many times they had seen me on national television. It was, of course, all a lie. But I got up there and played my signature songs, "Waitin' For The Robert E. Lee," and "Alabamy Bound"—and for some reason a peculiar banjo arrangement of the "Theme from Exodus." My chutzpah was in high gear and I managed to sell it night after night.

During the fall and winter, I would play banjo in the nightclubs of Kansas City with the great Dixieland bands of the day. Kansas City was a hot bed of live jazz and the downtown strips on Twelfth Street and Baltimore were filled with jazz clubs, conventioneers, streetwalkers, and a wonderful seedy, bawdy world that has long since disappeared, replaced by modern, sterile architecture.

In the middle of all of this craziness on Twelfth Street was the Folly Theater. This was one of the last true bump-and-grind burlesque houses to operate in America. It was a forbidden thing. My parent spoke of it in hushed tones (though I know for a fact they double dated there with another couple and were mortified to their dying day that they had ever set foot in this raunchy place). It was the bawdiest place in town.

Naturally, I couldn't wait to go. You were supposed to be eighteen to get in. At sixteen, my friend Dave Knapp and I decided to see if we could make it through the door. The admission price was 99 cents. The box office man, a cigar hanging out of his mouth, didn't even look up from reading *The Racing Form* as he took our dollar bill and threw a penny back. When we walked through the door we felt that we had somehow entered the most exciting place on earth. It was just like the stereotype of the old burlesque house: bald headed men sitting with raincoats in their laps, a five-piece band in a pit, all of them smoking, the drummer doing the obligatory rolls and rim shots for the bumping and grinding strippers. Onstage was a terrible emcee; a bad comedian spouting hackneyed jokes that were stale even then. There was a "candy man" who stood in the aisle during intermission selling an "erotic" book. He would tell details of the lurid plot that would make your hair stand on end as he tried to flog the cheap pulp novels under his arm.

Herb Kratoska, the man who taught me how to play the banjo. He had a long career as a musician and was a part of the famed radio KMBC Texas Rangers who went to Hollywood and appeared in a string of singing westerns. It was autographed to me in 1964. The photo was shot in the 1940s.

But it was, of course, the strippers that we came to see. Dave and I decided to sit in a box, which gave us a direct view down onto the stage, as well as the dreary audience. The strippers were old. Their breasts were sagging in spite of—or perhaps because of—tassel twirling and other feats of agility. They would toss out wisecrack remarks to the patrons. The law required pasties and G-strings. This was before the Supreme Court ruling on obscenity that unleashed modern pornography. The laws of the state insisted that the nipples and crotch be covered. In looking back it was rather tame. It is hard to imagine today that this was arousing to the nearly all male audience, but you make do with what you have—and in those days that was what you got for erotic entertainment. If I had waited until I was of legal age, I would have missed it all. It closed down a couple of years later and another whole form of American entertainment bit the dust. Soon hardcore porn and pole dancers in heels would replace this form of erotic entertainment.

A postscript to this story is that twenty years later the theater was completely restored as a jewel box of Kansas City history. It became home to jazz concerts, string quartets—and a travelogue series. In its first year operating as a restored performing arts hall, I was booked to show my film *The Great World Cruise of the QE2*. When I walked out onto the center of the stage and looked out at the audience, I couldn't help but gaze up at the box where Dave and I sat and think *if this audience only knew...*

During my years as the "The Wizard of the Strings," I worked the fairs and nightclubs but I also would be sent out on other gigs. On one occasion, I was to emcee and be the middle act between two "exotic dancers" at some lodge convention in St. Joseph, Missouri. I arrived at the hall where this was to take place. I went to the one dressing room we were all to share and brought out my music charts and started going over them with the pianist who was going to accompany my act as well as the two dancers. Midway into explaining my arrangements, one of the strippers walked in, chewing gum and being very chatty. I continued to explain the set to the pianist, turned around and saw that the stripper was stark naked. She was wiggling into her G-string and applying the pasties. Of course, she would have no compunction about taking off her clothes in front of me; she was going to take them off in front of two hundred inebriated men in a half-hour. At show time, I went out did an opening song and then introduced the first exotic dancer. She came out, did a ten-minute strip and then walked off the stage to the expected catcalls and whistles. Then I came out to do my banjo act. You have no idea how disinterested two hundred drunken lodge men can be over a banjo act sandwiched between two strippers.

It was about this time that I decided that while I loved show business, perhaps I should aim for a somewhat more attentive audience. The next day I saw an ad in *The Kansas City Star* for a travelogue film that would be shown the following Tuesday at the Plaza Theater. It was titled *Portraits of Austria* and it was to be narrated by the producer Curtis Nagle. I decided to check it out. And that decision changed my life.

At age seventeen; going to school during the day and working the Kansas City jazz joints at night. 1967.

CHAPTER THREE

THE TRAVELOGUE BUSINESS

The Plaza Theater was an old movie house (long since gone) that was built in the 1920s during the heyday of movie palaces. It was on the Country Club Plaza, a shopping district in Kansas City that was the first suburban shopping mall in America built in 1919 by J.C. Nichols. It was forty blocks south of downtown and was built as a duplication of the city of Seville, Spain. The architecture was authentic and beautiful, the shops elegant; it was classy when it opened in the early part of the 20th century and remains so today.

I would see advertisements on the entertainment page of *The Kansas City Star* for travelogues that were being presented at the Music Hall downtown and at the Plaza Theater. I had never seen a travelogue before and didn't have much sense of what to expect. But TWA flew to Vienna, so I decided to go see *Portraits of Austria*, being presented at the Plaza Theatre by filmmaker Curtis Nagel. There were three television stations in Kansas City and they had no travel programming. If you wanted to see programs about travel, you went to travelogues.

The classic travelogues were feature-length movies narrated live by the filmmakers. They were intended to be a full evening of entertainment, always with an intermission. The format really never changed over the forty years I did the live travelogue lecture circuit. There would be a spotlight on a microphone in the center of the stage. The host for the evening would come out from the wings and introduce me, telling the audience something about my background and credentials. I would then go center stage and make my opening remarks (which in the nomenclature of the business was called the "front talk"). I would usually speak for about five minutes.

This was my time to psych the audiences for what they were about to see. I would then ask for the house lights to be dimmed and move to the side of the stage. The spotlight and house lights would go dark, the curtain would open to reveal the screen and the film would begin. A music and sound effects track would run with the film but I would do the narration live from the side of the stage. At the end of the first half (usually about 45 minutes) it would say "Intermission" on the screen, the spotlight would come up and I would go center stage and take a bow as the audience applauded, acknowledging that I was narrating the film live. After the intermission, the process was repeated. I would speak for five minutes center stage, call for the lights, move to the side and again narrate live for the second half of the film. At the end of the program I would say "Thank you and good night," the center stage light would come up and I would walk into the spotlight to take my bow. Sometimes the applause was generous; sometimes less so.

The travelogue intermissions were originally built into the shows so the projectionists could change the film reels and the carbon arc. The old carbon arcs in the projectors would not last for a full feature-length film and most theaters had only one 16mm projector. The intermission also gave audience members a chance to talk with one another. The patrons were usually season subscribers and many of them knew each other. The travelogues, in many towns, were as much about socializing as they were about the films. The travelogue series provided a means to get out for the night, be entertained, learn something new, and see friends. Travelogues operated as subscription series much like the local symphony, theater, or opera companies did.

I am always asked "Why did you do the narration live?" It's true that sound on film was hardly a new thing. The narration could have been on the film soundtrack. But there was a presence about doing it live. Doing the narration live gave me, as a public speaker, a chance to connect with the audience directly. It's hard to describe but I know my programs were better because I narrated the films live than they would have been if I had put my narration on the film's sound track. Also, we were minor-celebrities in our day. People came not just to see the movie but also to hear directly from a travel expert, someone who knew the subject matter because he or she had been there and made the film. The ticket buyer expected a live show presented in an intimate and entertaining manner. And that is what I hope I delivered.

THE TRAVELOGUE BUSINESS

Travelogues were always part of a series of six to eight programs in a season running from September to April, and most of the patrons bought tickets to the entire season of shows. The programs were interpretive; one person's subjective view of the subject. One month Don Cooper would take them to Alaska, the next month Thayer Soule would take them to Spain, the following month Ken Richter would take them to Australia, and so on.

The great heyday of travelogues was not the 1920s and 1930s when Burton Holmes, the creator of the travelogue, was in his prime, but rather the 1960s, 70s, 80s, and early 90s. The middle class was beginning to travel. With deregulation of the airlines, travel was no longer something for just the wealthy. Average people could save up enough money for a two-week tour of Europe. Overseas travel became an activity nearly everyone in America could look forward to and there was virtually no place to see travel programming, hence the wide expansion of the classic travelogue series. In Burton Holmes' day, people came to travelogues to see places they would never go; by the time I started making films, people were coming to see places they were planning to visit the next summer.

At the same time, almost every city and town in America built a performing arts center. Sometimes they were brand new auditoriums, other times they were restored movie palaces. By the mid-1970s, there were hundreds of new performing arts facilities throughout the United States and they needed programming to fill their theaters. A travelogue series was relatively inexpensive, easy to put on, and they were popular with the public.

In its heyday, around 1980, there were over five thousand travelogue series in the United States. They were in auditoriums ranging from a few hundred to three thousand seat houses. We often had multiple performances of the same program and the theaters were often full. In the 1970s I would appear at the Seattle Opera House and show my film five times over three days in a house with three thousand reserved seats for the World Cavalcade travelogue series. This all started downhill with the advent of cable television and was accelerated by home video and subsequent technologies, which made the live-lecture travelogue largely unnecessary. Today some travelogue series still exists in a few places but it is a shadow of what it once was. But in their heyday, travelogues were a big business.

Meanwhile, back in Kansas City...

I showed up at the Plaza Theater and the auditorium was nearly full. I sat in the back of the balcony. A man name George Morgoulis, who operated the series as a for-profit business, came onto the stage and welcomed the audience. Then he introduced the speaker/filmmaker, Curtis Nagel. Curt had a thick Bostonian accent, he was short and rotund, and he had a "business partner" named Bill Moore. They had lived together for decades. Curt was pompous but loveable. He gave his introduction speaking of the wonders of Austria and whetting the appetite of the audience for what they were about see. He always called his films "Portraits of..." and he always finished his front talk with the same phrase "And now as we take our palette of color film we shall paint these portraits of Austria" (or Germany, or India, or New Zealand; whatever the topic of the evening was). The lights dimmed, the music came up, and the screen filled with beautiful images of a lovely alpine nation. Curt stood to the side of the screen and narrated the film live to the very end. Once the program was over, the audience applauded, Curt took his bows, and I thought, "Well that looks like a fun way to make a living," and for the next forty years that was exactly what I did.

The fact that I knew nothing about filmmaking, or even photography, didn't seem to faze me. I figured I could learn. It was, fortunately, a more innocent time and audiences were much more forgiving. I shudder at some of the material I foisted off onto audiences in my early years, but I did get better; my cinematography improved, and I was good on stage, and that counted for a lot.

As I walked out of the theater, I started trying to figure out how I could get myself into the travelogue business. Travelogues combined the two things I loved most in life, travel and show business. I had set out on a course and chosen a direction, but I couldn't imagine the wonderful life ahead of me as I left the Plaza Theatre that day.

Curtis Nagel, left and Bill Moore, right, on the set of their television show in Los Angeles. Curt presented the first travelogue I ever saw, *Portraits of Austria* at the Plaza Theater in Kansas City. The photo was shot in the 1960s.

Thayer Soule, Burton Holmes' protégé and my mentor. Thayer spent 55 years on the travelogue lecture circuit, first working for Burton Holmes, then going out on his own as an independent travelogue filmmaker. 1988.

CHAPTER FOUR

TRANS WORLD AIRLINES TO LONDON

The decision to go into the travelogue business was based on a love of international travel that already had a firm grip on my life. Because of my father's job with TWA, I had a passport filled with customs stamps and visas. By the time I graduated from college I had been to seventeen countries.

My first trip abroad was in 1966. I had just graduated from high school. I was eighteen and I decided to go to London. It was a good choice. There were no language problems (save for a few cockney phrases) and it was cheap. I was traveling with *Europe on Five Dollars a Day*, Arthur Fromer's bible for students and middle-class Americans traveling in the 1960s. I stepped off the Trans World Airlines jet at Heathrow and got into a black London taxi and headed off to my bed and breakfast in Bloomsbury. Today I would *not* get in that cab; the fare is over $100 to get into central London, but in 1966, a cab ride was inexpensive.

The taxi went flying into the city and I watched out the window with amazement as we passed sites I had only seen in pictures—Big Ben, Buckingham Palace, Piccadilly Circus—and all while driving on the wrong side of the road! The taxi pulled up in front of a run-down five-story bed and breakfast on Bloomsbury Street. A large woman greeted me. She was missing all of her upper teeth, save one (the British and their teeth). She took me to the top floor of this dingy B&B. I shared a bath with four other rooms. Breakfast was served on the first floor and was hearty. The place was dated (I particularly remember the cabbage flower wallpaper) but it was of little importance to me. I was young and planned to spend no time in the room except to sleep. I had London to see.

After a quick change of clothes, off I went. The Changing of the Guard, Madame Tussauds, the National Gallery, the Tower of London, the Crown Jewels, Fleet Street, Carnaby Street... somehow in five days I took it all in mostly by getting around on London's subway system, "The Underground" or better known as "The Tube." I quickly acclimated myself to British life. I learned to stop at four o'clock for tea and I had a suit tailored on Oxford Street. In the 1960s, this was a big thing to do when you went to London (or Hong Kong). The three-piece suit was custom made and shipped to Kansas City. It was, as I recall, 30 pounds, then about $75. The suit arrived in Kansas City a few weeks later and I wore it for years.

I was already a budding theater enthusiast by the time I arrived in London. I can thank my parents for this because every summer we would go see the big musicals at the Starlight Theater in Kansas City. It was an outdoor theater in Swope Park with 8,000 seats. All the seats in the last row were a dollar and that's where we sat. The people on stage were like ants but I saw everyone from Martha Raye in *Wildcat* to Giselle McKenzie in *Gypsy*, and Bert Parks in *The Music Man*. I still remember the very first show I saw at the Starlight: I was eight, it was 1956, and the show was *Plain and Fancy*, a musical about the Amish of Pennsylvania—and they raised a barn on the stage! What magic.

So on my first night in London, off I went to the theater to see *The Mousetrap*. This Agatha Christie murder mystery had been running at Saint Martin's Theater in London's West End since 1952. And it is still running today. It is the longest running play in the world. Two years later in 1968 I was back in London on another trip and I went to see *Cabaret*. Judy Dench played Sally. I didn't have much money so I bought the cheapest seat, 99 pence—about $2.40 at the time. The seat was in the upper, upper, upper balcony. London theaters were built with the class system in mind. The working classes sat in the balconies and made their way to their seats through separate entrances and stairwells. The upper classes sat in the stalls (orchestra seats in America) and were spared any chance encounter with the working stiffs. American theaters are egalitarian. New York theater balconies offer good sightlines and you go in and out with everyone else. But London theaters still reflect how engrained the class system was (and in some ways still is) in London culture. I climbed to the top of the Palace Theater up stairs so steep that if you stumbled you could have gone rolling out of the balcony and into the stalls. London theater balconies can be positively scary. I loved the show and it never occurred to me the experience might be more satisfying in a better seat.

And I went to the London Palladium, London's great variety theater. Today it is owned by Andrew Lloyd Webber and is a used for big scale musicals, but in 1966 it was still a vaudeville house with variety acts, performing several shows a day. The headliner was a popular British song and dance man. There were dog acts, a chorus line, a magician, singers, dancers, a big orchestra in the pit—everything I imagine the Palace Theater in New York City was during its vaudeville heyday.

I kept passing in front of The Talk of the Town on Leicester Square. It was London's best known nightclub, the equivalent to the Copacabana in New York. Everyone from Frank Sinatra to Judy Garland to Ethel Merman played The Talk of the Town. On my last night in London I decided I would go. I don't recall the price but it must have been reasonable since I didn't have much money. I can't imagine what the maître d' thought when I walked up and said "I'd like a table for one." But he was polite and led me to a table on the side. I was served dinner and watched a big splashy stage show (I distinctly recall showgirls descending from the ceiling). Vaughn Monroe, a popular British singer of the time, was the headliner.

The courage, some would say raw chutzpah, I had was notable. It never occurred to me that a person my age just didn't do these things. But I did, and because I did, I saw so much that would soon be gone. The Talk of the Town closed a few years later to be replaced by a disco and later a casino—and another chapter of entertainment history is only a memory.

I returned to Kansas City from London that summer in 1966 ready to see the world. I had my first passport stamp and I planned to fill that passport with as many stamps as I could. So where to next? Why not Bombay?

London: My first trip abroad on TWA. Ten years later in 1976, while filming *Royal London*, I would climb to the top of Big Ben to film the clock mechanism strike noon. 1966.

CHAPTER FIVE

TWENTY- FOUR HOURS TO THE OTHER SIDE OF THE WORLD

Bombay. It was halfway around the world. It was India. It was 1967. What an adventure.

I left Kansas City on TWA Flight #1. The plane stopped at JFK in New York for a short layover. I passed the time in the famous Eero Saarinen TWA Terminal. The place was shaped like a bird, and the building seemed to want to fly away. It was, for many years, the most famous international gateway in the world. I, and millions of other travelers, left for and returned from journeys to the farthest corners of the globe through that iconic terminal.

It was twenty-four flight hours from Kansas City to Bombay (today Mumbai). Flights to India tend to arrive in the middle of the night. The TWA flight left New York in the late evening, traveling over the Atlantic at night, and arriving in Paris in the late morning. By the time the plane had stopped in Rome, Tel Aviv, and Cairo, it would be approaching Saudi Arabia near midnight. The plane finally touched down in Bombay at 3:00 a.m.

The moment I walked off the plane I could feel the heat. It was like a sticky, hot oven even at three o'clock in the morning. After clearing customs, I boarded a bus that would take me to my hotel. The bus lumbered along through the outskirts of Bombay and soon we were in the middle of the city. The streets were lined with people sleeping on the sidewalks, thousands of them. I was told that in the morning a cart would come through and take away bodies of anyone who had died in the night.

I checked into the hotel, a rundown place that had been, in its day, a grand stopover for English aristocracy. It had seen better days. I looked longingly down the street at the Taj Mahal Hotel, the luxury hotel of Bombay then and still today. The air conditioning in my hotel was hit or miss and of course you could not drink the water or dare touch an ice cube. It was my first trip abroad where I had to watch everything I ate or drank. I managed to have the experience of traveling to India in 1967 without getting sick.

This is not to say there were no complications with the food. The hotel room rate included the meals. The first night I went into the hotel dining room and I ordered a dinner of mutton curry. The waiter said he would bring it with no spices. I protested and said I wanted an authentic Indian dining experience. Aiming to please the pushy young American, the meal was brought out and placed in front of me. I took one bite. There was a pause—like the slow motion of a car wreck—before I thought, *oh no, this is a mistake*. It felt like I had just poured battery acid down my throat. I looked around for water. There was none on the table. I was gasping. The waiter saw me and quickly brought a bottle of water that I chugged like a fireman putting out a blaze. The waiter quietly took away my plate and returned with another serving of mutton curry without the fiery spices. He was very gracious, typically Indian. When the Indians use spices they are serious. I was much more careful in ordering food after that first night.

I used the next day to explore Bombay on my own. I went to the Gateway of India at the harbor and wandered the streets of a city that still had many remnants of its British colonial past. The second day I hired a guide and driver. I remember the price, two dollars for the whole day for the driver, car, and guide. The guide, a middle-aged woman in a yellow sari, started by having the driver take us to the usual tourist attractions but I stopped her and said I didn't want to see the things I could see on my own. I wanted to see the things I could *not* see on my own. I had done my research. I told her I wanted to first see the cages.

The cages are a huge, sprawling squalid area of Bombay that houses prostitutes. It is the largest brothel in the world. The guide told me about the lives of the young women, many of them barely out of childhood. They stood in front of cramped rooms that had wooden cage doors on the front. They wore garish clothes, shockingly different from the typically colorful but modest saris Indian women wore. It was tawdry and sad. I was told a figure in rupees equivalent to one dollar would be adequate compensation for an hour of a young girl's time and body. We drove and drove and it seemed to go on forever. The cages have not gone away since my visit in 1967. Today there are over two hundred thousand prostitutes working the cages. It is a tragedy of the human condition, but also a part of the mosaic of Indian life.

I asked to see a Hindu funeral. The guide took me to a cremation as it was underway. We stood at a distance. The family was gathered around the smoldering pyre. Some whispered, others paced, everything was quiet and somber. The body on the pyre had been partially consumed. It takes several hours for a cremation to be completed. I can still recall the acrid smell. We left quietly after about thirty minutes. It was the first and only time I have seen a body burning.

Sensing that I was looking for the unusual, the guide asked if I would like to see the Towers of Silence. I asked what they were, she told the driver to head there and simply said to me "Come, you will learn."

Zoroastrianism is a religion that originated in Persia. In the 7th century, many practitioners migrated in India. Today their numbers are quite small, less than 100,000 in the world, about 70,000 in India. Its basic belief is to "be among those who renew the world… to make the world progress towards perfection," vague, a little hard to wrap your head around, but the practices of handling a corpse are unusual to say the least. My guide explained that after death, Zoroastrians consider the body to be polluted. Evil had overtaken the individual and was the cause of death (one assumes the soul has moved on). Burial is forbidden because it would pollute the ground, burning is forbidden, because it would pollute the air, so the body is left outside to be consumed by birds of prey.

We stood next to a large circular stone building. These were the Towers of Silence. She explained that there were stone tiers inside. The bodies would be placed on the tiers, and over time they would be consumed. As she was telling this to me, I looked up into the trees overhead. They were filled with vultures. In the middle of her explanation was a clamor of noise. The vultures all took off, wings flapping furiously as they headed into the stone tower. "A body has just arrived," my guide said. Later, she explained, lime would be used to dissolve the bones.

I can tell you this was pretty heavy stuff for a kid from a Lutheran family in Kansas. But it opened my eyes to a broader worldview. It made me appreciate that everyone has (or has not) a spiritual view of life and death and as a citizen of the earth it should be our goal to understand differing points of view.

I have been back to India a number of times since. I regard it as an essential travel experience. It is a kaleidoscope of the human condition. You do not see India without being changed. It gives immediacy to the phrase "how the other half lives." I have returned at different stages of my own life, but nothing stands in my memory quite as vividly as the images, the sights, sounds, and smells of that journey to Bombay when I was so young, so long ago.

More trips to Asia would follow, Sri Lanka, Bangkok, Hong Kong, and Japan. The wonders of the Far East were ahead.

The cages in Bombay, the world's largest brothel. I was not in Kansas anymore. 1967.

A part of the Grand Palace of Bangkok. A part of my early exposure to the Far East on TWA. 1967.

CHAPTER SIX

THE CLOCK WAS TICKING

Time was running out. That seems like an odd thing for a student to say, but my privileges of free travel on TWA would end when I graduated from the university. I was aware of this from my first trip abroad at eighteen. In four years I packed in a lot of trips, more than I can count or even remember.

There were several trips to Paris, one to Zurich, another to Geneva and one trip to Frankfurt, Koblenz, and Heidelberg. I made a long trip to Sri Lanka, Bangkok, Hong Kong, and Japan. Then Rome, Athens, and Lisbon and Madrid, several trips to Honolulu, and lots of stopovers in New York City, Los Angeles, and San Francisco.

The only money I had I earned as a banjo player working at nightclubs in Kansas City. After my college tuition was paid, all of the money I earned went to travel, which, fortunately, could be done on the cheap in the 1960s. I was so concerned about stretching my money that I pulled a crazy stunt to get from London to Paris. It couldn't have cost much to take the train to Dover and the ferry across the English Channel, but I was hungry and I needed a place to sleep for the night so—and I swear I am not making this up—I flew from Heathrow to JFK, had a nice meal en route, and turned around at JFK and boarded a flight for Paris. I had another nice meal and a good night's sleep on the plane. In those days you could often raise the armrests and use the three seats as a bed. The things you do when you're young and trying to save a buck.

And oh that first trip to Paris! I loved Paris from the moment I first walked along the Seine. I arranged a hotel room at the airport—Orly in those days. I can't imagine traveling today without reservations but for much of my travel as a student, I just went and never worried about finding a room. I booked a hotel near the Boulevard Saint-Germain, I settled into the fifth floor walk-up, and what was the first thing I did? The Eiffel Tower? The Louvre? The Champs Élysées? No. I was off to 32 Rue du Rocher to get a ticket to The Folies Bergère.

The Folies Bergère was legendary. Each night lavish music hall revues with topless dancers in massive headdresses went on at eight o'clock. Several of my father's friends at TWA had seen the show. They spoke of it in hushed conversation. It was considered taboo. Topless dancers—shocking! I went to the box office and, having little money, pointed to the lowest price on the sign next to the window. I expected to be seated far back in the balcony. Instead I was taken to the main floor and shown the back wall. I had unwittingly bought standing room; not that I minded particularly. Once the show started I slipped into an empty orchestra seat I could never have afforded. Every seat had an ashtray. Everyone smoked; cigars, cigarettes, plumes of smoke rose out of the orchestra. It's a wonder the place didn't burn down. The show, the costumes, the variety acts, it was the Paris Music Hall revue, something I immediately loved.

The "Can Can" number at the Folies Bergère. 1967.

Most of these trips I made alone. To be honest, I had a pretty lonely upbringing. While my parents were kind and endlessly supportive, I had few friends. I was the loner kid. I made puppets and built a marionette theater in my bedroom, and somehow pestered my parents into buying me a Montgomery Ward Stella guitar for $19 when I was nine. It was the start of rock and roll and the guitar was the instrument everyone wanted to learn to play. But even then I was different. I soon got a four-string banjo and I learned to play every Al Jolson song, but I never learned a single piece of the Beatles music.

In 1965, a year after I had gone with my parents to the World's Fair, my sister and I went to New York City together. It is the only trip we ever made as brother and sister and I remember the details vividly. New York City in the late sixties was pretty grimy but I was learning to love it. I loved the noise, the hustle, and the pace. It was the most exciting place on earth (and in some ways, still is). We flew into JFK and took a cab to the Astor Hotel at 44th and Broadway. It was demolished in the 70s to make way for a tall skyscraper, but in 1965 the Astor Hotel stood in the heart of Times Square.

At the time we lived on the outskirts of Kansas City, Kansas. Our neighborhood had not been annexed into the city, and our mailing address was Muncie, Kansas. As we rode into New York City in a yellow checker cab, my sister announced firmly that we were *not* putting down Muncie, Kansas on the hotel registry. We would be from Kansas City. I agreed and we both signed the Astor Hotel registry, with fountain pens, 31 North 78th Street, Kansas City, Kansas. The hotel desk clerk banged the silver bell and shouted "Front!" and the bellman appeared to take us to our adjacent rooms. I wonder what I gave as a tip? I'm sure it was not enough. Nonetheless, the bellman was gracious and we settled in for a four-day stay, my sister and myself, the toasts of Manhattan from Kansas City, Kansas. We went to the Museum of Modern Art and the Guggenheim. We saw the show at Radio City Music Hall, we went to the Village Vanguard and heard Miles Davis, and we rode the subway late at night. It's a wonder we weren't mugged.

One memory of the trip was going to see *The Tonight Show with Johnny Carson* in studio 6B at Rockefeller Center. As I remember, we just showed up at NBC before the taping began and walked into the studio. It was smaller than I expected; studios always seem larger on television. About an hour into the ninety-minute show, Carson introduced a new comedian. The guy had never been on television before. Carson ignored him while he performed and chatted with Ed McMahon, smoking non-stop. The comedian was not invited to come over to the desk and chat with Carson. His name was Flip Wilson, and he, of course, went on to a huge career and is perhaps best known for creating the character of Geraldine... "The devil made me do it!"

On our last night in New York, my sister and I walked around the corner from the Astor Hotel to the Shubert Theater on West 44th Street. We bought two seats in the back of the balcony for $3.75 each. We saw *The Roar of the Greasepaint, the Smell of the Crowd,* which starred Cyril Richard and Orson Bean. It was pretty heavy stuff, or so it seemed at the time. Certainly not a light musical—it was serious theater. And it was my first Broadway show. I saved the *Playbill,* and I have saved every *Playbill* of every show I have seen ever since. I have over 1,600 *Playbills,* including some classic flops. Next to travel, theater is my greatest love.

My sister became a fine photographer and an avid sports enthusiast. She appreciates the great outdoors, and does not share my love of cities. She has made a wonderful life for herself with her husband Art, splitting their time between a lake cottage near Traverse City, Michigan in the summer and a winter home in Tucson, Arizona. But on that trip we were a handsome young couple, Mister and Miss Jones, from Kansas City seeing New York and staying at the Astor Hotel.

CHAPTER SEVEN

COLLEGE DAYS AND GLEE CLUB GRIEF

My sophomore year of college I left home. I moved from an almost rural setting on the outskirts of Kansas City, Kansas over the state line to Kanas City, Missouri. I had my own apartment in a ratty, turn-of-the-century building on Armour Boulevard in the center of Kansas City's sleazy nightlife district off Troost Avenue. Today it is poor and abandoned, but in the 1960s it was a wild, hopping place.

I lived across from the King Arthur nightclub and I would often wake up in the middle of the night to bottles being thrown and fistfights underway. The cops never seemed to be around, or if they were it was always after-the-fact. It was a free-for-all night after night. I played banjo in the clubs and I remember working a joint on Troost when a full-scale brawl broke out. The bandleader shouted out "The Beer Barrel Polka!" Why we always played the "Beer Barrel Polka" when a barroom brawl broke out is still a mystery to me.

Most of my bosses were part of the Kansas City mob. Kansas City, in those days, was a great live-music town but it was also a mob town, and the mobsters owned the clubs. I worked the clubs until closing and went to college during the day. I attended the University of Missouri-Kansas City. It had been, for decades, Kansas City University and had only recently been taken into the MU system. It was an urban school and most of the students lived in apartments near the campus.

I blossomed in college. I left behind high school life and never looked back. I made new friends, I became a part of school life, and I was really happy. I majored in speech with an emphasis in radio and television broadcasting. My diploma says "Bachelor of Arts—Speech." I am probably one of the few people to ever get a degree in speech who actually made a living giving speeches.

The Broadcasting Department was housed in a series of small buildings that had been built by William Rockhill Nelson, the publisher of *The Kansas City Star*. The equipment was hand-me-downs from local television stations. We had a public radio station, KCUR-FM 89.3, and I would spin vinyl on the air. Public Broadcasting, in those days, was all about classical music. It was long before *All Things Considered, Morning Edition, Fresh Air,* and the great programing NPR offers today.

Edie McClurg, who went on to a notable career as an actress in Hollywood, managed the station and would coach (in the way that a Marine Drill Sergeant coaches) us in the correct pronunciation of all those tongue-twisting foreign names, composers, conductors, soloists—and we had to get it right. And if you thought nobody was listening—make a mistake and the phone would ring off the hook. I can still hear Edie screaming "Saaaaa Saaah!!!!" (Saint-Saëns) into the booth as I mangled the composers name.

What I remember about radio was that it was lonely. You were in that booth by yourself and while you assumed there were people out there listening, it was a lonesome job. I needed more human contact, which is why I never seriously considered staying in radio.

Almost everyone has one teacher who makes a difference in his or her life. It might be an elementary teacher, or a high school instructor. For me it was a college professor named Gaylord Marr. Gaylord had an intense interest in his students. He took me under his wing—as he did so many students—and he was really the person who made the single most significant impact on my life, outside my parents. He was a taskmaster but he got results. He turned out dozens of successful broadcasters; people who went on to major careers. And he always had time for you: his home was open to all of the students and we virtually lived on the third floor office of his home.

Gaylord Marr was passionate about popular culture and collected everything from records to books and, in later years, VHS tapes, DVD's, and scads of magazines and newspapers. Every day at 5:30 p.m. (this was the Central Time Zone) he would tape Walter Cronkite and the CBS Evening News on ¼" audiotape using an old Wollensak reel-to-reel tape recorder. I would come over and help him with the cataloguing and sometimes

I did the taping. By the time I graduated, the house was chock-a-block with stuff. Eventually, it outgrew the house and the entire collection was donated to the university. Today the Marr Sound Archives at the University of Missouri-Kansas City is considered one of the most important sound archives in the country.

In 2012 I returned to my alma mater for commencement. It was nice to be back on campus and see how my university had grown. During some free time, I drove by Gaylord's old house on Locust Street in the Hyde Park neighborhood. I knew Gaylord had died a few years before. I wondered if his widow, Olga, was still alive and if she still lived in this rambling house. I went up to the door, rang the bell, and Olga opened the door. She looked at me and she said "Doug Jones!" I had not seen her in nearly forty years and yet somehow she knew who I was. She invited me into the house and we talked for hours.

Most of the audio collection had been moved to the Marr Sound Archives on campus, but there was still a staggering amount of stuff in the house. She took me outside to a large building Gaylord had built in the back of the property. It was filled with racks and racks of every medium imaginable. Videotapes, ¼" tape, magazines, newspapers, maps, books, cassette tapes, eight-track tapes! Every form of recording technology from the invention of the television onward was piled up in this room to the top of the twenty-foot ceiling. "Gaylord kept everything. Let me see, you graduated in what year? 1970?" she asked as she opened a big black filing cabinet. "Yes, here you are." She brought out several fat manila folders that were filled with every paper I had ever written for every class I had taken with Gaylord Marr—complete with his critiques—and boy, was he kind. I started looking through them and yikes! It's amazing I ever graduated. Nothing is quite as shocking as looking at your academic efforts forty years after the fact. But there they were, every single paper—and at the back of the files I came across something touching.

In 1970, after four years of college, I needed 120 credits to graduate. I had managed to get 119 and decided to fill out the last one by taking Glee Club for a single 1-hour credit. This seemed easy enough, certainly no academic challenge. But the professor was a jerk. I was working every night playing banjo, and I had a standing contract to play at the Levee, a nightclub that still exists in Kansas City. The Glee Club professor announced that we were going to do a concert on such and such date at some auditorium. It was a Saturday night and I knew I had to work. I pleaded with him to be excused from the concert but he would have none of it. If I didn't show up at the concert, I would flunk. I had a union contract I had to fulfill. I didn't do the concert, I played my gig at the Levee, and I flunked Glee Club.

So there I was, one month before commencement, with 119 credits. I wasn't going to graduate. I went to Gaylord in a panic. He told me to come up with a proposal and he would create a one-credit, special-study class, for me alone. I wrote a long research paper on the travelogue business. He gave me an A, I got my 1-hour credit and I graduated in June of 1970.

And so here I was in Gaylord's storage building, his ghost no doubt standing by, in May of 2012 pulling my paper on the travelogue business out of a filing cabinet. Olga let me keep it. It was actually pretty good; it detailed what the travelogue business was like in 1970, outlined my own career blueprint, and it allowed me to graduate—after I achieved the distinct honor of being the only person in the history of the University of Missouri-Kansas City to *flunk Glee Club*!

Graduation day at the University of Missouri-Kansas City. I earned a diploma in radio and television broadcasting. I would leave for Paris the very next day. The picture is taken under the same sycamore tree in my parent's backyard that I was holding onto in an earlier picture at the age of two. 1970.

CHAPTER EIGHT

MY FIRST FILM CAMERA—THE SUPER 8

Inspired by Curtis Nagel's presentation at the Plaza Theater, I was determined to begin my career making travelogues. The fact that I knew nothing—and I mean nothing—about filmmaking didn't occur to me to be an obstacle. I would learn, and I did—slowly.

First, I needed a camera. Professional travelogues were made with 16mm cameras using huge amounts of 16mm film. I decided to start small so I bought a Super 8mm motion picture camera at the Katz Drugstore at 40th and Main. I bought a few rolls of film and took some practice shots around Kansas City. I decided I knew enough to make a film, so off I went to Portugal. The glory of that TWA pass. My father lent me his old wooden tripod. I was smart enough to know, even then, that steady shots were essential. Nobody wants to watch handheld movies.

Lisbon was lovely. It was sunny and warm and the Portuguese are friendly, hospitable people. I traveled all over the country by train and shot everything that I thought was worthwhile—or as much of everything that I thought was worthwhile that I could get onto 10 rolls of film. I was careful to count out the seconds as the camera rolled. Film was—and still is—very expensive. You did not just let the camera roll. You would count, 1-2-3-4-5-6-7 and then you stopped unless something really important was going on in the scene. Even after I started shooting digital later in my career, when film cost was no longer an issue, I still used the same technique. It made editing easier. Having too much material can almost be as bad as having too little. Know what you what, shoot it right, and don't overshoot everything.

I had no training. I read books, I asked questions, I picked up tips, but I was largely a self-taught filmmaker. Fortunately, I had a good eye. Having a good eye is something you don't learn. You either have it or you don't. You can refine it and improve it, but if you don't have a good eye for framing, composition, following motion, and capturing a shot, you are unlikely to ever be a great cinematographer.

Something I learned early on was the importance of light. Many people will tell you that composition is the most important element of photography. I would argue that is it light. Gilbert Grosvenor, president of the National Geographic Society, wrote years ago that you could shoot the greatest landscapes of the world under cloudy, dull light conditions and the shots would look drab no matter how important the subject matter was. Conversely, you could frame a red stop sign against a white grain elevator on a brilliant blue-sky day with puffy white clouds and strong front lighting and a simple subject would come to life because the light was right. I can't over-emphasize the importance of light and photography. Rembrandt knew it as a painter and great filmmakers know it when they look through the viewfinder.

I loved Portugal. I went to Sintra, a charming town filled with castles and palaces. I took a train to Nazare, a fishing village on the Atlantic Coast. Portugal was poor in the late 60's. It was a bit ramshackled, and when I went back in 2012, I found little had changed. It was charming as ever; a little rundown, but still one of my favorite destinations. Lisbon is like San Francisco, built on steep hills, a bridge that looks like the Golden Gate, trams that wander up and down the slopes like the cable cars, panhandlers, an occasional drug dealer, and backpackers (today's equivalent of 1970s "hippies") everywhere.

I shot the Belém Tower, the St. George Castle, men mending fishing nets, women baking bread, priests saying mass. I was starting to get a sense of what was needed to make a well-rounded film. You have to have people. Without people, travel films are pointless records of monuments and scenery. People are always what make any film come alive.

I returned to Kansas City and I sent the film in for processing. I have to mention what a nerve-racking experience this always was. Later as a professional I would go off on a shoot, sometimes with as much as 30,000 feet of 16mm film. I would shoot roll after roll and have no idea if I was getting anything at all. The camera could have a stuck shutter; there could be a hair

MY FIRST FILM CAMERA—THE SUPER 8

in the gate, an unforeseen bit of grit in the film path. You could come back and process the film and have nothing, or scratched film, or thousands of feet of footage with a wiggly hair running across the screen. Hollywood dealt with the problem by processing the film as dailies. Even on location, Hollywood filmmakers would send the film back to Los Angeles for overnight processing. But when I was on a ship, somewhere in the world, shooting a film, or on location in an obscure far-off country, this was not an option. Over my long career shooting nearly 500,000 feet of film, I had remarkably few problems. There would occasionally be a defective roll of film from Kodak or a reel that got too much light exposure in loading, but there were few serious issues. But that doesn't mean I didn't worry a lot.

So there I was back in Kansas City with ten measly rolls of Super 8mm film on Portugal. I had a crude little editing setup and a Super 8mm projector. Splices were made with tape. I cut the film—and this is a *huge* difference between then and now. With today's digital editing, you can't make mistakes because everything can be undone. When you cut film there could be *no* mistakes. Once that film was cut, you couldn't put it back together. You learned to be very careful with those scissors.

Somehow I managed to wrangle this footage into a twenty-minute film. I probably used 80% of what I shot. I wrote a script, recorded a music track on an old Weber tape recorder, and voilà! I had my first travelogue. It had to have been terrible. I haven't seen it since I made it. I am tempted to have it transferred to digital but I'm afraid I would die of shame that, on the basis of this amateur effort, I thought I was ready for the big time.

With the Portugal film in the can, I was ready to go all in. This meant buying a 16mm camera. In those days, the main camera in use was the Bolex. They were marvels of Swiss engineering: nearly indestructible and machined to perfection. I decided to buy an H-16 Rex 5 with an 18-86mm Vario-Switar zoom lens. The zoom lens was a relatively new thing for motion picture cameras.

So did I buy my camera at the local camera shop? No, I got on a TWA flight and flew to Zurich. I knew I could get the camera cheaper in Switzerland. How I figured out which camera shop to go to, I don't recall, but it was near the main railway station. The man was very nice and he sold me the camera and an aluminum Bolex tripod for a little over $500. I can pin point the date exactly. It was June 6, 1968. The reason I remember this is that I was eating breakfast in a restaurant on the Bahnhofstrasse and a man opposite me was reading a newspaper. On the cover was a picture of Robert Kennedy and the word "Tote." I looked at the man, confused, and he looked back and just said one word. "Dead." I was stunned. Like many young people, I viewed RFK with great idealism. His assassination, coming so soon after Martin Luther King's, was shocking. The assassination of Dr. Martin Luther King, the riots, Bobby Kennedy's assassination, the Democratic Convention in Chicago free-for-all, the dissatisfaction over the Vietnam war—1968 was a pivotal year in America. It was a year that changed who we were.

Back in Kansas City, I bought a few rolls of 16mm Kodak film which was much more expensive than Super 8mm. I bought editing equipment, rewinds, two thousand foot metal reels, a hot splicer, a Moviescope to view the footage, and a 16mm projector. I became familiar with all that equipment and soon I was ready to go out and actually shoot my first feature-length travelogue. I chose Belgium. Why? I truly do not know. TWA didn't even fly there. It was hardly a "hot" topic. It wasn't like travelogue promoters were clambering for the subject. The reasons behind the choice are lost in the gaps of my memory, like the missing eighteen minutes on the Watergate tapes. But I had decided on the topic and off I went. It was the summer of 1968. I turned twenty-one while I was shooting the film.

CHAPTER NINE

FILMING BELGIUM

Of all my travel memories you would think that my first big travelogue shoot would be among the strongest. It is not. Maybe I want to forget. Maybe I am still shocked that I could go off with so little money, so little knowledge, so little practical skill, and actually attempt to make a film that people would pay to see.

I was still at UMKC and it was between my sophomore and junior years. I had purchased my Bolex camera in the spring and now I had to come up with money to buy film. I had a 16-foot water skiing boat that I sold for $1,500. That bought me two cases of 16mm Kodachrome film—10,000 feet. A finished ninety-minute film was about 3,000 feet, which meant I was shooting 3:1, an incredibly optimistic shooting ratio for someone who had no idea what he was doing.

I was too young to rent a car so my father went along to help me get wheels. We flew from Kansas City to New York then on to Paris. In Paris we changed planes and flew Sabena to Brussels. We arrived very late at night and went to some cheap hotel off the Grande Place. It was up four flights of stairs and dreary beyond words. My dad and I decided we would sleep there that night and move on the next day, which we did. My father's comment was "Your mother would have a fit if she could see this."

The next day we got up, rented a car, and took off to Lier, a town not far from Brussels. It had a big town hall (as did every city in Belgium), a colorful astronomical clock, and a bunch of ramparts and castle walls. I started shooting.

Electric eyes were a new feature on cameras in the late 1960s. It's fortunate that my Bolex had one because I knew so little about photography,

I would have had trouble setting the f-stops. God only knows what images I would have come back with. By changing the f-stop, you increase or decrease the amount of light entering the lens. Squint your eyes and then open them. The f-stop setting does something similar. Eventually, I learned and I became adept at eyeballing the light and determining the correct f-stop setting. Today's digital cameras are a maze of complexity with their endless settings. On the old 16mm film cameras, it was very simple: focus and f-stop. That was all there was to set. The shutter speed was preset.

The only other variable was the "speed" of the film. I shot my first film on Kodachrome II. Kodachrome II had a "speed" of 25 ASA for daylight. If you used a filter to shoot interior scenes (artificial light has a different color temperature and required a filter) the "speed" went down to 16 ASA. These are very low film speeds, which meant you had to have a lot of light. Today digital cameras will shoot almost in the dark, but when I started shooting, the film stocks required a lot of light. I carried lights, aluminum stands, a tangle of electrical cables, and 220 voltage conversion boxes for shooting interiors. It was all clumsy and difficult to use, particularly working alone.

When I started, 16mm cameras were fairly large. If I set my Bolex camera up on my tripod, everyone knew I was a professional (or at least trying to be one). Filmmakers today can truly be a "fly on the wall" and get everything they need with no one even aware they are around.

From Lier, my dad and I drove to Antwerp where we spent two nights. I shot the cathedral, the Peter Paul Rubens House, many paintings, lots of gardens, and the general sights of the city. We went on to Ghent and Bruges. It didn't rain much, which is unusual for Belgium, so I got most of my footage under sunny skies. I shot a canal trip in Bruges, filmed some of the old master paintings, the Van Eycks, and the Memlings. We climbed to the top of the town belfry, where the carillon operator was happy to let me bang around on the levers, making a racket that boomed out over Bruges. I was trying to play "Heart and Soul" on a 16th century carillon. I have a vague memory that the bell keeper was drunk. And it was noon.

We ate a lot of *moules* (mussels) and a lot of *potage* (soup)—and an awful lot of *frites* (French fries). Frites seemed to be the staple of the Belgian diet. They were everywhere. Long before food trucks became the rage in America, Belgians were selling frites in paper cones out of rolling vans. The soup was always served in a tureen. You could ladle out as much as you could eat. It was a cheap way to fill your stomach. We went on to the North

Sea coast towns, Zee Bruges and Oostende, and then drove down to Ypres. Surrounding Ypres were lots of battlefields and war memorials. It was in the fields of Flanders that the worst battles of World War I were fought.

And it was there that I learned a valuable lesson. I had some general outline of how the film was going to flow, but I hadn't developed topic organizational skills and I was relying more on the "we go here, we go there…" school of shooting travelogues. But I was certain of one thing; that I was going to finish the film with a visual comment surrounding the poem *In Flanders Fields*.

I filmed cemeteries, gravestones, and the red poppies waving in the wind. I mixed it all together and closed the film with a montage and a recitation of the John McCrae poem. I still know it by heart.

> *In Flanders fields the poppies blow*
> *Between the crosses, row on row,*
> *That mark our place; and in the sky*
> *The larks, still bravely singing, fly*
> *Scarce heard amid the guns below.*
>
> *We are the Dead. Short days ago*
> *We lived, felt dawn, saw sunset glow,*
> *Loved and were loved, and now we lie*
> *In Flanders fields.*
>
> *Take up our quarrel with the foe:*
> *To you from failing hands we throw*
> *the torch; be yours to hold it high.*
> *If ye break faith with us who die*
> *We shall not sleep, though poppies grow*
> *In Flanders fields.*

I returned to Kansas City and began cutting the film from my meager collection of useable footage. I tried to get advice from other people in the travelogue field. Everyone was an expert on everything and, of course, every one of the travelogue filmmakers thought his or her way was the *only* right way to do anything. It was an arrogant lot of independent filmmakers and it was a challenge to maintain my own voice and vision.

All the speakers and all of the agents said the same thing. Kill the ending. It's depressing. People who come to travelogues are old and they don't want to be reminded of death. Axe it. But I didn't. I held my ground and kept the ending. It was the right decision. Looking back the movie was really pretty dreadful. It was filled with clichés, lots of religious festivals (the Belgians loved to trot out statues and parade them solemnly through the streets), plenty of castles and medieval towers, lots of religious art, a lacemaking school, glass blowing, and crystal cutting. But I had my ending. It was about the awfulness of war and the price young men paid. The images of the poppies waving in front of the tombstones, the canons on a hill overlook fields where horrific battles had been fought; it was all very sobering.

The first time I showed the film in public in Willow Grove, Pennsylvania, the audience was deeply moved as the film faded to black over a lonely poppy waving on the screen. I had learned how to manipulate the audience's emotions. And I learned that you could have eighty-five minutes of forgettable material, but if your last five minutes were good, that's all anyone would remember.

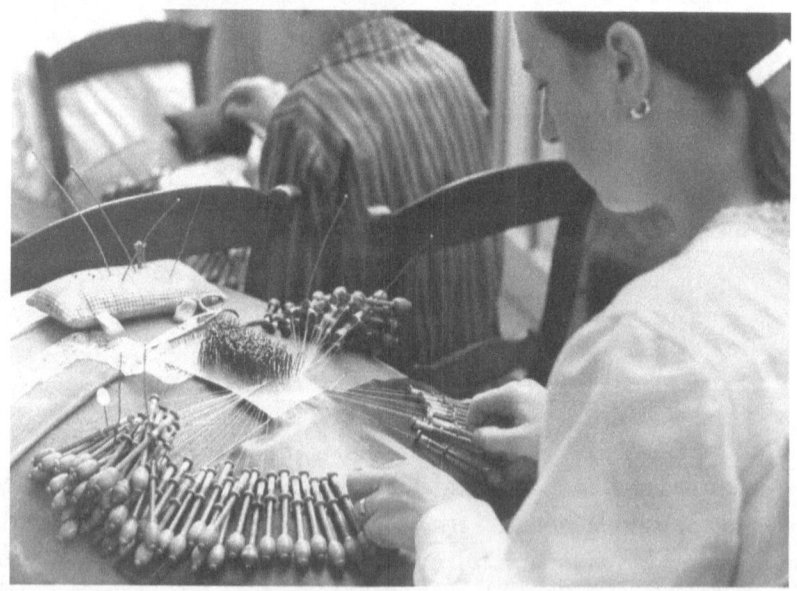

Lacemaking in Belgium. I was shooting Kodachrome II 16 mm film using a Bolex Rex-5. 1968.

Throughout my career, I started my filmmaking projects by deciding at the beginning of the research what the ending would be. The ending was vital. If I could make the ending great, I could build the rest of the film backwards from that point. I finished *Royal London* with a tribute to Winston Churchill and the Battle of Britain, *Sailing Down to Rio on the Queen Mary 2* with the Carnaval parades, *Great Cities of Europe* with the lights of Paris on a full moon night, and *New York City–Broadway USA* with the Statue of Liberty and haunting images of immigrants on Ellis Island. The audience will forgive a lot if you leave them with a cherished moment at the end. And thank God, because that first film on Belgium was pretty grim.

I was, of course, unaware of this fact until much later. I thought it was the best movie in the world. And since I had to stand on stage and narrate the film live, my confidence in the film was essential. I would walk out onto the center of the stage and basically imply "Listen up, you are about to see something great." Self-confidence is a requirement for anyone who walks onto a stage. The people seated in the theater had not only paid money to see my film and hear what I had to say, but they had given me their most valuable commodity: their time. Over my career, nearly four million people gave up two hours of their time to see my movies and hear what I had to say. I never forgot that fact.

Meanwhile, my father had returned to Kansas City to his job at TWA. I stayed on in Belgium continuing to work. Quite by chance, in a restaurant off the Grande Place in Brussels, I met a man named John Strong. John was an established travelogue producer and he was making a film on Belgium as well. He took me under his wing—well sort of—in the way a condor might protect a small animal it was about to consume. We did a lot of things together, shot side-by-side sometimes, and became friends—or so I thought.

Once I had the film edited, I tried to get some traction in the travelogue business. I went to see a filmmaker named James Metcalf who was showing a film on the Virgin Islands at the Music Hall in Kansas City. I went up to him afterward, introduced myself, and told him about my film. I don't remember the exact chain of events, but I ended up flying to Chicago and meeting him at an auditorium in Villa Park, Illinois. He finished his show that night at 10:00 p.m. and we went to the Dupage County Airport where Jim's Cessna 172 was parked. He flew me to his home in Dowagiac, Michigan. It was my first time in a private plane. Jim flew his plane to all of his shows. In those days, as speakers, we had to wear tuxedos on stage. Jim hated wasting time so he would leave the stage in his tux, bum a ride to the airport, and take off. *AOPA Magazine* (The Aircraft Owners and Pilots Association) gave him an award for logging the most hours flying an airplane in a tuxedo!

I could never have imagined how that short forty-minute hop on a winter night across the south end of Lake Michigan would affect me. I would not get my pilot's license for another twenty years, but once I had it, my life changed. Ultimately, I flew my Cessna 310 to every state in the continental USA showing my films. I logged 2,900 flight hours and saw America from a front row seat at 14,000 feet. (I still have a Cessna 310 as of this writing and I still fly coat-to-coast by myself).

But that would be years away. For the moment, the goal was for Jim to get my Belgium film reedited into something showable. He was like a taskmaster yelling at me to "cut that out, you don't need anymore freakin' flowers!" You have to remember that "cutting it out" was very literal: you had to physically cut the film and splice it together. Cuts were final. We were shooting and showing original Kodachrome—not a print. The reason was that original Kodachrome was gorgeous on the screen; the prints made from it were not.

Jim helped me recut the film and he pushed hard to get a man named Cecil Houghton to book me. Cecil ran a company called Ralph Windoes Travelogues. They were based in Grand Rapids, Michigan and they held the keys to the kingdom: 6,000 shows scattered across the country. It was where all the travelogue people started; it was boot camp for film lecturers. Jim arranged for me to preview my film *Belgian Panorama* for Cecil Houghton so I flew to Grand Rapids. John Strong, who I had not seen since Belgium, happened to be in town. John had wasted so much of his time in Belgium that he had not finished his film. He purported to be interested in helping me and extended a hand of friendship and assistance. The next day John took me to Cecil's office on the 13th floor of the McKay Tower in downtown Grand Rapids. I showed the film, all ninety minutes of it, to Cecil and the office staff. Afterward, Cecil went into a tirade of criticism. Cecil was a combination of P.T. Barnum, Napoleon, and Hitler. He was a tyrant, but he was passionate about travelogues and had built his business into a small empire. After degrading me in front of the office staff, he finished by saying "But in spite of all of that, we will hire you for next

Editing *Belgian Panorama* at Jim Metcalf's house in Dowagiac, Michigan. Notice the white glove on the left hand holding the film. Digital filmmakers don't have to worry about fingerprints when they edit. 1969.

Jim Metcalf, my early champion, getting ready to leave on his travelogue lecture tour in his Cessna. Twenty years later I would be doing the same thing in my own plane. 1970.

season." I was elated and left Grand Rapids on a cloud. I was being hired by Windoes Travelogues! I was on my way.

And then a week later I got a letter. It was short and succinct.

We are withdrawing our offer of employment for the 1970-1971 season.

Sincerely,

Cecil Houghton,

President,
Ralph Windoes Travelogues.

I was dumbfounded; I was in shock, what had happened?

The answer would not come out for twenty years. Two decades later, I was in my apartment on West End Avenue in New York. The doorman rang my apartment and said a man named John Strong was in the lobby to see me. Bewildered, I told the doorman to send him up. John walked into my apartment—I had not seen him since that day in Grand Rapids—and plopped himself down on the sofa. He proceeded to tell me he had sabotaged me with Windoes by revealing a secret he knew about me, because he was afraid I would get all of his Belgium film showings since he had not finished his film on time. He then stood up and left. The whole encounter lasted about thirty minutes. I am still as dumbfounded today as I was when he showed up in 1988. I always wondered if he was in a twelve-step program and trying to do the "make amends" step. If so, he did not act particularly remorseful about sabotaging the budding career of a twenty-one-year-old.

But oddly enough it was a blessing in disguise because instead of starting at the bottom, and Windoes Travelogues was the bottom; long drives, small towns, low fees, lots of shows, I actually started at the top.

Come... See this exciting and unusual view of Belgium

BELGIUM, PANORAMA

Presented in person by a bright new personality in the travel field

Doug Jones

Why Belgium? Because a trip to Belgium is like a grand tour of the continent. In 90 minutes Doug Jones shows you why Belgium is really "Europe in Minature" as he takes you on an exciting, historical journey that looks at this country from the beginning of the middle ages into tomorrow. You will stroll through medieval castles, meet the King and Queen of Belgium, learn how to operate a windmill, visit a crystal factory, see the "Virga Jesse" Festival — held once every seven years, visit the battlefields of Flanders "where poppies grow"... along with much more!

3 Shows – 2 Nights for the Entire Family
TONIGHT at 7:30 p.m.
and SATURDAY at 6:45 p.m. & 9 p.m.
Central High School Auditorium

A newspaper ad from the *Kalamazoo Gazette* for one of my first showings of *Belgian Panorama*. They got the title slightly wrong but they described me as "a bright new personality in the travel field"—they should have added "as green as grass." 1969.

CHAPTER TEN

MY BIG BREAK IN THE TRAVELOGUE BUSINESS

Windoes Travelogues fired me before I had even gotten started. Anyone familiar with the travelogue business in those days would have said, "get that banjo back out, you're going to need it."

Everyone new to the business started at Windoes Travelogues. You did 150-175 shows a year, driving to the dates, hauling a projector, traveling great distances, and working in mostly small towns. Their business model was using travelogue series as service club fundraisers. The local Kiwanis Club would sponsor a travelogue series of six programs, each presented by a different speaker on a different topic. The Kiwanians would sell the tickets, rent the auditorium, pay the speakers, and hopefully there would be a profit at the end of the season to fund community projects. Some of these service club travelogue series were very large. The Downtown Grand Rapids Kiwanis Club ran a travelogue series at the Civic Auditorium and they had five performances of each show in a large 3,000 seat theater and generally the shows were full.

Working for Windoes was like a training camp. You endured a lot. The goal was to rise out of the Windoes circuit, get an agent, and get booked on the big independent travelogue shows that were presented, often as profit ventures, in large auditoriums. In the 1960s, many of these privately operated travelogue series had grown into sizeable operations.

About the time I arrived on the scene, the major speakers were all complaining that they were not being paid enough (and they probably weren't). A group of travelogue speakers got together and formed an organization: The Film Lecturers Association (FLA). It was by invitation only and it represented the most important names in the business. There were about thirty members. Some people felt the organization was aloof. It was true that FLA represented the best talent and they did not want the minor players. The main purpose of forming the group was to negotiate with the big sponsors and try to raise the speaking fees.

The travelogue sponsors, of course, hated the speakers for forming this organization and having the audacity to want more money. So the travelogue sponsors formed their own organization called The Professional Travel Film Sponsor Association (PTFSA). It was made up of about twenty-five members. They were a combination of people who ran shows for large institutions (the Chicago Geographic Society, the Carnegie Institute in Pittsburgh, the Denver Museum, Michigan State University) and the private for-profit promoters who often booked other musical attractions and theatrical events. All of these people had a vested interest in putting a stake in the heart of the speakers and their new organization.

So while the Film Lecturers Association was having its meeting in Chicago in November of 1969, the newly formed travelogue sponsors association decided to meet in Detroit. At their first meeting they solicited new travel filmmakers to come and show samples of their wares. They did need new talent, but what they really needed was to be able to go the Film Lecturers Association and say, "See, we can get speakers who aren't members of your price-fixing organization."

Enter me.

Word somehow filtered down that there was going to be this meeting. I managed to get on a plane to Detroit and arrived on Sunday afternoon, just as this august group was to begin its first new filmmaker previews. There were only three new travelogue producers who had heard about this. I was fortunate that I was last and the first two were not very good. I showed fifteen minutes of my *Belgian Panorama* film. I had a lot of enthusiasm, and I was young, and I was new—and I would probably work cheap.

After I did my presentation I was surrounded by sponsors, each lauding their own importance and the importance of the series they represented. The speakers were an egomaniacal bunch, but the big sponsors were just as bad, if not worse. Several people chatted me up at the same time. In the midst of this crush, a man tapped me on the shoulder. I turned and he handed me his card. He didn't say a word. I put the card in my pocket and resumed my conversation with the people surrounding me. Later, back in my hotel room, I looked at the card. It said "A.K. Gee World Adventure Tours, Winnipeg, Manitoba." I had no idea who this was but I would soon learn.

A.K. "Bill" Gee ran the World Adventure Tours travelogue series across Western Canada. His family had gotten their start promoting classical music concerts. Toscanini, The Vienna Boy's Choir, Rubenstein, Horowitz, they all came to Winnipeg under the banner of A.K. Gee. He was the Sol Hurok of Western Canada. The Gees were a lively bunch. Bill had a son named Bruce who would eventually take over the business with his sister Nancy. Bill's brother Ed—"Uncle Ed"—introduced the shows and was more often than not, plastered when he walked on stage. Bill himself was prone to hitting the bottle.

They operated World Adventure Tours in the biggest auditoriums of Western Canada with multiple performances in each hall; the Centennial Concert Halls in Winnipeg and Saskatoon, the Jubilee Auditoriums in Edmonton and Calgary, the Queen Elizabeth Theater in Vancouver and the Pantages Theater in Victoria. It was quite a run. They had close to 23,000 subscribers across four provinces.

After the Detroit meeting, I returned to Kansas City and a couple of weeks later I got a letter and a contract from Bill Gee to do the World Adventure Tour series with my film *Belgian Panorama*. It was the single biggest series and largest travelogue prize in all of North America and it was my very first contract. I was paid $5,000 for seventeen shows. It was probably a lot less than he was paying the established speakers but for me it was a fortune, and, oh by the way, it was for the following season in *February!*

I still remember getting off of that plane in Winnipeg in February of 1972. I had never been that cold in my life. The corner of Portage and Main Street in Winnipeg is called the coldest street corner on earth for good reason. Taxis used propane and the trunks reeked of the fumes. Their windows had plastic bubble pieces to help the driver see out the back and side. Standard defrosting did little in this cold. Every car had a heating element that went down the dipstick and attached to an electrical outlet to keep the engine block from freezing at night. It felt like I had arrived to perform at the North Pole.

"Uncle Ed" met me at the airport reeking of alcohol. I let him drive me to the hotel that day, but on another tour two years later he was so loaded I had to take the keys and drive myself to the hotel and send him home in a cab.

The following day I was to do two shows, the first at 6:00 p.m., and the second at 8:30. But before I could go to the auditorium to do the sound and film checks, I had to go to the censor. Canada would not allow any film to be shown that was not cleared by the censor. The entire film was screened before the man stamped the fiber case with "Approved for All Audiences." From there I took a cab to the stage door and met the projectionist, the soundmen, and the lighting people. They were professionals and I have good memories of the crews. I went back many times and the crews became like family.

The audiences were loyal beyond words. They would let nothing stop them from showing up. In the dead of winter, in a place like Winnipeg, there wasn't a lot to do. Having an excuse to get out of the house and into a nice auditorium for a couple hours was probably more the reason for the success of the World Adventure Tours than an undying interest by the audience in travel movies.

Many years later, I was appearing in Winnipeg in January with *The Great World Cruise of the QE2* and Nancy Gee came backstage to tell me about a phone call she had just received. A woman had called the box office and said that her husband had died. She was wondering if it was OK to bring a neighbor and use her husband's season ticket. Nancy said of course it was OK; the ticket could be used by anyone. The woman said, "Oh thank you. I appreciate that. But we may be a little late because we are still waiting for the funeral home to pick up the body." Now *that* is a loyal season ticket subscriber.

After the shows in Winnipeg, I boarded a flight to Saskatoon. I stayed at the Bessborough Hotel and did my shows before moving on to Edmonton the next day. The flight was delayed due to the weather, but eventually it took off. We had to circle Edmonton for some time while the runway was cleared of snow. I was becoming more nervous by the minute. I had two shows that night at the Jubilee Auditorium. 3,000 seats and both shows were nearly sold out.

Finally, the plane landed around 5:45 p.m. The first show was at six o'clock—in fifteen minutes. There wasn't a taxi in sight, so I wildly flagged down a pickup truck. I opened the door, jumped in, and told the poor dazed Alberta man that I had to get to the Jubilee Auditorium ASAP! In the United States I probably would have been thrown out of the truck, but this man, sensing my franticness, managed to get through the snow filled streets and deposit me at the front door of the Jubilee Auditorium at exactly 6:00 p.m.

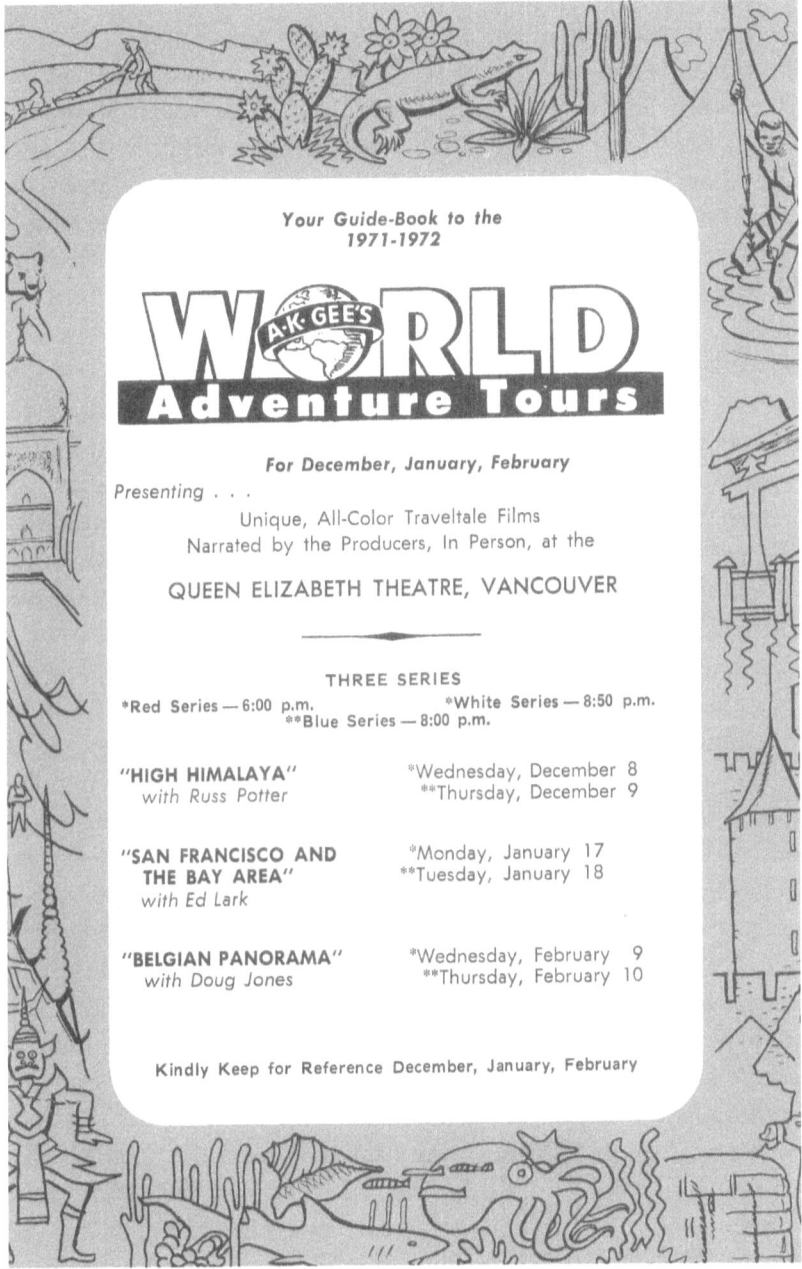

A program from the Queen Elizabeth Theatre in Vancouver for my first appearance with *Belgian Panorama* on the A.K. Gee World Adventure Tours series of Western Canada. I was there on February 9th and 10th. I had just come from ten shows on the other side of the Rockies starting in Winnipeg. I still shiver thinking about the cold. 1972.

I ran in the front door. A man on stage was saying, "Ladies and Gentleman our speaker is not here. We have not heard from him, we have no idea where he is so unfortunately, we must..." I knew there was no time. This was not a moment to be subtle. So I shouted from the back of the house "Stop! I'm here!" The entire audience turned around and stared. You could hear a pin drop. I slowly started trudging down the aisle with my film in hand and slowly the applause started. The audience cheered and I milked it for all it was worth. I did two shows back-to-back and finally got to my hotel room exhausted at 11:30 p.m. The next morning, it was on to Calgary. There wasn't a moment to catch your breath.

From Calgary I flew over the Rockies to Vancouver and the temperatures climbed dramatically. It was still February, but a chilly rain will beat minus twenty degrees any day. In Vancouver I worked at the Queen Elizabeth Theater and the next day I took the BC Ferry to Vancouver Island and traveled on to the Victoria Pantages for the last shows of the run.

I did the Gee series sixteen times. I have great memories of those huge audiences and the friendliness of Canadians. But they were also willing to speak up. Once, I was showing my film *New York City–Broadway USA* in Vancouver at the Queen Elizabeth Theater. It was at the beginning of the film and I was talking about the history of New York. I said "The English controlled New York for 118 years..." and a woman in middle of the orchestra shouted out, as loud as she could, "British, not English, you fool... British!" That was not a mistake I ever made again.

So I was off and running. I had done the Gee series. I was getting bookings for other big auditoriums and the future was looking bright. Everyone else had an agent, but I managed to negotiate the contracts and create my schedule without representation. Everyone assumed it was because I didn't want to pay commissions. Actually, it had little to do with the commissions. I wanted control over my schedule. I managed to work steadily for almost my entire career without a booking agent. Ironically, as the travelogue business was winding down, I went back to where I had originally been fired and worked for Windoes Travelogues in the final years of my career.

Before doing the Gee series in Canada, in my last year of college I had seven lecture dates with *Belgian Panorama*. They were the result of a speaker falling ill, getting in a car wreck, or some other unfortunate incident. In those days, the established speakers were booked solid so there weren't a lot of people to call on when an emergency occurred. But I was available, ready, willing, and (sort of) able. My very first show was in Willow Grove, Pennsylvania outside of Philadelphia. Sasha Schemel, who was an adventurer who made films about tigers and lions in the wild—and had the scars to prove it—fell ill. He was in his late 80s, and he never returned to the stage. He died shortly afterward. Cecil Houghton, who had so succinctly dismissed me and had sworn I would never work for Windoes Travelogues, was in a bind. He had two dates of Sasha's that he could not get filled. But Cecil was pragmatic. He needed a speaker fast. He called me and asked if I could do the shows, and I got on the first plane to Philadelphia.

I arrived a day early. I was still flying standby on my TWA pass and I didn't want to risk missing the shows. I had little money so I checked into the Philadelphia YMCA. I was aware that there was a large travelogue series at the Academy of Music on Broad Street run by the Philadelphia Geographical Society so I decided to drop into their offices, unannounced, and introduce myself. A woman named Emily Rosser was the executive secretary. She ran the office and oversaw the organization, the travelogue series, and the sale of the twenty-five hundred memberships. There were no single ticket sales; you bought the whole package with a membership or you didn't go.

I told her I was in town to show my film *Belgian Panorama* the following evening in Willow Grove. It was snowing like crazy that day. The city was starting to grind to a halt. She became wide-eyed. "You have a film on Belgium?" I soon learned they had a program that night with a filmmaker named Russ Potter who was scheduled to show his film *Belgium of the Masters* but Russ was stranded someplace waiting for a plane to take off. She had a backup. She said, "Where are you staying?" Being too embarrassed to say the Y, I fumbled and said "The Hilton." I can still remember her scowl and the tone of her voice as she stared at me and said "There's no Hilton in Philadelphia!" Rule number one; know your facts before you lie. I had to fess up. She didn't seem too bothered. She told me to be at the Academy of Music at 6:30 and to bring my film. I went back to the YMCA and tried to take a nap but I was too excited about the possibility of being Ruby Keller in *42nd Street*. "...You're going out there a kid but you're coming back a star!"

I showed up at 6:30 p.m. Russ Potter wasn't there. I gave my film to the projectionist, but at about ten minutes to 8:00 p.m., Russ came flying in the stage door. He had made it and I was, like Cinderella, back in the pumpkin. I did stay for his show. Russ was a fine filmmaker and his take on Belgium focused around the great master painters.

And the hall! The Academy of Music on Broad Street in Philadelphia is one of the most beautiful horseshoe-shaped theaters in America. Built in the 1850s, it was still home to the Philadelphia Orchestra. The house was full that night. Everyone was well dressed. Being a member of the Philadelphia Geographical Society was, at the time, a mark of social standing in the city.

Russ finished his program and I met him backstage afterward. He thanked me for being on standby. We later became friends. His wife Maggie Potter ran the World Geographic Society shows at the Wilshire Ebell in Los Angeles. I would work for Maggie many times over the years.

Three years after I sat eagerly in the Academy of Music that night waiting for Russ Potter to not show up, I returned to Philadelphia and did the first of what would be fourteen performances in that hall. The first film I showed there was *Paris of the Parisians.*

And, oh, by the way, I made it out to Willow Grove the next day and did my *Belgian Panorama* show, and people liked it. I went on to Erie, Pennsylvania, then returned to Kansas City. The next month I worked for the Ad-Sell League at Peony Park in Omaha and the Highland Park Woman's Club outside of Chicago. And I also did shows that season in DeKalb and Canton, Illinois and a show at Emporia State Teachers College in Emporia, Kansas. And for each of the shows I was paid two hundred dollars. Not bad for a kid in his last year of college.

It was this meeting of the Film Lecturers Association in Chicago in 1969 that indirectly got me my first job. FLA represented the top talent in the field. This group photograph includes spouses and agents as well as filmmakers. From left to right: Top row; Ruth Butler, Curt Nagel, Dr. Gerald Hooper, Ed Lark, Stan Midgley, Clay Francisco, Bob Davis, Arthur Twoomey. Center row; Bob Longe, Don Parker, Phil Walker, Alfred Wolff, Jeanne Porterfield, Lisa Chickering, Don Cooper, Eric Pavel, Constance Midgley. Front row; Bunny Kamen Longe, Jim Metcalf, Thayer Soule, Willis Butler, Ken Richer, Hjordis Kittle Parker, Nicole Smith, Maita Pavel.

CHAPTER ELEVEN

GRADUATION AND THE DREADED DRAFT

So I was off and running with *Belgian Panorama*. But to have a successful career in travelogues you had to constantly be producing new films. It was time to decide on my next topic. I chose Paris, which remains one of my favorite places on earth. If I could have improved my French I would have stayed and never come back. But sadly, for all my world travel, I am not a gifted linguist. I have tried. Believe me, I have tried.

I had made my film on Belgium while I was still at university. I graduated two years later (with no help from the Glee Club) and I left the following morning, after commencement, heading to Paris to make *Paris of the Parisians*.

But there were a couple of snags I would have to deal with first.

Graduation marked the end of two very big things in my life. One was my Trans World Airlines pass. Once I was no longer a student, it was over. From here on out I would be paying my way to fly TWA.

The other more problematic issue was the end of my student deferment from the draft. The Vietnam War was raging at its height and the draft was in effect. Troop requirements increased by the month and by June of 1970, when I graduated, they were drafting everyone except women and children. I did not want to go to Vietnam. I had two friends come back in body bags. I saw no point to the war (and ultimately neither did President Gerald Ford). We were told it was our last chance to stop the spread of Communism, to disrupt the domino effect. The end result was tragic; thousands of American and Vietnamese lives lost, and little accomplished—certainly none of the U.S. goals. But in 1970 our government was embroiled and needed able-bodied men. So I used my trump card: I told them I was gay.

This is not something I did lightly. I had come to realize this about myself sometime after I entered college. By the time I was a sophomore, I was pretty certain this was simply who and what I was. Coming out was not a horrible experience. It happened gradually. One day a light bulb went on in my head and I said to myself "Oh, this isn't just a phase, this is who you are." From that moment my life became easier. I had a better sense of who I was and who I would become.

Don't get me wrong: being gay in Kansas City in 1970 was not easy. It was not something you went around shouting out loud. Gay life was underground, often found through mutual friends. Bars were hidden. You went in through back doors. It was a hush-hush existence. But as bad as that might seem, it was also sort of cool. You felt like you belonged to a secret club. Like old lodge men with their coded handshakes, we had our own ways of identifying each other. There was "the glance" that occurs between two people where the eyes lingered just a fraction of a second longer than usual. There were certain codes, certain questions, as you carefully attempted to find out if someone was "a friend of Dorothy." We actually used that question. It was a coded comment based on the enthusiasm many gay men had for Judy Garland. It referred to Dorothy in *The Wizard of Oz*. You would be at a party, talking to another person. You would eye someone across the room and ask your conversation mate, "Is he a friend of Dorothy?" It seems so quaint today, back then you had to be careful. LGBT people were not accepted by society at large. We have progressed enough that today people come out much more easily. That's not to say that every young person who comes out has no problems. But, in general, it's easier to come out and be open about who you are in the 21st century that it was in the 20th.

At some point, probably my sophomore year in college, I was questioning my sexual orientation and decided to seek some counseling. This was not something I would have gone to our family doctor about, so I went to Western Missouri Mental Health. This was a state run mental health facility in downtown Kansas City. Today it may be a fine institution, but in 1970 it seemed like it was only one step away from a snake pit. They were so behind the curve it was shocking. I was given an appointment to see a doctor who was clearly too squeamish to even approach the subject.

GRADUATION AND THE DREADED DRAFT

So I asked for another doctor. The next doctor was not unwilling to talk about it but he told me in the first session: "I will counsel you as long as you want to change but don't come here and tell me you want to accept being a homosexual. I cannot help you do that. It is a terrible life."

Well how's that for openers! I saw this doctor maybe three times. He was a strident man, filled with some silent rage about gay people, warning me of the miserable life I would face if I could not change my ways. By the time he suggested electrical aversion therapy, I decided I'd had enough. I was not unhappy about being gay. I met interesting, creative, people, I got laid now and then; what was so awful about this? So I walked out of the doors of Western Missouri Mental Health and thought I would never return.

But I did.

As the draft loomed, I decided to "check the box." It was a question on the draft medical form that asked if you had any homosexual tendencies. It was a serious decision. I knew that by checking the box, I would probably have to be self-employed for the rest of my life. 4F draft status stated you were unfit for military service. If I applied for a job, I would be asked the reason for my 4F status. If I lied I could be in trouble. If I told the truth I would never be hired. In 1970, there was no job protection for LBGT people, and I don't think there still is in Kansas or Missouri.

My travelogue business was doing well and I was confident I would succeed. I would not have to answer questions about my draft status because I would be self-employed. But it was still a *big* decision to check the box.

The war was so unpopular, the draft so disliked, that thousands of straight men checked the box and attempted to convince the draft board they were gay. The draft board wasn't buying this anymore. If you were going to use the gay "get-out-of-jail-free" card, you had to *prove* you were gay. And this is what took me back to Western Missouri Mental Health and the homophobic doctor who told me never to come back unless I wanted to be "cured." I made an appointment and I went in to see the doctor. I told him I had been called for my military physical and I needed a letter stating that I was homosexual. He stared at me with contempt. But he told me to come back the next day and the letter would be waiting at the front reception. I returned the following day and the letter was there. I still remember what it said.

To whom it may concern:

I have seen and attempted to treat Douglas Jones. I have deemed his case untreatable. Mr. Jones is an incurable homosexual.

So there it was in black and white. I was an "incurable homosexual." Not something I was overly upset about when facing the draft and the Vietnam War. Two days later I went to the Army Physical Examination headquarters on Main Street with my letter. Because my file contained "sensitive information," I was told I had to hand-carry my own file. And to make matters worse, I saw all my old high school friends who had also been called up, and they wanted to know why I was carrying my own file.

That experience ranks as one of the most degrading experiences of my life. There were about fifty men, all between eighteen and twenty-two. Everyone was lined up and told to drop their drawers and spread their cheeks. A doctor walked along with a flashlight checking for hemorrhoids. Then each of us had to endure the dreaded hernia test with the same doctor sticking his figure into our groins. This was all handled with barking and screaming; general nastiness that was somehow supposed to prepare us to serve our country.

Finally, I was called into a cubicle. The doctor I had been assigned was actually pretty decent. He looked at my "proof" that I was an "incurable homosexual," stamped my forms and said to me "I hope you find someone nice and settle down and have a good life." I wish I could find that doctor today and thank him for his kindness. It meant a lot.

In more recent times the issue concerning gays in the military has been a part of a national conversation. "Don't Ask Don't Tell" was a terrible policy that required people to lie about themselves—how un-American. Dropping that hated policy and opening the military to LGBT people was a long, hard-fought battle but it has been good for the United States. It shows us to be progressive and it strengthens the troops by including talented people who choose to serve.

In looking back on my life, I can't claim much discrimination. Beside my early mishap with Windoes Travelogues—the reason Cecil Houghton vowed I would never work for Windoes was because John Strong had told him I was gay—being declared unfit for military service was one of the few times in my life I can say I was discriminated against. But with the Vietnam War raging, and Paris only a week away, it was discrimination I could live with.

CHAPTER TWELVE

PARIS AND THE PARISIANS

I had no sooner flipped the tassel on my mortarboard than it was time to leave for Paris. I was packed; the cameras, the tripod, four cases of Kodachrome II—20,000 feet of film—four light rigs, and clothes for three months. And this was before anyone had even thought of inventing the rolling suitcase. My parents took me to the airport in Kansas City and I was off, first to JFK, then on to Orly International Airport, and Paris—the City of Light.

I was no longer eligible for free travel on TWA, but I was already working the angles. In those days, airlines would pay travelogue filmmakers a fee equal to the airfare to put a shot of one of their planes in the film. I had a contact with the public relations department at TWA and they agreed to do this. I booked the flight and paid for it with the check I got from Trans World Airlines. TWA paid me $750 to include a shot of a TWA Boeing 707 jet arriving in Paris at Orly International Airport. About half way through the Paris shoot I drove out to Orly early one morning, I went up in the control tower, set up my Bolex camera on the tripod beside the air traffic controllers, and waited. I can't even imagine what clearance it would take to get me into the tower at Charles de Gaulle Airport today, but in 1970, I just knocked on a door and someone took me up in an elevator. Soon a Boeing 707 appeared coming in for landing. My shot of the TWA plane with its bright red logo was the opening shot of the film... arriving in Paris on TWA. It was an early version of product placement.

Paris was magical. I rented a car and spent twelve weeks in the city driving everywhere. I settled into a hotel in Neuilly-Sur-Seine, out past the Arch of Triumph. The room was amazing. It was covered in wild Chinese wallpaper that matched the draperies, the bedspread, and the upholstery—the room was psychedelic. Waking up in the morning was like being on an acid trip.

I did the quick Parisian breakfast of coffee and croissants and off I would go to shoot what was on my agenda for the day. I had devised a theme for the film—a week in Paris. The film would be broken into seven sections, one for each day of the week. The film opened on Sunday with shots of the empty parks. Slowly people arrived and the city came to life. From the parks the film moved to Notre-Dame, its vast interior and stunning stained glass, bells ringing from the towers announcing the start of mass. On Sunday afternoon the film moved to Longchamps Racecourse for the steeplechases and then a boat ride down the river Seine under the bridges that unite the city's right bank and left. Monday was about getting to work and included scenes on the Paris Metro and a contrived, but clever, sequence in a taxi that was supposedly caught in the traffic circle around the Arch of Triumph, and a ride to work in an elevator—to the top of the Eiffel Tower. Tuesday was a day spent with the artists of Paris in Montmartre and inside an artist's studio. Wednesday was Bastille Day, France's equivalent of the Fourth of July. I started the sequence at Versailles where I was given open access. The French Government Tourist Office had made the arrangements and the guides at Versailles couldn't have been more helpful. After a short film sequence on the French Revolution, I added a shot of Place de la Bastille where the prison once stood, then moved the story to the modern day with the Bastille Day Parade. I shot the parade from the press stand on the Champs-Élysées. Fighter jets flew overhead at the beginning of the parade; the colors of the French flag, the Tricolour, plumes of blue, red, and white smoke trailing overhead. George Pompidou was president at the time and he was standing at attention in full regalia across from me.

For the Thursday sequence of the film, I went to a family in Montparnasse. It was common to include family sequences to show how local people lived. I was introduced to a family and spent several days with them, following the wife to the market, the husband to work, the kids to school, and home for dinner. These sequences, while somewhat trite today, were important at the time. They gave American audiences a chance to see real people going about their lives in different cultures around the world. Friday was spent with a young couple wandering through the romantic city.

The Eiffel Tower at night with the fountains of the Trocadero. I fell in love with "The City of Light." 1970.

The Sacré-Cœur atop the hill of Montmartre. One of dozens of sights I filmed for my travelogue *Paris of the Parisians*. 1970.

The final day in the theme of the film was Saturday and it was spent with a couple that was celebrating their anniversary. They went shopping; I filmed them at Christian Dior, they had dinner at Le Grand Véfour, one of Paris' most famous restaurants, and finished up the night at the Folies Bergère. In point of fact, they never went to the Folies Bergère. I shot the footage separately. The Folies Bergère would never have allowed me inside. I snuck my camera in. In those days, it was considered acceptable to do what you had to do to get the shots. The Folies Bergère should be glad I filmed the footage (and I actually did it again in 1988 for *Great Cities of Europe*). The operation shut down in 1989 and I think my shots may be some of the only existing footage of those remarkable shows.

At some point in the summer my parents came to visit. They were interested in watching me work, and they both loved Paris. I took them up to the observation area on the top of the Arch of Triumph. My mother looked over the edge at the swirl of traffic below and said with amazement, "Look at all those little foreign cars!" then laughed at the absurdity of her comment. One night I took them to the Moulin Rouge where Toulouse-Lautrec painted his famous posters of the Can-Can dancers. The champagne flowed freely. Recently, I was cleaning out some files and came across this picture taken that night. It is clear I was feeling no pain.

I spent three months in Paris and when it was finally time to come home I made a decision that would have a big impact on my life. I decided to scrap the remaining portion of my round-trip ticket on TWA and sail home on the brand-new flagship of the Cunard Line, the *Queen Elizabeth 2*. The ticket was $400 and I shared a room on the lowest deck with two total strangers. It was my first time on an ocean liner and I loved it. The cramped berth on the waterline didn't bother me because I spent no time in the cabin. I made friends and stayed up until all hours. It was my first time on the *QE2* but not my last. Over the next forty years, I would spend over four hundred days at sea on the ship, and I produced four different travelogues aboard her, including *The Great World Cruise of the QE2*. I sailed on her final crossing in October of 2008. As I left the ship the very last time that autumn day, I kissed her hull. It was my way of saying goodbye to a ship that had been very good to me. The two things that influenced my travel life the most were Trans World Airlines and the *QE2*.

Back in Kansas City, I sent the film in for processing and got to work editing the picture. I already had dates booked and the film had to be ready

I took my parents to the Moulin Rouge to see the Can-Can revue during their visit while I was shooting *Paris of the Parisians*. The champagne bottle is empty and my face shows why. 1970.

by January 5th when I would first show it in Easton, Pennsylvania. I had a decent amount of material to choose from, my film shots had improved since Belgium, I had a storyline built into the program, and I felt much more confidence in this film.

As I was finishing up the final editing of the film, I was invited to watch the lighting of the Country Club Plaza for the Christmas season. This was a Kansas City tradition and it was at this party that I met a man named Ben Solomon.

A newspaper ad for *Paris of the Parisians* at the Van Wezel Auditorium in Sarasota, Florida. 1972.

CHAPTER THIRTEEN

THE INDIANAPOLIS YEARS

The lighting of the Country Club Plaza in Kansas City for Christmas is an annual event. Since its inception, the Plaza has been covered with lights during the holiday season. Each of the Spanish buildings are ringed and outlined in thousands of colored lights. The tradition of lighting the Plaza on Thanksgiving night continues today.

So... I was seeing a guy who owned a dry cleaning business. He knew two guys who had an apartment above the Plaza with an expansive view. On Thanksgiving they would throw a party for the Plaza Christmas lighting ceremony. There were probably forty people there. I began talking with a guy; his name was Ben Solomon. He was a friend of the hosts and he was in town from Indianapolis where he was the curator of decorative arts for the Indianapolis Art Museum. I shamelessly dumped my date and gravitated to Ben.

Ben was nice looking, not overly handsome, but he had a distinctive face. And he was cultured. I was not. My parents had done their best to bring the arts into our lives: they took my sister and me to The Nelson Atkins Museum to look at the paintings, but none of us had any knowledge about what we were seeing. Ben knew. In fact, he knew a lot about several narrow fields. He was incredibly knowledgeable about furniture and decorative arts. He had a large collection of antiques. He knew history and he was able to talk about art in relation to historical events. I latched onto him because I wanted to better myself.

I decided to pick up and move to Indianapolis. I suppose part of the reason was a desire to live someplace new, and perhaps to cut the ties with my parents as well. I didn't give it much thought I just did it. I told my parents I was moving because Indianapolis would be more central to where my future travelogue lecture dates would be, and that was true. But I don't think I ever considered the impact it would have on their lives. My sister had moved to Michigan several years earlier with her husband who got a professorship at Michigan State University. I was the only one my parents had left to see and interact with on a regular basis. And I just picked up and moved. If I could do it over again, I would not have changed the decision but I would have been kinder and gentler to my parents when I left. But you can't change the past.

Ben and I rented an apartment in a marginal section of the city, but it was a great apartment. It was the penthouse at the Piccadilly at 28 East 16th Street in Indianapolis. And it was a true penthouse, complete with huge terraces and a double height living room with a giant arched window overlooking the skyline. We rented it for $350 a month, which was a lot of money at the time. I returned to Kansas City, packed up my stuff, and called a moving company. Ben would have preferred that I burned it all. But you drag stuff around because you are attached to it. "Stuff" is often a statement about who we are. The movers arrived and packed everything up and I got in my car and drove off to "Naptown" to start a new life.

When we leased the penthouse it was all white. When I arrived back in Indianapolis one week later, I took the elevator up to the penthouse, (you had to have a key because the elevator opened directly into the living room) and it was now terra cotta orange—and the dining room was jet black. I was dumbfounded. "How could you do this without at least discussing it with me?"

Ben's response was "Oh, I wanted to surprise you!"

This was typical of the seven years we spent together. We clashed constantly.

Once, I was on the road doing lectures, and I came back to Indianapolis and a friend said, "Did you see the paper?" I was puzzled and I said "No." He brought out a copy of the Sunday *Indianapolis Star* with a full-page story complete with pictures about "Ben Solomon's Piccadilly Penthouse." My name was not mentioned. It was as though I didn't even exist.

Ben had more antiques, more chairs, paintings, porcelain, crystal, and silver than you could imagine. His home today is like an overstuffed antique store. The last time I was in his house, I counted over 100 chairs.

Ben Solomon in the dome car of the Rheingold Express traveling through Germany, 1974.

I knew from the beginning that if Ben were faced with choosing between the furniture and me, the furniture would win.

Ben left the Indianapolis Art Museum and went into the decorating business with a crazy character named Jack Holland. Jack was a piece of work himself. They got into some gigantic fight—and bang—Ben was fired and out of a job. He couldn't go back to the museum so what now? Together, we pooled $12,000 and started Solomon/Jones Antiques. When we opened our store at 38th and Meridian, we spaced out the inventory our meager investment had bought and opened the doors. We reinvested every dollar we took in and gradually the shop grew into a large operation.

Ben and I moved out of the Piccadilly in 1974 and I bought the Vonnegut House on Pennsylvania Avenue. I don't remember why Ben didn't participate in the purchase, but he did not. It was probably because he had lousy credit. We did not comingle our money (thank God!). The Vonnegut House was a large 1920s French Normandy home with a slate roof. It was where the author Kurt Vonnegut Jr.'s aunt and uncle lived.

We were pioneers in taking on this house. The neighborhood was dicey and semi-dangerous, but we were young and all we could see was a big house with a lot of potential. We lived there only two years because I had my eye on another prize. The old Booth Tarkington home at 4270 North Meridian was for sale. A family bought the derelict property and quickly got in over their heads. It was on Indianapolis' most prestigious street—North Meridian—a few blocks from the Governor's Mansion. It was built in half-timber English Tudor style in 1911.

Booth Tarkington was Indianapolis' most famous writer. He won two Pulitzer Prizes for *The Magnificent Ambersons* and *Alice Adams*. He wrote dozens of books and plays. And the entire world passed through his home. When Alfred Lunt met Lynne Fontanne and they were playing the English Opera House on the Circle downtown, Lunt brought his fiancé to 4270 North Meridian to meet Tarkington. Garson Kanin and Ruth Gordon, Winston Churchill, Mary Martin, the list of people who passed through this house was a who's who of the world of show business, politics, and literature.

I bought the house in 1976 right before I left to make *Royal London*.

We constantly had to restock the antique store. We had various sources for inventory. One source was a dealer in Chicago, Don Rose Galleries. Don, a true eccentric, was the single largest purchaser at the MGM and

Sitting in the living room of the penthouse atop the Piccadilly, 28 East 16th Street in Indianapolis, reading *Program Magazine*, the trade publication for the travelogue business. 1971.

20th Century Fox back lot sales. In the 1970s, both movie studios closed their back lots and sold off huge collections of art and furniture that were used as studio props. Don bought truckloads.

One piece that he got from the MGM sale caught my eye. It was a 17th century Dutch painting of an old man, attributed to Jacob Backer. There are Backers in the old masters collections of major museums throughout the world. He was a student of Rembrandt, and ultimately a competitor. They were contemporaries in 17th century Amsterdam. I bought the painting for myself, with my own money. The painting never went into the store inventory. The Wallace Collection in London had one. I wrote and sent a picture of mine, thinking it might be the pair to the female Backer the Wallace had. They wrote back and confirmed that my painting was indeed a Jacob Backer but not the pair to the one in their collection. Years later, a man named Peter Van den Brink was doing a retrospective of Backer's work at the Rembrandt House Museum in Amsterdam. A curator at the Wallace Collection came across the photograph of my Backer and wrote me by snail mail asking if he could forward my information. He included Peter Van den Brink's email address and the communication immediately became electronic. I forwarded a picture of my Backer. Peter wrote back in less than an hour "Ah, yes I have been looking for your 'old man' for some time." He knew the entire history of the painting, its sales records from the late 1700s until 1926 when the trail went cold. (This was obviously when MGM prop buyers in Europe bought the painting). He told me it was painted in 1637 and that the previous year Backer had done a similar painting with the man's wife. That double portrait was hanging in the Hôtel de Ville in Reims, France. My painting was included in the museum show, identified as being in a private collection in Los Angeles.

I had owned the painting for four decades and knew almost nothing about it. And with the speed of an email and an attachment, the entire history of a 400-year-old painting was in front of me. The Backer still hangs in my Los Angeles home.

By 1977, Ben and I were in a stagnant relationship. We had the store and we lived together but clearly we had different goals. One evening, after dinner, we sat in wing chairs on either side of the fireplace in the living room of the Tarkington House. A fire was going and I posed the question: "What do you want your life to be like in ten years?" Ben spoke at length. His dreams were based on his life, personal and professional, in

The Vonnegut house on Pennsylvania Street in Indianapolis.
A wintery day in early 1975.

Indianapolis and the future that he hoped for. After he spoke he posed the same question to me. I waxed on about a life in New York, and a life spent traveling the world. We looked at each other and realized it was over. We had spent seven years together and we each grew from the experience. But it was time for us to go our separate ways.

I loved my time in Indianapolis. It's one of America's great cities. I loved sitting on the first turn of the Indianapolis 500 on race day, I loved having dinner in the King Cole Room off the Circle, and I loved going to Clowes Hall for Broadway shows. But it was time to move on. I sold my interest in the shop to Ben. I put the Tarkington House on the market, it sold quickly, and in April, all that I owned was put on a truck bound for 465 West End Avenue on the Upper West Side of Manhattan. And my life was about to get very interesting.

The Booth Tarkington House, 4270 North Meridian Street in Indianapolis, on a snowy day in February 1977.

The living room of the Vonnegut house. On the right wall is the Jacob Backer portrait painted in 1637. I still have it today in Los Angeles. 1974

CHAPTER FOURTEEN

FILMING NEW YORK CITY, HAWAII, AND VENICE

In June 1971, shortly after arriving in Indianapolis to find my apartment painted orange and black, I had to turn around and leave. I had a lecture date in Columbus, Ohio on the campus of Ohio State University to show *Paris of the Parisians* at Mershon Auditorium. The following day I was driving to New York where I was going to start shooting my third travelogue, a film called *New York City–Broadway U.S.A.* No one in the travelogue business had made a film on New York in decades. Frankly, no one wanted to. By 1971, New York was a grimy, dirty, graffiti ridden, unsafe mess. But I thought the project would be challenging and I set out to do it.

I had never driven in New York City before. I arrived late at night after a long haul on the Pennsylvania and New Jersey Turnpikes and made my way through the Holland Tunnel on the lower end of Manhattan. I emerged into chaos—taxis, buses, trucks, cars, and pedestrians everywhere. No one paid any attention to lanes, stoplights were merely suggestions, and here I was bouncing up the pothole-filled West Side Highway and onto Eighth Avenue in a 1968 gold Cadillac that screamed, "Steal me."

I stayed with a friend I knew from college on the Upper West Side for a few days until I managed to get a sublet at 91st and Broadway. This apartment would be my home for the next ten weeks while I shot the film. Throughout my stay in New York I parked my car on the streets. It had an alarm, which was always going off and driving the neighbors crazy. The police once stopped me because they thought I had stolen it.

The old pre-war apartment was in a very marginal neighborhood. The Thalia revival movie theater was around the corner, the subway only a few blocks away. The city was crazy, loud, crumbling, and at its nadir. A few years later the city was officially bankrupt. After the infamous *New York Daily News* headline about President Ford being asked to help the city out—"FORD TO CITY: DROP DEAD"—the city hit its bottom. (In fairness to Gerald Ford, he never said those words; it was tabloid headline writing). It was not until the 1990s that New York City began its long climb back to being the preeminent city of America and the world. Today it dazzles, but in 1971 it could be spooky.

I set to work. I had devised a simple theme of following Broadway from the tip of Manhattan to the Bronx. The film started with a brief history, some early footage of New York that I had scoured from the National Archives, and then an approach by water to Manhattan on the Staten Island Ferry. The World Trade Center was under construction. Tower One was finished, Tower Two was about halfway done. Over the years I shot the Twin Towers eight different times for various films. The last time I shot the World Trade Center was August 11, 2001—one month before the 9/11 attacks and the shocking collapse.

I got onto the floor of the New York Stock Exchange. I filmed a ticker-tape machine and traders wildly calling out buy and sell orders. I filmed the garment district and at Abe Schrader's, a high-end women's fashion label. I shot Times Square, the theater district, Radio City Music Hall, Rockefeller Center, Fifth Avenue, Lincoln Center, Central Park, and I tucked in many different human-interest stories throughout the film. I finished the program with a story of immigrants; a montage of early Ellis Island pictures, the Statue of Liberty, and the famous Emma Lazarus poem,

> *"Give me your tired, your poor,*
> *Your huddled masses yearning to breathe free,*
> *The wretched refuse of your teeming shore.*
> *Send these, the homeless, tempest-tossed to me,*
> *I lift my lamp beside the golden door."*

For the 1972-1973 lecture season, I started my tour by making my second appearance at the National Geographic Society with my New York City film. Gilbert Grosvenor, president of the society at the time, came up afterward and complimented me on the film. My first appearance for the National Geographic Society had been with *Paris of the Parisians*. I ultimately appeared for them fourteen times. The National Geographic Society used to present speakers and their films at Constitution Hall in Washington D.C. which had 4,000 seats. I did a show on Thursday night and two on Friday.

A woman named Joanne Hess ran the travelogue series for the National Geographic Society. She was unmarried, reserved, a bit stiff, but she could open up once you got to know her. Her personality represented the tone of the National Geographic Society. The organization had evolved out of an elite group of academic and society people and included the families of Alexander Graham Bell and Gilbert Hovey Grosvenor. It was a stuffy and rigid organization, but very prestigious. They would pick me up in a limousine and deliver me to the stage door of Constitution Hall.

Constitution Hall was owned by the D.A.R.—the Daughters of the American Revolution—and is infamously known as the place where Marian Anderson, the African-American opera singer, was barred from appearing. The D.A.R. tried to claim that it had merely been a misunderstanding, but a person at the National Geographic Society told me that, for decades, their contract with the hall specifically stipulated that only Caucasian people were allowed onto the stage.

Putting finishing touches on the marquee in Lincoln, Nebraska for my showings the following day of New York City–Broadway U.S.A. 1973.

After I made the film on New York, I turned my sights west to Hawaii. In June of 1973, I headed off to Honolulu to make *The Hawaiian Adventure*. I was taken with the James Michener book *Hawaii* and tried to follow the same idea in creating the film, starting with the ocean at dawn, volcanoes exploding, and telling the story of how the Polynesians arrived. The Hawaii film was fun to make, the weather was perfect, and it was an easy place to work. Hawaiians are generous of spirit, cooperative, easy going, and friendly. I shot on the five main islands and I pieced together a well-rounded program.

In 1974, I headed back to Europe to make *The Magic of Venice*.

Earlier in the year I appeared on *The George Pierrot Show*. George Pierrot was a Detroit television personality with a big regional following. He would have travelogue filmmakers show their programs and be interviewed on the air. It was live and anything could and did happen. George was a colorful, Jabba the Hutt-looking character. He loved off-color jokes and filthy limericks that he would tell during the commercial breaks so the punch line would hit just as we went back on the air, challenging the guest and studio crew to hold back laughing.

While I was in Detroit doing the show, I met a man named Mike Mitchell. Mike was working for WWJ-TV where *The George Pierrot Show* originated. He had a friend in Washington. D.C. he wanted me to meet. His name was Charles Sedgwick. I met Charles after one of my appearances at the National Geographic Society.

Charles was from the famous New England Sedgwicks. His family had come over on the Mayflower and he was quick to let you know. He was very old school. He was with the State Department and was the official French translator for four presidents: Eisenhower, Kennedy, Johnson, and Nixon. When Kennedy went to Paris to meet De Gaulle, it was Kennedy, De Gaulle, and Charles in the room. He also spoke fluent Italian and had contacts in Rome and Venice, so I asked Charles to come along when I made my film on Venice and act as my translator. He agreed and we flew out of Dulles on a TWA jet headed for Rome. In Rome, we transferred to Alitalia and flew to Venice where all our bags, equipment, and film were loaded into a boat—and off we went. I can still remember seeing Venice for the first time as we approached the city from the water. Charles was sitting at the stern in his coat and tie, smiling, hair floppy in the wind; it was like a scene out of a Visconti movie.

A newspaper ad for my appearances with *The Hawaiian Adventure* at the Music Hall in Kansas City, 1975.

6,702 persons attend
Travelogue depicts Hawaii

Film lecturer Doug Jones showed 6,702 Spokanites a Hawaii of white-water surfing, roller-skating parrots and lush greenery laced with waterfalls at the travelogue sponsored by Spokesman-Review Charities, Inc., Tuesday.

In his 4 and 7:30 p.m. presentations at the Spokane Coliseum, Jones included a geological history of the islands' formation from volcanic eruptions.

Settlement of the islands by Tahitians, native arts of lei-making and poi-pounding, the once-dominant whaling industry in the town of Lahaina on the island of Maui and sugar cane and pineapple harvesting all were depicted in Jones' film.

pools of Maui, the leper settlement on the island of Molokai, the black lava sands of the "big island" of Hawaii and the orchid gardens of the island of Kauai.

The audience watched parrots play poker, ride a scooter, pedal a small bicycle and roller-skate at the Paradise Park Bird Show in Honolulu. The audience also peered underwater to watch strangely striped and puffer-bellied fish in Sealife Park.

Jones sandwiched historical background between scenes of current-day Hawaiian life.

Among his most unusual sequences were actual films of the Japanese attack on Pearl Harbor, captured from

Japanese forces and available for Jones' use through the National Archives in Washington, D.C. He balanced the scenes with descriptions of the gallantry of Hawaii's Japanese who served in U.S. forces during World War II with distinction.

Jones paid tribute to the racial and cultural mix in Hawaii which he described as having produced a "beautiful people."

The next Spokesman-Review Charities, Inc., travelogue will be Feb. 3 when film lecturer and producer Bill Madsen will present "Wonderful Mexico." Performances are slated at 4 and 7:30 p.m. in the Spokane Coliseum.

A newspaper review from the Spokane *Spokesman-Review* in 1975 after a showing of my film *The Hawaiian Adventure*; 6,702 people attended the show. It was a *big* business. The middle-class was starting to travel and they wanted to see where they were going. 1975.

George Pierrot, the Detroit television personality. His travelogue program *The George Pierrot Show* was broadcast live at five o'clock each day on WWJ-TV. 1974.

Charles Sedgwick. Charles was my translator during the Venice shoot. He had aristocratic contacts in Italy. He was with the State Department and was the official French translator for four presidents. His family, the Sedgwicks of Stockbridge, Massachusetts, traced their lineage to the Mayflower. 1973.

Shooting footage for *The Magic of Venice* with my trusty Bolex, the Grand Canal and the Rialto Bridge in the background. In the early days, I wore dress clothes to shoot. Later I wore nothing but jeans. 1974.

The boat pulled up alongside the San Toma vaporetto stop and our bags were unloaded. A team of porters hauled the luggage, equipment, and film through the narrow lanes of the Dorsoduro to our flat. Charles had arranged for us to rent the top floor of a palazzo on the Rio Novo right off the Grand Canal. It was six flights of stairs up and six flights of stairs down, but I was young, and it was stunning inside. I rented it from a Contessa in Rome that Charles knew and we had the flat for the whole twelve-week stay in Venice.

There was (and still is) a large ex-pat community of Brits and Americans who live in Venice. Charles had entrée to them and I was able to tag along. I would have had no way of entering this world, but because of Charles, I found myself at these daily cocktail parties with the likes of Peggy Guggenheim, the artist Vedova, assorted Counts, Countesses, and the moneyed rich from America and the U.K.

In 1974 Venice was crumbling and the flooding from the lagoon was becoming destructive. Several American based groups, Save Venice and The International Fund for Monuments, tried to help. Efforts were gaining traction and I was able to film a lot of the restoration work that was in progress. But all of it was meaningless without a solution to the flooding. Plans were developed in the late 1960s to build inflatable locks on the three entrances to the lagoon. These could be closed during high water to stop the destructive flooding. Five decades after the proposal was originally made, they have still not been built. The fact that Venice continues to flood year after year, and with greater frequency due to global warming and rising sea levels, is simply a disgrace. It is fixable and the fact that the Italian government has done nothing about it is unconscionable.

While I was there, I was given access to almost everything. The Italian Government Tourist Office was very cooperative. Tourism is vital to the city. Venice was not filled with hordes of tourists as it is today. They needed publicity and American tourists. My film was seen as a way of encouraging travel to Venice and they thought it made sense to help me. I returned to Indianapolis and edited *The Magic of Venice*. I showed it throughout the country for several seasons.

If I think about it, I can still hear the sound of the water lapping at the base of the palazzo on warm summer nights sleeping with the windows open in a Contessa's apartment in Venice in 1974. It is one of my most indelible memories.

A newspaper ad in the *Atlanta Constitution* for my appearances with *The Magic of Venice* at Symphony Hall. 1975.

A new headshot done by J.J. Kriegsmann, the Broadway portrait photographer. 1974.

CHAPTER FIFTEEN

ROYAL LONDON

By June of 1976, I had finished my sixth season of lectures and I was fairly well established in the travelogue business. I had 165 shows that season including an appearance with World Cavalcade in Seattle. This was a prestigious set of shows at the Seattle Opera House. The series was a for-profit business operated by Elizabeth Saunders. She ran a classy operation with reserved seats, a formal introduction, and the speaker and introducer always wore tuxedos. The house held 3,000 people and she had almost 13,000 subscribers. There were five performances of each show. It was dates like this that were so much fun to do.

After Seattle, I returned to Indianapolis. The season had ended and it was time to shoot the next picture. I decided to make a film called *Royal London*. I was going to show London from a perspective of British history and the monarchs who had ruled.

I had planned on ten weeks in London and decided to rent a flat rather than stay in a hotel. I rented a flat in Lancaster Gate on the north side of Hyde Park. The following morning, after I arrived, I rented a Morris Mini. This was when the Mini was a real Mini—they were like toy cars. I had never driven on the left before and learning in central London traffic, with a stick shift in my left hand, was challenging. But I was surprised how quickly I adapted and how fast I learned the crazy quilt of one-way streets. Today, traffic in London is terrible but in the summer of '76, I zoomed all over London in that Mini.

A man at the British Tourist Authority named Peter Finch Hodges was helpful in setting up whatever I needed. I gave him an ambitious list of things I wanted to film and, one-by-one, he made all the arrangements.

I wanted to film in Westminster Abbey. Done. Off I went with my lighting rig. The Abbey was closed and here I was running cables and setting up lights in the Chapel of the Order of the Bath by myself. I filmed the throne where every King and Queen of England has been crowned since Edward the First. It was a rapturous experience being in the Abbey alone. When I was finished, I found a guard who let me out and before I left I took one last look back at this place where so much British history had taken place and thought, I was lucky to have had this all to myself for a brief moment in time.

The next morning, I was standing at the entrance to the Tower of London. A Beefeater guard met me and showed me around. I got a chance to film inside the Tower before all of the tourists arrived. I pleaded to film the crown jewels but got a definite "no." It was one of the few things I was ever refused in my years of shooting.

I filmed various country houses, including Blenheim, the seat of the Duke of Marlborough. These country houses, the Brighton Pavilion, Syon House, Ham House, were woven into the story. At Blenheim, I filmed the main dining room, which was set up with a full dinner service of Royal Worcester china. I had my lights set up on the lightweight (and somewhat flimsy) aluminum stands. I went to move a light and I got my leg tangled in the cord and the light went smashing down, missing the edge of the table and the priceless Royal Worcester china by inches. I was alone in the room at the time and no one saw this happen, but I was shaken at what trouble I would have been in if I had left Blenheim with a half a dozen pieces of Royal Worcester china in shards.

Once the storyline moved into the 20th century, I was able to add archival footage. I had film of George V and his son Edward VIII. I included a sequence on the abdication crisis in 1936 when Edward VIII renounced the throne for "the woman I love." That woman was Wallis Warfield Simpson, who had caused a stir in Britain by being divorced, twice no less, before setting her sights on the Prince of Wales.

One of the best experiences of that trip was going to the top of Big Ben. I thought it would be interesting to film the clock mechanism striking twelve noon. I asked permission to do this and I was told to be at a certain spot at the base of the tower at 11:15 a.m. Ben Solomon had flown over for a couple of weeks to help me. I asked, "Where's the elevator?" and the guard scowled. "There is no elevator, sir." Ben and I looked at each other, sighed, and divided up the equipment: a case of lights, the main camera, a heavy tripod, and off we went up 366 stairs.

We got to the top and it was impressive: the huge mechanism, the glass clock faces, the pendulum ticking away swinging in the shaft, the giant bells of the Westminster chime and of course, Big Ben, the thirteen-ton hour bell for which the clock is named. Time was literally ticking away as I quickly set up my equipment to grab the shots of the chime striking 11:30 a.m. and 11:45 a.m. I got the spinning governors and the hammers banging down on the four chime bells. Then, at noon, the chime went through its four-part cycle and I turned the camera to the hammer banging down on Big Ben itself. The sound was deafening beside the bell. Shortly after noon, it was all over. We packed everything up and made the climb back down.

Inside the clock room atop Big Ben waiting for the clock to strike twelve noon. 1976.

Peter Finch Hodges was apparently pleased with my work and one day called me into his office and handed me some papers and said, "You'll enjoy this. Be at the main gate of Windsor Castle on Wednesday at 11:00 a.m." I had an invitation to see and film the induction of Sir Harold Wilson, a former Prime Minister, into the Order of the Garter. Being made a member of the Order of the Garter is one of Britain's highest honors. The entire royal family would be there. I was escorted into a private apartment in the main tower gate where a small group of people had gathered. We were served a pleasant lunch and then we went out onto the ramparts to watch the spectacle. The Queen, Prince Phillip, the Queen Mother, and Prince Charles—everyone was there, processing along in their Garter robes. It was British pageantry at its best.

This happened a few days before Britain's biggest annual event: the Trooping of the Colour, the Queen's official birthday parade which takes place along Pall Mall. The Queen's actual birthday is in April but since the weather is so dreary then, her "official" birthday is the second Saturday in June when the weather is more likely (but not guaranteed) to be cooperative. I was on the press stand as the procession began. The Coldstream Guards, the bearskin caps, the brass bands, the horses, and the timpani; all of the pageantry was simply stunning. Everything moved along to Horse Guards Parade at Whitehall where the Queen would review the troops. It was two years before the Silver Jubilee, the Queen's twenty-fifth year on the throne, and on year twenty-three she was still riding her steed sidesaddle.

To close the film, I did a sequence on Sir Winston Churchill and the Battle of Britain. I shot Chartwell, Churchill's country home in Sussex, his artist studio (he was an avid painter), and intermixed all of this with footage of the Battle of Britain and Churchill's voice delivering "The finest hour speech."

"But if we fail, then the whole world, including the United States, including all that we have known and cared for, will sink into the abyss of a new dark age made more sinister, and perhaps more protracted, by the lights of perverted science. Let us therefore brace ourselves to our duties, and so bear ourselves, that if the British Empire and its Commonwealth last for a thousand years, men will still say, This was their finest hour."

The war footage that I had acquired through the National Archives was chilling. London burning; Edward R. Murrow reporting, "This is London..." Churchill touring the ruins, the stiff upper lip, keep calm and carry on. The close of the film was a tribute to the British spirit that had endured throughout the war. London, England, and Britain survived. They rebuilt and prospered. I was pleased with the film's ending and it did genuinely move audiences. *Royal London* was my most successful film to date.

The next project would be more difficult.

In front of Chartwell, Winston Churchill's home in Kent.
Filming for *Royal London*. 1976.

A newspaper ad for *Royal London* in Monroe, Louisiana. I appeared on stages in all fifty states over the course of my career. 1977.

The University Auditorium at Michigan State University with an audience of nearly 3,000. That night I was showing *Royal London*, which I had been recently finished. East Lansing, Michigan. 1977.

CHAPTER SIXTEEN

OFF TO EGYPT

After the experience of making *Royal London* in 1976, I decided to do something more exotic. No one had made a film on Egypt for years. I decided to make a film and call it *Egypt–Gift of the Nile*. The title was lifted from a quote by Herodotus, the Greek historian, who said, "Egypt was the gift of the Nile."

I traveled to the Middle East on Trans World Airlines. It was a long flight and I was exhausted by the time we arrived. As I stepped off the plane in Cairo everything hit me—the heat, the noise, the chaos. Egyptian summer is not for the faint-hearted. I did the film shoot in June because my lecture season had run into late May. No one in their right mind goes to Egypt in June for pleasure, much less work, but there I was.

I gathered my bags and equipment and hired a taxi that took me to the Nile Hilton where I was based for my seven-week stay. The ride from the airport to the hotel was a madhouse of donkey carts, camels, men in flowing robes, hawkers, buses, trucks, fumes—the wild mosaic of Egypt.

The Nile Hilton was a refuge for those seven weeks. Travelers are often criticized for staying in plush, western hotels. The conventional wisdom is that you can get a more authentic experience by staying in local establishments and there is truth to that. But a pleasant, comfortable bed and a decent shower can be a blessed respite from dealing with challenges that come from working in developing countries. The Hilton faced the Nile River; Tahrir Square was a short distance away. I was in the bustling heart of Cairo.

Egypt's infrastructure was horrible (and it probably still is). The telephone service was so bad that if I needed to talk to my contact at the Egyptian Government Tourist Office, it took less time to leave the hotel, walk the twenty minutes to his office, and climb the stairs (the elevator never worked) than it did to get a call to go through. Egypt was, in some ways, the Arab version of India. It was crushingly poor, the sense of futility was pressing, and yet the Egyptians seemed oddly content (at least in 1977). They lived by the phrase "in sha'Allah." It means, "If God is willing." And they use it constantly. It ends virtually every sentence. It is both a blessing and a curse. It allows people to accept their lot in life, but it also prevents people from taking initiative to change things. I find a similar nature among Indians who, as Hindus, live with the sure hope of reincarnation and a belief that things will be better the next time around. They are coping mechanisms. People all over the world use different techniques to get through life. In Egypt it was the phrase "in sha'Allah."

In 1977, the tourism that made up the backbone of Egypt's economy was at a near standstill. It was only four years after the 1973 war with Israel, and Americans were still reluctant to travel there. Those who did travel to Egypt during this period were treated like royalty. Egyptians expressed great affection for Americans. Tourist officials hoped my film would increase American tourism to Egypt. There were enough serious travelers going to travelogue programs that they felt it was worthwhile to help me.

Egypt was calm in the late 1970s. Anwar Sadat, probably Egypt's greatest ruler of modern times, was in power. He brokered a peace with Israel when no one thought it could be done. He had a genuine concern for the plight of the poor. He was beloved by everyone I spoke with. But there were disgruntled elements, zealots even then, and his assassination in 1981 sent Egypt on a downward spiral with the dictatorship of Hosni Mubarak and the uncertainty that followed.

But when I was there, it was a peaceful place in a crazy, noisy, nutty sort of way. The traffic was unbelievable. People would hang off buses like apples dangling from a tree. Everyone seemed to talk at once and they spoke with their hands as much as their lips. Men walked hand-in-hand, a curious trait of the Middle East that in no way implies homosexuality. It is a gesture of friendship, nothing more. At night the giant movie palaces around Tahrir Square would be packed with men; women were rarely seen after dark. But during my time in Cairo, women tended to wear western clothes. You did not see the hijab, the long black covering, until you went up the Nile into the countryside and villages. Cairo was a lively city and sophisticated in a distinctly Middle Eastern way. Nightclubs did not even open for business until midnight and the main attraction, always a famous belly dancer, would not come on until well after 3:00 a.m.

Each morning, my guide and driver would pick me up at the hotel shortly after dawn. We would head out to shoot whatever was on my agenda for the day. By 11:00 a.m. we were back at the hotel. I would have lunch, nap and then go back out again about four o'clock. The midday heat was intense and you simply had to take a break. There were few tourists in the country during that summer. I remember wandering around the Pyramids and the Sphinx by myself; 5,000 years of history standing before me with no one else in sight.

I made a side trip to a Coptic Christian monastery at Wadi El Natrun, I traveled to Port Said and the Suez Canal, and I trekked out to the Fayoum, a huge oasis about sixty miles southwest of Cairo. The Fayoum is fascinating. Giant waterwheels bring water from the Nile to the irrigation canals using methods that remain unchanged since the days of the ancient Egyptians, who figured out how to use the water of the Nile to irrigate the desert.

I needed to get the film shot by the end of July because I had to edit the picture and get it ready for shows in early September. This concept of working on a set schedule was completely baffling to the Egyptians. A deadline? The idea was not even part of their thought process. It was a case of needing to get a project done according to a western timetable in a culture that had no concept of a timetable.

This was particularly frustrating the day I went to the Fayoum. I saw countless things I wanted to film but before I could get to work, I had to be taken to the office of the tourism director for the Fayoum. Introductions were made, polite conversation was exchanged, tea was served, it was all very civilized—and it was eating into my limited time.

Finessing your way through these situations can be challenging. You have to accept a certain amount of wasted time as part of a culture where life moves at a slower pace. On the other hand, none of that helped me with the fact that I would have over a thousand people in an auditorium for the first show in three months. Somehow I got out of the director's office and got what I needed shot that day. It was some of the most interesting footage I filmed during my time in Egypt.

From Cairo, I traveled by plane to Luxor. The airlines were spooky. If they couldn't manage to get the telephones to work, or a door properly hung, you couldn't help but wonder about their aircraft maintenance. My experiences in Egypt up to that point didn't give me a lot of confidence.

Luxor is awesome. The Temple of Karnak, the Valley of the Kings, the Colossi of Memnon, it's everything you would expect it to be; a remarkable travel experience in an ancient land. I was in Luxor for a week and I was able to travel out to villages and fields to shoot farmers using ancient agricultural methods. I went to a camel market and an alabaster factory; I filmed the Son et Lumière show at Karnak and took sunset trips in feluccas down the Nile. It was blissful.

From Luxor, I traveled on to Aswan in Upper Egypt. Aswan stands on the first cataract of the Nile. It is also the site of the Aswan Low Dam built in 1902. In the 1950s, General Gamal Nasser announced that Egypt would build the Aswan High Dam. It was completed in 1970, largely with the help of the Soviet Union. It was controversial then as it is now. The dam disrupts the natural flooding of the Nile each spring. But Egypt needed power, and the hydroelectric plant generated a significant amount of electricity for a nation that was far behind western countries in providing the comforts of modern life for its citizens.

From Aswan I flew to Abu Simbel, one of the great archeological wonders of the world. Once plans for the Aswan High Dam were announced it became apparent that hundreds of ancient sites would be flooded with the rising waters of the new Lake Nasser. It was decided to concentrate on preserving Abu Simbel, a massive temple complex carved into the walls of rock that bordered the Nile. A dozen nations participated in the project and the entire complex was cut into thousands of blocks and moved like a puzzle to higher ground. Without international help, the temples would not have been saved.

Back in Cairo, I was wrapping up my work but I had one final day of shooting left. I had been waiting for approval to film the treasures of King Tutankhamen in the Cairo Museum. Permission was finally

The Luxor Temple, from *Egypt–Gift of the Nile*. 1977.

granted. On a morning that the museum was closed I went to a side entrance. A guard took me into the rooms where the treasures stood. He turned on the lights and simply left me there. I spent three hours in those rooms among the treasures of King Tutankhamen alone. The world was a simpler and more trusting place in 1977. I stood in front of the gold coffin, my Bolex camera whirring away, and I wondered what it must have been like when Howard Carter, the British archeologist who discovered the tomb, cracked the seal in 1922. Reportedly, his excited assistants shouted out, "Can you see anything?" and Carter replied, "Yes, wonderful things." Egypt was, and remains, a pinnacle destination, and a place any serious traveler should see.

From Cairo I left for Indianapolis by way of London and New York. Once home I began cutting the film and preparing for the 1977-78 lecture season. *Egypt–Gift of the Nile* premiered in Indianapolis at the Murat Shrine, a grand old theater downtown. I had a nearly full house, and from there I left for San Francisco to start my seventh season of lectures on the travelogue show circuit.

The solid gold inner coffin of King Tutankhamen in the Cairo Museum. I was left alone to film these priceless treasures. 1977.

Cutting *Egypt–Gift of the Nile* in my editing room on the third floor of the Tarkington House in Indianapolis. 1977.

A newspaper ad for *Egypt–Gift of the Nile* for the Walker Lecture Series in Concord, New Hampshire. 1978.

CHAPTER SEVENTEEN

MOVING EAST–INDIANAPOLIS TO NEW YORK

After a lecture tour of 184 shows, I returned to Indianapolis in May of 1978. My last show was at the Bushnell Auditorium in Hartford, Connecticut, a giant barn of a theater with a great pipe organ. It was fun to stand in the wings of those theaters listening to the wheezing and noise as these monster instruments produced such a big sound. I think I was showing *The Hawaiian Adventure*. Why the organist chose to close the preshow with "Chattanooga Choo Choo," I don't know, but it put the audience in a good mood. There were several places that had these great theater organs: the Pasadena Civic Auditorium, the Oakland Paramount, and the Palace Theater in Marion, Ohio come to mind.

Back in Indianapolis, life was not so good. Ben Solomon had moved on. He had a new boyfriend and we were clearly headed for the rocks. I remember how causal the breakup seemed at the time. I think we both thought we would find someone else and duplicate the experience—less the headaches we had with each other. Of course, it doesn't work that way. You really never repeat that first relationship. By the second (or third, or fourth) both parties have acquired a lot of baggage, both physical and emotional. It was hard for me to find someone willing to put up with all the issues I brought to a relationship, including a traveling job. But at the time we didn't think that far ahead. Ben moved out of the Tarkington House and I was by myself in that giant property. The loneliness set in immediately.

So there I was, living alone in this rambling house in Indianapolis. And then I became sick.

I was on lecture tour in Albuquerque, appearing at Popejoy Hall at the University of New Mexico. I went back to the hotel room not feeling well, and flew home to Indianapolis the next day. Eventually, I became sick enough that I went to Winona Memorial Hospital. The ER doctor took one look at me and said, "You have hepatitis." I was apparently bright yellow but I couldn't see that the color of my skin was any different than usual. (A sidebar fact about me: I am color blind—which doesn't mean I don't see any color but I see it differently. My parents first realized this when I was coloring the faces in my coloring book green. I have classic red-green colorblindness).

You would not normally hospitalize someone for hepatitis but I had no one to care for me, so I was admitted. I had a particularly vicious case and I was scheduled the next night to be in Philadelphia at the Academy of Music. It was the first time I had ever canceled a show. André de la Varre, a colleague, filled the date. But more on my mind was the fact that I was scheduled at the Seattle Opera House in a week's time. I had to get out of that hospital. Two days passed and I was still yellow and incredibly weak. I announced I was leaving. I signed papers stating that I was leaving the hospital AMA—against medical advice. I got out, went home, and in three days packed and headed to the airport. I was not going to miss the Seattle World Cavalcade shows. They were too big. I couldn't leave Elizabeth Saunders and her ticket holders in the lurch.

I slowly got over the hepatitis. I was told that once you had hepatitis B you would never get it again. I would find out in time this was incorrect. I did recover and I continued on the road with my lecture tour. I was in and out of the Indianapolis, trying to pick up the pieces of my life after the breakup with Ben.

I was remarkably awkward socially. That might sound strange given my work and my life on stage, but I was actually shy when it came to making new friends. And I was hopeless at dating. After the split with Ben, the friends disappeared. Most of them had been couples. Ben had a new boyfriend. Friends chose sides and they mostly chose Ben. He was a great Indianapolis gadfly and party giver. He had more to offer than me. I was pretty much hung out to dry by the people I had known during those years.

In 1978, if you wanted to meet someone, there was little else you could do other than to go to bars and dance clubs. I went, but I was the quintessential wallflower. I somehow checked all of my self-confidence at the door and became the worst dance-bar patron ever. One night, I decided I was going to go to the main dance club in Indianapolis and I was determined

I was going to speak to someone and get someone—just one person—to dance. It was the age of disco. I went into the club dressed in some John Travolta Saturday-Night-Fever outfit (it was 1978—oh, the clothes!). I'm sure my desperation was showing, not unlike the title character of Booth Tarkington's Pulitzer prize-winning novel *Alice Adams*, which had been written in the very house I owned. No one would talk to me or dance with me. Finally, I went home. I was dejected but I was also angry. I felt I deserved better than this. I laid awake all night.

The following day, I packed a bag and drove straight to the airport in Indianapolis. I walked up to the TWA counter and said, "I want to be on the next flight to New York." In 1978, you could do this. Airfares were regulated and there was little security to speak of at the time. "We have a flight leaving in 30 minutes," said the ticket agent. "I'll take it," I replied. Out came the credit card and off to the gate I went. Two hours later, I was in a taxi heading to my New York City hotel, the Royalton on West 44th Street. This was when the Royalton was a somewhat down-at-the-heels hotel, long before Philippe Starck turned it into a haven of hipster modernism. I had stayed there so many times, they knew me by name. It was the only hotel in the world where when I walked in, they would look up and say, "Hello, Mr. Jones."

It was a Sunday night. I unpacked my bag, took a "disco nap," and headed to the Ice Palace on West 57th Street. It was one of the big discos of New York City back in the day. I walked in with confidence. I spotted a guy, asked him to dance, he said, "Sure," and I might as well have gone to the pay phone and called the Mayflower Moving Company that moment. The wheels were set into motion. My Indianapolis days were over. My New York City years were ahead. In some respects, I should have been there all along. From my childhood days of drawing pictures of the Copacabana, I was destined for New York. I spent three days in the city, met people, stayed out until dawn, and I felt instantly at home.

Back in Indianapolis, I called a real estate agent and put the Tarkington House up for sale. The house sold quickly and I had to move quickly. The house was filled—and I do mean filled—with stuff: antiques from the store, mountains of film and equipment, and various things collected along the way. I was downsizing and moving to New York. Tons of stuff went to the auction house.

Now the big challenge: finding a place to live in Manhattan. There is no bigger obstacle for anyone considering a move to New York than the dreaded subject of housing. I had to be out of the house in Indianapolis and I had to do something fast. I saw an ad in the *The New York Times* classifieds for an apartment for rent at 465 West End Avenue. I went to look at it. It was big, but the building was ratty. The whole Westside was very rundown. In the 1970s, the Upper West Side of New York had the highest concentration of homeless, mentally ill people in America. And it was into this neighborhood that I moved.

I assumed I would just get a lease and it would be my apartment as long as I paid the rent. Such was not the case. New York City had a maze of housing laws and regulations. Technically, I was not renting the apartment from the landlord. He had "rented" the apartment to his nineteen year-old niece and I was "subletting" the apartment from her. This was done to get around the rent regulations so he could charge more money. Everyone in the building *hated* me. The man below me was paying $326 for exactly the same apartment. He had been there since the 1920s. I was paying the hated landlord multiple times more than everyone else. I just wanted a place to live, but I was viewed as an evil outsider coming in and helping the landlord rape them all. The adversarial relationship between New York City landlords and tenants is legendary.

I quickly figured out that I needed to get the lease into my name. So I bribed the landlord. I offered him $5,000 to put the lease in my name and he agreed. He wanted no check, cash only. The teller at the Chase Manhattan Bank counted out $5,000 in one hundred dollar bills, and the landlord handed me a lease for apartment 9C at 465 West End Avenue with my name as the lessee. Was it ethical? No. Was it wise on my part? Yes. I could see what was happening all over the city. Apartment buildings were being converted from rentals into cooperatives. The "insiders," those people already living in the building, were given deals to encourage them to buy. It was all anyone talked about. "Are they converting your building?" "What is the offering plan?" "What is the insider pricing?" New Yorkers became obsessed with home ownership. A lot of people were left in the dust, but ultimately it did improve New York's housing stock. It turned most Manhattan residents into owners instead of renters. People had a stake in their property and buildings rapidly improved.

Our building was another matter. The landlord was so hated that the tenants in the building went on a rent strike. We put our money into an escrow account and withheld it from the owner. He followed suit by shutting off the heat in the dead of winter. The tenants eventually strong-armed him into selling us the building en masse. We had a 100% participation co-op conversion in 1982 and the prices were insane. I bought an eight-room, twenty-three hundred square feet apartment for $42,000. Even in 1982, this was a ridiculous, crazy low price for the space.

So now I owned an apartment in New York City. The Upper West side was starting to improve and the city—well, it was magical. I was in my 30's, one of the best decades of my life. I never walked out of the apartment without feeling a sense of wonder; I was living in the most exciting place on earth.

People often ask me what my favorite thing is about New York. I always tell them it's not Broadway theater, the museums, Central Park, Fifth Avenue, or any of the standard iconic attractions. The single greatest thing about New York City is just walking down the street. In a thirty-minute walk on any street in Manhattan, you will see a thousand little daily dramas played out in front of you. It is sensory overload, one of the greatest shows of humanity on earth.

I fell into a circle of theater people. They were fun, funny, bright, and all they talked about was Broadway. I started going to Broadway shows the way other people would go to the movies. I saw all the big hits and all the big flops. My most cherished *Playbill* is for *Moose Murders*. It is considered the most legendary of all Broadway flops. It starred Eve Arden, who did only two performances before she walked—and I saw one of them.

New York was endless fun. You didn't live in your apartment. You lived in the city. You didn't need the same amount of space that other people across the country had. New Yorkers can—and do—function in remarkably small spaces. I was lucky to have a large space; most of my friends lived in studios or one-bedroom apartments.

I spent nights at Studio 54, The Saint, Xenon; the disco era was an exhilarating time in New York. The Stonewall riots of 1969 opened the doors of gay liberation. People had been in the closet for so long that when we collectively did come out, we did it with a bang. We partied until we dropped. It never occurred to any of us that the all-night partying would have any consequences. But lurking around the corner, like a pin ready to burst our balloon, was an invisible virus that would eventually be called HIV. The AIDS crisis was about to arrive.

CHAPTER EIGHTEEN

FILMING THE NATIONAL PARKS

After the Egypt shoot, I was ready for something easier. Egypt had been fascinating and eye opening, but also grueling. The heat was exhausting and the hustle even more so. Throughout the Middle East, there is a continuous hustle about everything. Someone is always trying to get something from you, whether it is the rug merchant following for blocks trying to entice you back into his shop, or the camel driver that saw me as an American movie maker and couldn't differentiate between me and MGM—and wanted to be paid accordingly. I loved Egypt, but I was also relieved when I left. It had been my hardest film shoot to date.

After *Egypt–Gift of the Nile* was finished and I took it on the road, I made my move to Manhattan. That first summer in New York I decided to give myself a break and shoot something in the U.S. It was my tenth year in the travelogue business and I decided to make a film in homage to two of my mentors.

Jim Metcalf, my earliest champion, had made a film many years before called *Wings Across America–The National Parks*. He flew his Cessna 172 to shoot the film. His national parks film was successful because of its use of aerial footage, which was still a novelty at the time. Jim had shot his film nearly twenty years before. I felt it was OK for me to put my own stamp on the subject.

Curtis Nagel, who showed the first travelogue I ever saw, *Portraits of Austria*, had become a good friend. He was retired so I took his "Portraits of" motif and used it for my film. I paid tribute to Curt in the front talk by finishing with his signature phrase "…and now as we take our palette of color film we shall paint these Portraits of America."

I spent two years shooting. I included winter sequences in Yosemite and Mount Rainier. I traveled as far west as Hawaii and as far south as Florida, to fourteen of what was then a system of thirty-nine national parks.

I used a new Canon Scoopic, a 16mm camera developed in the late 1960s for use in television news. Long before videotape, television stations would send cameramen out with 16mm film. They would shoot local events, process the film in the station, and put it on the air immediately. The phrase "Film at Eleven" came from those days. The Canon Scoopic was considered lightweight; it weighed eight pounds. Today's high-definition cameras often weigh less than three pounds. The Scoopic's best features were its built-in handle and thumb-operated shutter trigger. It was much easier to use than my clumsy Bolex. The Scoopic never really caught on, but I loved mine. I ran almost 400,000 feet of film through the camera over several decades, a hundred feet at a time.

I started the shoot in Maine at Acadia National Park. Acadia is not a dramatic place like the western parks; the scenery is gentle. But there are craggy rock formations along the sea, crashing waves, New England lighthouses, and flora and fauna distinctive to Maine. I went out with a lobster fisherman at 4:00 a.m. as he checked his traps. The fisherman checked about a hundred traps before we returned to the dock at noon where he went about the business of selling his catch to the commercial buyers on the pier. The subject of lobster fishing was a stretch to include in the Acadia National Park sequence, but human-interest stories made the film less static.

From Maine, I flew to Denver and then on to Jackson Hole, Wyoming. Jackson Hole was the jumping off point for Yellowstone National Park and the Grand Tetons. Yellowstone was a visual feast. Spouting geysers, Old Faithful, Yellowstone Falls, Mammoth Hot Springs, bubbling pots of mud, steam, hissing sounds, and buffalo wandering freely. Yellowstone was fairly empty back then. I had a cabin at the Yellowstone Lodge. In those days it was austere: no television, no radio, just a bed, but it gave me a chance to think, read, and pull back from the modern conveniences we all take for granted.

Along the way, I started my shoot of Grand Teton National Park, which is adjacent to Yellowstone. The Tetons were still covered in snow in June; Moran Lake mirroring the peaks. It was some of the most beautiful natural scenery I had ever seen.

From Jackson Hole, I flew south to Bryce Canyon in Utah. I rode by horseback to the bottom and was grateful for the handheld feature of the Canon Scoopic on that shoot. At the end of the day, during the last hour of light known by photographers as "magic hour," Bryce Canyon takes on a yellow glow. It was named for an early pioneer named Ebenezer Bryce, who made the unromantic observation that it was "a hell of a place to lose a cow."

I traveled on to film Arches National Park in Utah, the largest collection of natural arches in the world, fifteen hundred in all. They stand on a plateau and represent millions of years of rain, wind, and erosion.

Next I made my way to Mesa Verde. The Native American cliff dwellings show an advanced way of life that these Southwest tribes developed. Nearby was the Durango Silverton Railroad, one of the world's best known narrow gauge steam trains. Like the lobster fisherman in Maine, it was a stretch to include in the National Parks film, but it added variety to the Mesa Verde sequence and was fun to shoot. There is nothing like hanging out of the coach of a steam-pulled train and feeling the coal cinders flying by.

From Mesa Verde I went to the Painted Desert in Arizona, then Carlsbad Caverns in New Mexico. Filming deep in the cave was a challenge. I had to use "fast" film: film that was sensitive enough to capture images in the dim light. Today those light issues don't exist; you can film in virtual darkness with digital cameras. But when I was milling around in those cold caverns in 1978, I was shooting film that would have to be "pushed" at the laboratory, a process that would bring out more of the image.

I filmed the Great Smoky Mountains in North Carolina, and I returned to Hawaii to shoot Hawaii Volcanoes National Park. I got to film a major eruption of Kilauea. Standing near the lava flows at night, feeling the power of nature right in front of you, is quite an experience.

I traveled to the Everglades in Florida to shoot the subtle beauty of America's great marshland. I filmed alligators, pelicans, herons, and I got shots from the front of an airboat skimming over the swamp. Great fun.

One of the last parks I filmed was Yosemite. Having already shot winter scenes in the park, I returned in spring when the waterfalls were running at peak capacity and the Merced River was nearly overflowing. The meadows were filled with wildflowers, the birds were nesting, and the whole sense of renewal that spring brings was sublime.

But I saved the best for the last: the Grand Canyon. The Grand Canyon is one of those bucket list items. Everyone should see it. Standing on the South Rim, you look out and can't help but ask the question—what happened here? There are various theories, but however it came to be, it is one of the top natural attractions of the world. I filmed the mule train going to the bottom of the canyon. It's an exhausting but exhilarating experience riding down Bright Angel Trail. At the bottom, on the banks of the Colorado River, you look up. You are a full vertical mile down from the rim.

Back in New York City I began cutting the film. I was on a deadline. My first showing of the film was at the Grand Rapids Civic Auditorium for the Grand Rapids Kiwanis Club travelogue series. *Portrait of America–The National Parks* proved to be popular, and I had my largest audiences to date with that film. And I was traveling on my lecture tour with a new boyfriend. Burt Rendflash. In ultra-conservative, Dutch Reform, Grand Rapids, this was not looked upon kindly.

The marquee in front of the Seattle Opera House for *Portraits of America–The National Parks*. A part of the World Cavalcade Series. 1982.

Travel

THE WELL-MADE TRAVELOG

Filmmakers hit the trail with safaris in hand

by Judy Thorne
Special to The Times

The lights of the Opera House were dimmed and the film began to roll. At the corner of the stage, behind a softly lit podium, stood our guide, resplendent in tux and tails.

It was a smooth-talking Doug Jones, winner of the Film Lecturer of the Year Award, bidding us to "pack our duffel bags and be on our way."

We were off to see "Portraits of America," a cinematic glimpse at 14 national parks. Jones had researched, filmed, edited, wrote and set it to music. Now he was narrating it, too.

Jones is one of the 100 or so filmmakers who make a living at creating travelogs and taking them on the road to present to hundreds of audiences every year.

Last year, he presented 237 programs in 44 states, from large cities to small. One audience numbered 5,500, another, in a private club, only 100.

"It can be a lonely life," Jones said. "I go from airports to hotels to stage doors and back again. Sometimes I fly every day on the way to another lecture. Sometimes you're treated like the hired help; other times you feel like an honored guest. That's the way it is in Seattle."

For Jones, the stop in Seattle was a favorite. Because his World Cavalcade booking was for five

Doug Jones
Guide on a celluloid trail

"The timing on a travel film is critical," he said. "So I use my voice and manner, never the wording, to change the mood."

Because travelog films are created entirely by one person, they are a personal statement by the filmmaker.

The filmmaker chooses the topic, researches it, makes the travel arrangements, totes the camera, shoots the film and processes and edits it, selects the music score, and writes the script. When all that's done, he or she narrates it.

The lecture season runs September to May. Then there's pres-

A World Cavalcade show draws a good crowd to the Opera House in Seattle. Travelogs play to enthusiastic aud

films have a specific life to them," Jones said. "I have to retire them after about five years because clothing styles, cars and other objects tend to date them."

His film on the national parks, which have no cities, no cars, no fashions and only outdoor shots — "The Grand Canyon just doesn't change" — will have greater longevity.

What do booking agents look for in a travelog presenter? George Carlson, who has worked with travel films since his days as host of KOMO-TV's long-running

Matching slide shows and a

Want to be the guide on an armchair tour of your favorite vacation spot? To show your own travel films and slides to an appreciative audience?

Flora Lee Allen, a senior citizen with boundless energy, for 15 years has been matching frustrated slide show-ers with groups looking for interesting programs.

"All I do is put people together so that everyone's doing what they

enjoying what they're seeing."
Her personal project began when she and her husband took a trip around the world. "He couldn't decide whether to take movies or slides, so he did both," she said. "Then when we got home and no one asked him to show them, he was terribly disappointed. So we arranged something at our church and it all began there."
Now Mrs. Allen works with

from
Seattle
she's
doesn'
acts a
both p
She
helpful
staff r
of fri-
pants.

My shows got good newspaper coverage: A piece in the *Seattle Times* for *Portraits of America–The National Parks* at the Opera House.

CHAPTER NINETEEN

SAN FRANCISCO–THE CITY AT THE END OF THE RAINBOW

Burt and I had been together about a year at this point. We met through friends in New York. He was a hundred and eighty degrees from Ben Solomon. He was passive, quiet, and went along with anything. He was very handsome and was, in reality, an aging concubine. He had been the kept boy of a famous older tenor at the New York City Opera. Once he had "aged out," the tenor moved on to another young, cute thing and Burt found himself in his late thirties with no job skills and past his prime. He floundered. When I met him he was crashing in an illegal sublet, working for a shady real estate broker, and barely able to put food on the table. He did have a biting sense of humor, flowing blond hair, and he was perfectly happy to devote himself to making me happy. For a time it worked.

When it became time to decide on my next film subject, I chose San Francisco. It's one of my favorite cities and it had not been filmed for the travelogue circuit for many years. I did the shoot in the fall of 1980. Summer in San Francisco is impossible: there's too much fog. The best months for sunshine are in the autumn.

You can't make a film on San Francisco without the cable cars. In 1980, the cable car system was hanging on by a thread. By the end of the 1970s, they were in terrible shape. I knew money had been allocated to close the system down for a complete two-year overhaul. I wanted to beat the clock and get my footage before the shutdown began. I was paranoid about this. We got off the plane at noon and headed to 899 Pine Street where we had rented an apartment for two months. Burt hauled the suitcases and film cases up to the apartment and I went right down to Powell Street and started shooting. It was a beautiful day and the cable cars were operating on schedule. I shot the cars at twelve different vantage points from the slot on Market Street where the cars are turned around all the way out to Fisherman's Wharf and Ghirardelli Square. I went into the cable car barn and filmed the giant spinning wheels that move the cables under the streets of the hilly city. By the end of the day, I had shot 700 feet of film and wrapped the cable car sequence. I could relax. They could close the system down.

It was actually 1982 before the system shut down for overhaul. Today, the cable cars are still the city's best-loved attraction. Whenever I go to San Francisco I still ride on a cable car. I always take the position on the running board at the front and hang out over the street as the cable car makes the steep ascent to the top of Nob Hill. A trick if you are going to ride a cable car: wait until late in the evening. At 9:00 p.m. or even 10:00 p.m. the car will be making its last run and there are fewer passengers. Riding on the cable cars during the day usually involves a long wait but I have rarely seen the cars crowded late at night, and in some ways the experience is more romantic. The dark city passing by while you hang off of the running board, the clanging bell, the rattling of the wheels, the noise of the gripman yanking back the levers that grab the cable that takes the car almost into the heavens. It's a travel experience everyone should have.

I shot all of the obvious things; the Golden Gate Bridge, the Bay Bridge, Alcatraz. I stood inside a solitary confinement cell and had the Park Ranger close the door. It was chilling to stand in that pitch-black space and imagine what it must have been like for the prisoners. I took the ferry to Sausalito, filmed Fisherman's Wharf, the colorful murals, and the ethnic districts: Chinatown, Japantown, and the Mission.

Making a ninety-minute film on a single city requires stories with greater depth. One of San Francisco's well-known products is sourdough bread. I went to the Parisian Sourdough Bakery early one morning and filmed a sequence on baking the bread. The original batch of dough dates back to the Gold Rush days. I filmed a sequence at Levi Strauss on the making of blue jeans, the seismology laboratory at UC Berkley, and the house painters doing the colorful paint jobs on the Victorian gingerbread homes.

I did not do a sequence on the Castro district, which is San Francisco's well-known LGBT neighborhood. I chose to address the "gay issue" of San Francisco in my lectures during the front talk to the second half of the film.

I started showing the program in the winter of 1981. It was nerve-racking to walk on stage in places like Birmingham, Alabama and talk about San Francisco's gay community. I did not "out" myself but I'm sure many audience members could figure it out. By discussing The Castro in my front talk rather than the film itself, I could adjust what I said for the audience I was speaking to. If you are standing on stage in New Holland, Pennsylvania and 70% of the audience is Mennonite, you are not going to discuss gay life in the same way that you would in front of an audience at the University of Wisconsin in Madison. I had to have the latitude to adjust what I was saying for the place where I was speaking.

I filmed the colorful and noisy Chinese New Year parade. I shot the old Broadway night club district that blazed with neon signs advertising topless revues, drag shows, and the famous Carol Doda sign with her flashing neon breasts. All of that is gone now, but it was a colorful, bawdy district that recalled San Francisco's famous days of the Barbary Coast. And I filmed Halloween, San Francisco's favorite holiday. There is a huge parade in the Castro, which I did not film, but I did film the Exotic Erotic Ball. This is an annual event held in a big dance hall on Fisherman's Wharf. It was crowded, but I managed to move through the mob and film the craziness. One of my favorite shots was of two people dancing with unicorn heads. I thought it was so imaginative. I featured the shot at the opening of the Halloween sequence. I showed the film all over America at places like the National Geographic Society, the Harvard Club, in small towns, and even at religious institutions like Calvin College in Grand Rapids.

Ten years later, once VHS had become a reality, I decided to add soundtracks to my films so they could be released on home video. I recorded the audio post-production at Juniper Sound Studios in Burbank with my sound engineer Steve Sharp. I was narrating in a sound booth as the videotape ran on a monitor and the shot of the unicorns came onto the screen and Steve goes "Whoa!!!" "What are you stopping for?" I asked. Steve, who had a sharp eye, said, "The unicorns' horns are dildoes!" He backed up the tape and sure enough, my shot of the two unicorns dancing had bouncing eight-inch dildoes on their heads. Suddenly, I had this panic about all of the conservative places I had shown the film, the thousands who had seen it, and I wondered how many people had noticed this. I had shot the film, edited the film, and I watched the movie over two hundred times from the stage and I never picked up on this at all.

When Burt and I first arrived in San Francisco, we looked at each other and said, "Why are we living in New York?" San Francisco was so beautiful. So many of the problems of New York did not exist here. Both of us thought about picking up and moving. But after about six weeks, I looked at Burt and said "I miss watching an old lady having a fight with a bus driver." That intensity of New York was missing. For all of San Francisco's beauty, I missed the fast paced human drama of Manhattan. So Burt and I packed up and left San Francisco and returned to West End Avenue. I got busy cutting the film. I was starting my lecture tour late that season. I would go on the road to start showing *San Francisco–The City at the End of the Rainbow* in January 1981. I would start in Sarasota on a circuit of twenty-four shows for a company called Travelventure Travelogues. And it was on that trip that Burt and I had an evening off and chose to take in a kitschy local tourist attraction that would give me the idea for a new film.

CHAPTER TWENTY

THE WORLD CRUISE OF THE QUEEN ELIZABETH 2

The origin of the idea was so improbable.

I was showing *San Francisco–the City at the End of the Rainbow* on the Travelventure series in Florida in the winter of 1981. We were staying in Sarasota. All the shows were on the Gulf coast. I had a matinee in Saint Petersburg at the Bayfront Civic Center Auditorium. It was Sunday and I had managed to find a copy of *The New York Times*. I was sitting in my dressing room before the show, scanning the travel section, when I saw a small ad, only a couple of columns wide and maybe two inches high, for the 1982 World Cruise of the *QE2*. I had been on the *Queen Elizabeth 2* twice, the first time in 1970 returning from Paris, and again in 1976 when I made a crossing to London. I enjoyed the journeys but I hadn't thought much about ship since. The idea of a world cruise was intriguing.

I had the evening off and, after the matinee, Burt wanted to go on a dinner cruise on a funky tourist boat that sailed around Sarasota Bay. We boarded the boat and sat at a table by a window. Dinner was served, a pianist played, the sunset was lovely, the boats in the bay passed by, and the experience was charming—but I couldn't keep from thinking about this simple experience in Sarasota in bigger and grander terms; the *QE2* sailing around the world.

The idea was hatched and I set out to sell the film and myself to the Cunard Line. I certainly couldn't pay for the cruise; it was $30,000 per person. I had to get Cunard to comp me in exchange for the publicity value of the film. That was going to be a big sell.

How to reach customers was always an issue for travel businesses back then. Travelogue shows were considered a good method to reach travelers with money. Many tourist agencies, airlines, and cruise companies were willing to give perks in exchange for the publicity. Those perks usually involved free transportation, hotels, guides, and general assistance.

After some effort, I got an appointment with a man in the publicity department of the Cunard Line at 555 Fifth Avenue in New York. I went in, introduced myself, and placed a clippings book in front of him and just started turning the pages. The book was filled with newspaper stories, theater programs, and magazine clippings of shows I had done all over the country. This piqued his interest. Cunard had cooperated with the National Geographic Society in the mid 1970s on a television program call *Twilight of the Superliners*. It featured the *QE2* and basically indicated that all of it was coming to an end—soon. While Cunard was grateful for the publicity, they were not happy to have a program out there that suggested the ship was on its last legs. The ship had made a significant comeback but that was not newsworthy. They had to deal with this depressing television program that wouldn't go away.

So, I come along and offer to make a feature-length film on the World Cruise of the *QE2* at no cost to Cunard. I had the audiences, all I needed was a cabin—granted, a very expensive cabin. After several meetings and negotiations, Cunard agreed to provide a complimentary cabin for the full world cruise in exchange for the publicity value I could generate with the film.

This set into motion a whirlwind of planning. The ship would be stopping at twenty-four ports. I would have limited time in each port and I was going to need guides and drivers along the way. One by one, I contacted the government tourist agencies of every port the ship would visit. The arrangements had to be in place before the ship sailed on Jan. 17th, 1982. It was a staggering logistics project. I ran all over New York, going into meetings with the tourist agency representatives of Barbados, Martinique, Brazil, South Africa, Mauritius, Sri Lanka, India, Malaysia, Singapore, Thailand, Hong Kong, Korea, Japan, Hawaii, Mexico, Colombia, and Curaçao. My desk was flooded with brochures, maps, letters, lists of things to film; I nearly went nuts trying to put it all together.

To complicate matters, Cunard was slow to issue the tickets. I pushed them to issue our documents and they kept delaying. The ship was not sold out. But I knew that if the ship did fill up and they could sell our cabin before the gangway was pulled, they would do it in a heartbeat.

The *Queen Elizabeth 2*, the ship that took me around the world. 1982. Photo courtesy of the Cunard Line.

Burt Rendflash and me boarding in New York to start filming *The Great World Cruise of the QE2*. 1982.

Finally, the day arrived. Burt and I left the apartment with more luggage than I have ever taken on a trip. I had 30,000 feet of film, extra cameras, tripods, lighting rigs, and all the clothing, including tuxedos and formal attire that would be needed for an eighty-day trip around the world. And we still did not have our tickets. We picked up our tickets at the pier *an hour* before sailing. Until the lines were thrown and the ship was out into the Hudson River, I feared Cunard would throw us off because they had found one more paying customer at the last minute.

I had arrived early to film the provisioning of the ship. The chief chef, John Bainbridge, was inspecting a meat order of one million dollars. Fruits and vegetables were bought along the way, arranged by local shipping agents, but all the meat went on in New York.

There were musicians hauling on instruments, crewmembers crawling over the hull making last minute repairs. It was a sight to see, and the temperature was eleven degrees below zero. *The New York Post* had said it was the coldest day of the century. The ship was frozen into the berth and Cunard had to use ice cutters on tugboats to break her free.

Meanwhile, people were arriving to board. It was a flurry of limousines, mink coats, and Louis Vuitton luggage. In 1982, the world cruise was still a travel experience for the rich and famous. George C. Scott and his wife Trish Van Devere, television network anchor Harry Reasoner, Norman Vincent Peale, Ruby Keller, Rex Reed, it was an amazing assortment of people coming onboard. Alice Marshall, the head of publicity for Cunard, was watching me work as I filmed arriving guests on the red carpet. She looked wary, wondering it this had been a good idea.

In those days, passengers were allowed to invite guests onboard for the bon voyage party. The ship was packed with people. I was busy filming while the party was in full swing. The Joe Loss Orchestra played in the Double Down room, the passengers danced, and the champagne flowed.

At 3:30, the purser made the announcement "All ashore that are going ashore;" though it was said in Cunard-speak "Those not sailing on *Queen Elizabeth 2* shall make their way to the gangway on the port side, deck two." At four o'clock, the *QE2* pulled out of her frozen berth into the icy Hudson River. We sailed passed the Statue of Liberty and I looked back at the World Trade Center and realized we wouldn't be back for eighty days. I thought to myself—"How lucky am I?"

The ship sailed south and stopped first in Port Everglades, Florida to board additional passengers. I went off to film Miami Beach for the day. From Florida we made our way to Barbados and Martinique. In both ports the guides showed up as arranged and the filming went off without a hitch.

From the Caribbean, *QE2* sailed on to Brazil. We were at sea for five days before arriving in Salvador de Bahia. We started making friends. Within a few days, alliances were struck and we had a circle of people who would stay with us for the rest of the cruise. We also "crossed the line." It was my first time over the equator. This called for a ceremony known as "The Court of King Neptune." It's a hazing ritual for pollywogs, people who have never been over the equator, to turn them into shellbacks, people who have had the experience. The ceremony still takes place on ships today, but it tends to be pretty tame. In 1982, it was a madhouse. The passengers were covered in god knows what, and for the crew it was even worse: motor oil and chicken fat. In the end, everyone had to "kiss the fish," which meant literally kissing a giant dead fish before being thrown into the pool. I've seen the ceremony many times, but it was never more outlandish than on my first equator crossing in 1982.

In Salvador de Bahia, Brazilian guides showed us the great baroque architecture. It is Brazil's oldest city, settled in 1501 by the Portuguese, who built plantations and brought over slaves. Then we moved on to Rio de Janeiro. To first see the city from the water at dawn is mystical. It has one of the most beautiful natural settings on earth; dramatic mountains surrounding Guanabara Bay.

Rio de Janeiro has a large gemstone industry. There are dozens of major and minor gemstone firms and Cunard had to deal with a nagging problem. The jewelry firms would send handsome, cunning men to board the ship in New York. These men, "the jewelry mob" as they were known, would glom onto rich, widowed, women on board. They would dance with them (it was before the days when the line hired "gentlemen dance hosts"), whisper into their ears, and make their way into their cabins late at night. Once in Rio, the gigolos managed to coerce these wealthy women off the gangway and directly to their stores where they would part them from staggering amounts of money. The next year, Cunard put a halt to the whole thing and stopped allowing jewelry representatives to book passage to Rio. But it was fascinating to watch. When we sailed out of Rio, all the "jewelry mob" men were gone and the women were left alone—but with fabulous jewelry! And who knows, maybe memories of a great night or two at sea.

Ruby Keeler, the early Warner Brothers star, was onboard and Burt and I became friends with her. She was long retired from her movie career and she would go on long cruises, meet people, have her old films shown onboard, and be interviewed by the cruise director. One day, in the middle of the South Atlantic, heading toward Capetown, Ruby gave a talk and spoke of her life with her husband Al Jolson, and her career as a star for Warner Brothers working with the great choreographer Busby Berkeley. That night they showed her 1933 film *42nd Street* in the ship's theater and I was asked to escort her. There I was in my tuxedo, escorting Ruby Keller into the theater for a showing of *42nd Street*. When we walked in, the entire audience stood and applauded. We sat down and the great tap dancing epic filled the screen. The plot is simple; it's a movie about staging a Broadway show. The star gets sick at the last minute and the girl in the back of the chorus—Ruby—is chosen to go out on opening night. When Julian Marsh, played by Warner Baxter, shouts the classic line "You're going out there a kid but you're coming back a star!" I squeezed Ruby's arm, and she just looked at me and smiled. It was one of those travel moments I'll never forget.

As the ship made its way to South Africa, I got a chance to film the Captain on the bridge. Captain Peter Jackson was the master of the ship. And fortunately he was a great ham who loved being filmed.

When you boarded the ship for the world cruise, you turned in your passport. This was so the manifest officer could get all the passports cleared for each port in advance. In some places, the customs officers flew to the preceding port and sailed with the ship. In South Africa, two customs officers came on board by helicopter. We were about fifty miles off shore from Capetown when a helicopter approached and hovered over the helipad. Two men—in suits no less—were lowered down by rope. They went to work stamping the passports and when we tied up in Capetown, we just walked off of the ship.

South Africa was still under the racist policies of apartheid in 1982. I made contact with a man named Peter Van Dam who had a tough job. He was in charge of publicity for South Africa when the country was the outcast of the world. Peter would do *anything* to get good publicity. I was not going to make a political statement (though I wished that I could). I was there to film the natural beauty of South Africa so I got great assistance. Burt and I left the ship in Capetown and rejoined four days later in Durban on the east coast. It was common for people to do overland trips on the world cruise and rejoin the ship later in the voyage.

Greeting Captain Peter Jackson, master of the *QE2* during the World Cruise. He gave me open access to the bridge and loved being in front of the camera. 1982.

After two days in Capetown, Burt and I flew to Johannesburg and then took a small plane to Nelspruit to visit Mala Mala, a large private game reserve. Mala Mala was a great experience. We slept in a tent, the sounds of the wild all around. The next day, a guide took us out to film the animals. It was inspiring to see these great beasts, giraffes, zebras, wildebeests, gazelles, all roaming.

By the end of the day we still had not seen a lion. Another guide said on the CB radio that a pair of lions had been spotted a short distance away. We drove awhile and then pulled into this shaded spot and there they were, a male and a female resting side by side. The guide told us to be absolutely silent. I had my camera mounted on a tripod on the back of the jeep. I shot my film as quickly and as silently as I could. When I was finished I took my camera off the tripod. The "click" of the clip disengaging caused the male to rise up on his haunches, ready to lunge. Our driver pulled out a gun and pointed it directly at the lion and told us all to freeze. About ten seconds later the lion backed down and returned to his resting position. The guide kept the gun aimed as he put the jeep in gear and slowly drove away. It was the longest ten seconds of my life. The footage is in the film and I still find it chilling.

From Mala Mala we flew to Durban and re-boarded the *QE2* and then we set sail for Mauritius in the middle of the Indian Ocean. The island is famous for its giant lily pads in the Pamplemousses Gardens and elaborate model ships. I was taken to Curpipe, in the center of the island, to film the model ship makers. All the young girls in the factory were giggling. The owner told me that they had never seen an American before.

Next we docked at Colombo. Sri Lanka was idyllic. The peaceful nature of the island was in contrast to my experiences in India. It was calming. I was driven to Kandy to film the Temple of The Tooth. The temple holds a relic that is said to be a tooth of Buddha rescued from the burning funeral pyre. Along the way, we passed the elephant pools. Sri Lanka has large herds of Asian elephants that are used as beasts of burden. They are primarily used to move lumber. It is ironic that they are used to destroy the forests that make up their habitat. The elephants are bathed in the pools and well cared for, or at least it seemed that way to me.

I filmed the Kandyian Dancers and the fire-eaters, as well as a snake charmer. After I filmed the cobra lifting itself out of the basket, I was distracted by someone behind me trying to sell something. I wanted to get rid of the peddler so I packed up my camera and got ready to leave. I turned around and the snake charmer had the cobra in his hand directly in front of my face. I had forgotten to pay the photo fee and he wasn't letting me out of there without something. I still remember Burt saying "Doooooug… give him some money!"

Next: India. The *QE2* docked at Madras and all I had to do was set up my camera and start shooting. Cows wandering the streets, camels pulling giant carts, pedicabs everywhere; India is life on steroids. People, people everywhere. From Madras we flew to New Delhi, where a driver took us to Agra. It was late at night and the driver drove at breakneck speed, right down the middle of the two-lane highway. There were people and animals everywhere on both sides. I have never seen so many people and so much activity outside in the middle of the night. You had to drive in the center of the road to avoid killing someone or something. When the headlights of an approaching car appeared, no one slowed down. At the very last second, both cars would swerve around each other and continue barreling down the center of the highway. It was a continuous game of "chicken."

We finally arrived at Agra and checked into the hotel. I was to film the Taj Mahal the following morning. The Indians view, rightly so, the Taj Mahal as their greatest asset. I had been given permission to film the site. But the director of operations at the Taj had a different idea. Before I could enter the grounds, I had to go to his office.

Oh yes, I would be allowed to film, but I could not use a tripod. To use a tripod required a separate license. It was all a ruse to get a bribe. I offered something—I've forgotten what, probably $50—and the man just laughed and shook his head. I felt like I was being extorted, which I was, and I refused to be strong-armed into this bribe when I had made all the arrangements far in advance. So I left my tripod in the car and headed in to shoot the Taj handheld. Shooting something like the Taj Mahal without a tripod is a real challenge because the shots must be rock steady. I mostly laid flat on my stomach and use my arms as a wedge to support the camera and hold it dead still. My footage of the Taj Mahal looks good considering it was shot without a tripod. I also had to do it fast because word had come down that the authorities had changed their minds and I was not going to be allowed to film at all without some rupees changing hands. I worked quickly and within forty-five minutes we were gone. I had traveled to the farthest corner of the globe to see one of the grandest sites of the planet and I was in and out in less than an hour. Sometimes I had to work so quickly that I didn't have a chance to simply stop, breath, and take in the wonder of what was in front of me. I had to wait until later, when I viewed my own film, to appreciate what I had seen.

From Agra we traveled back to Madras and re-boarded the *QE2* and we sailed on to Malaysia and Kuala Lumpur. The Sultan of Selangor, the constitutional ruler of Malaysia, was a passenger on the *QE2*. When we arrived in Kuala Lumpur, his Rolls Royce and half the nation's military were there to meet him. He was off to his own palace for lunch with a group of people he had met onboard. Late in the afternoon, the Sultan walked back onboard looking content, the passengers invited to accompany him for lunch looked dazed from the extravagance and excess.

John Schlesinger, the Academy Award winning film director (*Midnight Cowboy*), was onboard. He and I spoke about the sights to see in Kuala Lumpar. I met John again years later in Palm Springs and reminded him of our conversation and our time on the *QE2*. I could see in his eyes the memories coming back from so long ago.

Jim Bailey, the female impersonator known for his Judy Garland act, boarded the *QE2* in South Africa to entertain the passengers with several shows. He got off in Kuala Lumpur and I wondered how he explained the contents of his suitcases, with all the wigs and Judy garb, to the Malaysian customs officials. The night after his Judy Garland show, I overheard a conversation in which a woman asked, "Did you see the Judy Garland show last night?" and the other passenger replied, "Oh, is she on board?"

From Malaysia we sailed to Singapore. I am always conflicted about Singapore. Sir Stanford Raffles founded Singapore in 1819 as a British trading post when almost no one was living on the island. By the end of World War II, it was in sad shape. It had been occupied by the Japanese, and it was crime ridden, poor, and battered. The British decided to let the residents have a council of representatives. The Peoples Action Party took forty-one of the fifty-three seats and chose Lee Kuan Yew to be the Prime Minister. He ruled Singapore with an iron hand and today his son has succeeded him and continues to run the country.

Lee Kuan Yew turned Singapore around. Today, Singapore is one of the best-run places on earth, literally. There is no poverty. Everyone is employed. All health care and education is paid for by the state. The standard of living is the highest in Asia. The place is spotlessly clean, the infrastructure excellent, but it is a one party system. There is no freedom of the press. It is notorious for chewing gum being illegal, and God help you if you bring in any drugs. Execution is standard punishment. If you ask Singaporeans why they don't rebel against this authoritarian structure, they look around and say, "Why would we?" You have to accept that other cultures have different values and if their systems work you have to acknowledge that too.

Singapore was the halfway point on the world cruise. That's when the "forty day fights" began. The crew told me it happened every year. About halfway into the journey many passengers had just had enough of someone's behavior. People who had been civil over dinner for forty nights decided that they had heard enough about a tablemate's politics, or religion, or snobbish life. This was the point where you were tired of putting up with the sloppy drunk that had been at your table for forty dinners. The maître d' would get busy and there would be a scramble to rearrange the dining room. People would be moved to new tables and new alliances would be made. As the trip went into the last forty days, people's tempers calmed down, but I remember a tense five or six days in South Asia when everybody wanted to strangle somebody.

Our next stop was Thailand. The *QE2* docked at Pattaya, and Burt and I took a car into the city. I had been to Bangkok twice before. Although I love the Thai people, they are gracious and very kind hearted, I am not particularly fond of Bangkok. Whenever I think of Bangkok, I think of choking fumes, noise, and ungodly traffic. What makes all of this worse is the fact that Bangkok really has no center. I can't think of another city in the world that lacks a central gathering place, a public square, or some spot that is defined as the central meeting point. The Chao Phraya River is the closest thing to a "center" Bangkok has. The river divides the city, like Paris, but much more profoundly. Boats and river buses zigzag up and down and people cross the river using water taxis. Still, the attractions are amazing. The Grand Palace is stunning. The floating markets teemed with activity. Bangkok has the largest collection of Buddhist temple architecture in the world. The long boats roar by in the canals powered by engines with shafts that extend out into the water. To steer the boat the helmsman swings the entire engine.

From Bangkok, the ship headed north to Hong Kong. The *QE2* docked in Hong Kong for five days. This gave everyone a chance to explore what was then still a British Crown Colony. In those days, Cunard would have the ship painted in Hong Kong. The moment we docked, the ship was covered in ropes and scaffolding and painters went up and down the hull painting the signature white top and blue-black bottom. I filmed the attractions I had seen on earlier trips; the dazzling neon signs of Kowloon, a point-of-view shot from the top of a double decker bus lumbering up Nathan Road. I shot the new subway system and Aberdeen, the floating city filled with thousands of permanent residents living on Chinese junks. I filmed an herbalist shop and next door was a store selling snakes as the ingredients for that night's dinner. I had a suit tailored; I filmed the cutters and sewers. And I shot a lavish culture pageant that included stick puppets spinning plates. Very cool.

From Hong Kong we sailed to Pusan, South Korea. It was still chilly and spring had not yet arrived. I filmed at Bulguksa, the Temples of Buddhaland. Many Koreans in traditional dress circled the temples and stopped to pray. We had a typical Korean lunch, not necessarily to my taste, and we had a government guide, who, for some odd reason, was completely obsessed with sex. He would ask the most pointed and inappropriate questions. He lacked any understanding of boundaries.

Next was Japan. We made two stops. The first was Kagoshima on the southernmost island of Kyushu. Dancers, musicians, and drummers welcomed the ship. And adding to the excitement, a large eruption of Sakurajima was underway. Clouds of smoke and ash billowed out during our stay. I filmed a very Zen-like tea ceremony, and I shot in a Pachinko parlor. Pachinko is like a pinball machine except you have no real control over the dropping balls or the score you amass. And if you do win, you'll get something exciting like a bar of soap or a bag of candy. But the Japanese love the game and the parlors are major centers of social life.

From Kagoshima we sailed on to Yokohama and docked there for three days. Our guide took us into Tokyo and put us up in a nice hotel, although the room was no larger than a closet, which is typical in space-starved Japan. The next day I filmed the great Shinto Shrines at Asakusa, the Imperial Palace, the Ginza, the Tokyo subway, and we traveled out to Kamakura to shoot the great Kamakura Buddha. The Japanese are pragmatic. Shintoism is the primary religion of Japan, but it has no concept of an afterlife. The Japanese will often use Shinto rituals to mark births and marriages, but as life draws to a close, they will often turn to Buddhism with its concept of reincarnation. It's a spiritual version of covering your bases.

Japanese culture is fascinating. It is a homogenous society; everyone is Japanese. Because of this homogeneity, there is a general belief that what is good for the group is more important than what is good for the individual. It's very noticeable in how the country operates and how people interact with each other.

Finally, we left Tokyo and returned to the dock at Yokohama where we nearly missed the ship. We had a hard time getting through the crowd to board. The Japanese love ocean liners and the *QE2* was the most famous ship in the world at the time. When we sailed, 100,000 people (I'm not exaggerating) were on the dock to watch the ship pull out. On the Promenade Deck I filmed this mass of humanity; a solid crowd of people for as far as the eye could see. It made me realize how important the *QE2* was in the travel dreams of people all over the world.

From Tokyo, the ship set out on its longest journey; six days straight across the Western Pacific to Hawaii. This is one of the largest bodies of open water in the world, and the swells can be over a mile long. Because of this, the ship was in constant motion, rising and falling on these giant swells. While I don't tend to get seasick, I do get tired. Being in a constant swell means that everything in your body, all your internal organs, is constantly moving. The net result is exhaustion. I was worn out by the time we pulled into Honolulu.

In Hawaii I filmed many of the same places and images I had shot in 1974 for *The Hawaiian Adventure*. I already knew where to set up the camera.

Honolulu to Los Angeles was another long leg. I used the time to film the galleys of the *QE2*, which were pretty amazing. It was a twenty-four hour a day operation. Bread was baked early each morning and the meals had to come out of the galley three times a day. There were eighteen hundred passengers onboard and a staff of twelve hundred, so three thousand people had to be fed. Nine thousand meals a day, 720,000 meals for the full world cruise.

From L.A., we sailed to Acapulco where I filmed the cliff divers at the El Mirador hotel. I also went parasailing. They hooked me into the harness and the speedboat pulled me off the platform and into the air. I went soaring up and over the wide beach at Acapulco. I was brought back down and landed on the floating platform and didn't break either my legs or my neck. Burt and I had lunch at the Las Brisas Hotel, famed for the pink jeeps and rooms with individual swimming pools.

Next was the Panama Canal. At 4:00 a.m., the ship slowed and the Panama Canal pilots boarded while I got off. I had arranged for a car to drive me alongside the canal so I could photograph the *QE2* as she made her transit. Earlier Cunard ships could not sail through the Panama Canal. They were too long. When the *QE2* was launched in 1967, she was intended to be both a transatlantic liner and cruise ship. She was shorter than the *Queen Mary* and the *Queen Elizabeth*, and designed specifically to fit through the Panama Canal. The clearance was eighteen inches on each side. The ship fit into the locks like a foot in a shoe. There were inevitable scraps and dings on the hull because the clearance was so tight. At the time, the *QE2* was paying the highest transit fee of any ship in the world—$100,000. Conversely, the lowest transit fee ever paid was 36 cents in 1928, when Richard Halliburton swam through the canal.

I filmed as the Miraflores locks filled with water and the ship rose on the Pacific side. The *QE2* then sailed across Gatun Lake and descended on the Caribbean side through the three Gatun locks. I went into the control rooms and watched the gauges going up and down as the men opened the locks and flooded the chambers. The tractor-like engines that pull the ship are called "mules" and they ran on tracks on each side of the locks pulling the ship in and out of the chambers. After the ship left the last lock, it proceeded on and docked at Colón on the Caribbean end of the canal. I re-boarded the ship at Colón and we sailed on to Cartagena.

This was my one and only time in Colombia. It was lovely but there was an eeriness about the place. I had never seen so many armed soldiers on the streets. You had the sense that the world of the drug cartels was not that far away.

Finally, we stopped in Curaçao. At the time it was a part of The Netherlands Antilles. It was charming with its Dutch gabled pastel shops. The island is known for Curaçao liqueur made from a local bitter orange.

From Curaçao we began the final journey back to New York. In those last days of the cruise, you traded phone numbers and addresses and said goodbye to people who had become close. Everyone swore lifelong friendship and that we would all see each other on shore. It didn't really happen much. Once off the ship, people went their separate ways. But sailing back into New York, under the Verrazano-Narrows Bridge, past the Statue of Liberty, and toward the World Trade Center, I took a moment to reflect. It had been a truly life-changing experience. I rank the 1982 World Cruise of the *QE2* as the single greatest travel experience of my life. Nothing I had done before nor have done since ever came close.

I made three more films on the *QE2*, and when Cunard retired her and sold her to Dubai in October of 2008, I made her final crossing. It was a tandem sailing with the *Queen Mary 2* out of New York. The *QE2* sailed from the 55th Street Pier on the Hudson River. The *Queen Mary 2* sailed from the Brooklyn Pier in Red Hook. We met in the harbor in front of the Statue of Liberty, two great ships, fireworks exploding overhead, horns blasting, and thousands of people onboard and on the shore to see the *QE2* leave New York City for the very last time.

THE QUEEN ELIZABETH 2

Standing in front of the *QE2* as she begins her transit of the Panama Canal at the Miraflores Locks; toward the end of the World Cruise. 1982.

Seven days later, our passage across the North Atlantic nearly complete, the two ships came to a halt beside each other ten miles off Land's End. Everyone on the *Queen Mary 2* was on the port side of the ship and it listed noticeably. Everyone on the *Queen Elizabeth 2* was on the starboard side and I'm sure she was listing as well. There was silence. Then, the two ships began a formal exchange of horn blasts. Each ship blasted five times in three cycles and finally the *QE2* gave the final blast. It was the signal that the *QE2*'s days were over. There were three thousand passengers and crew on the *QE2* and four thousand passengers and crew on the *Queen Mary 2*—seven thousand people adrift in the ocean and all you could hear was the sea lapping at the hull. It was pure silence. It was one of the most profound moments in my life of travel, saying goodbye to this ship I had loved so much. There is a part of my soul that stayed onboard that ship and never really left.

Cunard sailed the *QE2* for forty years, longer than any other ship in their history. She sailed more miles, carried more passengers, and visited more exotic ports of call than any other ship in the history of the world. She was and remains the last true ocean liner, the last great lady of the sea.

The marquee of the Embassy Theater in Fort Wayne, Indiana. *The Great World Cruise of the QE2* was my first really big success. The audiences were the largest I had ever drawn. 1986.

A new film required a new headshot; done by Ken Duncan, the famous ballet photographer. His work was popularized in *After Dark* magazine. 1982.

CHAPTER TWENTY-ONE

THE PLAGUE

Where to begin.

Burt and I returned home from the World Cruise in April of 1982. While the ship was transiting the Panama Canal, an astonishing announcement was made. The British government was requisitioning the ship for the Falklands War immediately upon its arrival in New York. Argentina had invaded the Falklands in a long-running dispute over sovereignty and Margaret Thatcher decided the Brits were not going to let them get away with it. She sent the British Navy to the South Atlantic and requisitioned the *QE2* as a troop ship.

Back in New York, I was worried that the ship would be sunk and not only the lives of the sailors on board would be lost—but my film as well. No one was going to be interested in seeing a film called *The Great World Cruise of the QE2* if the ship was laying at the bottom of the sea. It nearly happened. The only thing that saved the ship was the fog. The Argentinians made several flyover attempts to bomb the ship, but the fog was so thick they could never get a clear shot.

The war started April 2, 1982. Seventy-four days later it was over. The British won and they kept the Falklands (and their honor which seemed to have been much of the issue) and the *QE2* returned to Southampton. Back home, she was refitted. For some unknown reason they decided to paint her pearl gray. When she arrived in New York with this ugly hull, everyone knew it was a mistake. Ships' hulls take a beating and blue-black hides the rust. The pearl gray hull showed everything and she looked terrible only months after the new paint job was applied. Within a year, the *QE2* was repainted in her signature blue-black.

Before we left on world cruise, Burt had a friend who had gotten ill suddenly and died. In July of 1981, *The New York Times* wrote a short story about a "gay cancer" that had been seen in New York and Los Angeles. Forty-one mysterious cases appeared almost overnight. In time it was named GRID, Gay Related Immune Disorder. That moniker stayed with the epidemic for about a year until a friend of mine, Dr. Bruce Voeller, suggested at a National Institutes of Health meeting that it be renamed AIDS, Acquired Immune Deficiency Syndrome, to remove the stigma it was placing on gay people. Soon, the retrovirus was discovered and it was called Human Immunodeficiency Virus, HIV. And ultimately, we saw that it was much more than a gay disease. Before you could turn your head, it was like a bonfire out of control.

It seems so long ago. Today HIV infection is a chronic but manageable condition much like diabetes. HIV carriers live normal lifespans and die of heart disease, stroke; the typical illnesses of aging. But in the early 1980s that was not the case. You would have dinner with a friend and he would be full of laughter and life. Then you would run into the same person two months later and they were gaunt and drawn. You knew immediately. We called it "the look." We were terrified because we knew any one of us could be next.

In 1979, two years before the plague really hit, I produced an Off-Broadway play called *Newsboy* at the Players Theater. It was about a politician who had a gay son and he was trying to keep that fact out of the newspapers. It was no Pulitzer Prize winner, but it was a good play. John Glines had produced it in a small space. How I got the rights for this Off-Broadway production I don't recall. I dealt directly with the author whose *nom de plume* was Arch Brown but whose real name was Arnold Brueger.

As the producer, I made one fatal error. I broke the one sacrosanct rule of producing—I put my own money into the show. Well, that was a mistake. The show opened, the audiences did not appear, and within a couple of weeks I had to close it down.

In those days, a producer had to count the "deadwood" (the unsold tickets) and reconcile the receipts with the box office treasurer. It was a depressing affair because so few tickets were being sold. One night I was running late to the theater. I went into the subway at 79th and Broadway to catch the #1 train downtown. As I went down the stairs, I saw the train on the platform so I ran to the turnstile. I dropped the token in and tried to ram through. Unfortunately, I didn't allow the split second for the token to drop and I hit the turnstile mid upper leg with full body force. The pain was instant and horrible. The token dropped, the turnstile opened, and I rushed onto the train in excruciating pain.

Somehow I made it to the theater and went over the receipts with the box office manager, but I was getting very sick. My leg swelled to the size of a football so I went to Roosevelt Hospital where they told me I had a hematoma. Blunt trauma. They gave me pain medication, kept me overnight, and sent me home the next day.

Over the next week, the hematoma went away but I kept getting sicker. I had a fever of a hundred and four degrees each night that would last for an hour or two. I was becoming weaker and weaker. I lived alone (this was before I met Burt) and I was trying to keep *Newsboy* open but my health was fading fast. Finally, I decided to close the show. I posted the closing notice and gave the cast their final checks. I tried to sort out the closing financials that had to be done before we could shut down the production but I was too ill to do it so the box officer treasurer kindly did it for me.

After having been sick for over a week, I went to my doctor, Jacob Bornstein. He took one look at me and called Lenox Hill Hospital and had me admitted. I was in the hospital for almost three weeks. Every test imaginable was done. They couldn't figure out what was wrong. Eventually, they sent me home, but the spiking fevers still occurred like clockwork at 6:00 p.m. each night. Nobody knew what I had, nobody had any idea what was wrong, and my doctor and the staff at Lenox Hill were baffled.

In 1981, the first recorded AIDS death occurred in New York City. In the years to come, tens of thousands would die. But there were non-progressors. People, men primarily, who acquired the HIV virus but whose immune systems did not collapse.

In 1985, the HIV test was developed to confirm infection. I tested positive. I was not surprised. My doctor believed that my bout of illness in 1979 was probably one of the earliest cases in the epidemic, but somehow my system fought it off and the disease never progressed. I have been HIV positive for nearly forty years and I have never had an opportunistic illness or suffered any of the complications that come with AIDS. Why was I spared when so many of my friends were not?

By the time Burt and I came back to New York from the world cruise, the epidemic had turned into a conflagration. The phone would ring and another friend would be sick, or dying, or dead. I spoke at so many people's funerals that I had a standard speech I would give, just change the name and a few pertinent facts; it was an all encompassing, all purpose eulogy for my brothers who were gone.

It is impossible for anyone who did not live through this time to understand what it was like. Gay people had only recently come out of the closet. We were starting to live open and exciting lives. And just as we were starting to celebrate our creativity and contribution to American culture, along came a virus that nearly toppled a generation.

I can't count the number of friends I lost. And they were the brightest and the best. They were the artists, the musicians, the singers, the dancers, the actors, and the writers. They were the people who brought life to Broadway, the opera, television, the movies, the forms of popular culture the world adored. And they died as if a firing squad had shown up in Times Square, lined up the greatest generation of creative people in history, and mowed them down. I will spare you a recitation of the names. Many were famous, others unknown. The pain of the times lived in the souls of gay people across America as the unending tragedy spread.

People were desperate. They would try anything. Every quack cure that came along was worth a shot. The pharmaceutical industry worked furiously. They were trying to find answers, not necessarily for noble reasons, but because they knew there were billions of dollars to be made if the right medicines could be produced. But nothing worked. People were treated with toxic drugs, often prescribed in doses that made the illness worse. The body count increased, and the nation looked away.

Ronald Reagan may be a hero to fiscal conservatives and small government advocates, but ask any gay person who lived through the AIDS crisis and they will tell you that Reagan's refusal to acknowledge the epidemic, much less do anything about it, was the single greatest obstacle to stopping it.

So LGBT people took to the streets. We formed ACTUP—The AIDS Coalition to Unleash Power. We protested, we fought, we did outrageous things—but we finally got some attention. Drugs trials were shortened, new therapies were developed, and we empowered ourselves to be a part of finding the answers. And we joined together as a family. Relatives and friends often shunned HIV/AIDS sufferers. It was within our own community that we found our family. People took care of the sick and dying, and they often did it with no blood relatives to support them.

Then in 1995, Saquinavir, a new type of drug called a protease inhibitor, showed promise in trials. It was used in combination with two other drugs and in less than a year the AIDS deaths virtually came to a halt. The illness did not go away, but the sword of death that hung over everyone was gone. People started getting better and they did so quickly. The costs of the drugs were outrageous. People with good health insurance got the drugs quickly, while those without waited. Eventually, programs were put in place to help the uninsured receive the medicines they needed. They were frightening times. We looked around at everyone we knew and wondered who would survive. Many did, many did not. Tens of thousands died.

Burt and I remained together for another year. Our relationship was not destined for longevity. He died of AIDS eight years later in 1991. He was one of many dear and cherished people who were taken from me by one of the greatest health plagues of the 20th century. It was our holocaust. America did not want to deal with a disease that affected people on the margins of society. It is important to remember the price we paid for that indifference.

Today we have same sex marriage, federal benefits for same sex couples, and LGBT people adopting and having children. But there is a backstory. These advances did not come easily. They came about because of a generation of men and women who fought for justice, for health, and for the right to be true to themselves. My generation built the foundation on which gay people are able to prosper and be accepted today.

CHAPTER TWENTY-TWO

UNLUCKY IN LOVE

My career did not make for a stable home life. At one point, I realized that if I had one more "committed" relationship I would be tied with Elizabeth Taylor. But I kept trying. Part of me wanted a real relationship, a real coupled life, but twenty years would pass before this would happen. In the two decades that followed, there would be a string of crazy, failed, chaotic relationships. But for all the problems each entailed, they left me with some indelible memories, both good and bad.

In 1982, after Burt and I returned from the world cruise, he moved on to California and I was once again a single man. One evening in the summer of '82, I drifted into an Upper West Side bar called Boot Hill. A man named Bill Less was sitting at the end of the bar. (Note: I am using a pseudonym to protect his identity. You'll soon learn why).

We struck up a conversation and he invited me back to his place. He lived at 79th and Riverside Drive. We walked out of the bar and instead of heading uptown, he turned and walked toward a black limousine. He had a limo and a driver. This was a good start.

The driver pulled away from the curb and headed to 79th Street, turned left and drove to the Hudson River. I soon found out that Bill lived on a boat, a motor yacht, called the *Stella Maris*. I liked this.

Bill was smitten with me so I decided to give this relationship a try. Mind you, all of this sounds much more fabulous than it really was. Bill had delusions of grandeur. Yes, he had a limo, but the limo was missing two wheel covers and had a big dent in the passenger side. Yes, he lived on a motor yacht, but it smelled like diesel fuel and was a horrible mess. Boat people fall into one of two categories. They are either fastidious or they are slobs. Bill fell into the latter—big time. The boat was a mess, clothes everywhere, dirty dishes in the galley, but I had visions of cleaning it up, and Bill was so kind and caring it seemed a project worth undertaking. Bill was a commercial insurance broker with a booming business in the financial district. But the glamorous life he wanted did not come naturally.

Shortly after we started seeing each other, we decided to take the *Stella Maris* to Five Towns out on Long Island. I had friends who summered there and we were going to meet them at the marina. We sailed out of the New York harbor on a beautiful day. It was idyllic. A boat all to yourself to go wherever you wanted. I loved the idea.

We arrived in Lawrence, Long Island and docked next to the jewelry designer Ken Lane's 80-foot yacht, which was unpretentiously named the *Ken Lane*. I saw that boating could be much more glamorous than the scow I was on. Arthur and Marvin, two guys I had met on the *QE2*, came down to the dock to greet us. We had drinks on the boat, went out for dinner, and then Bill and I spent the night sleeping in the master berth with that gentle rocking that a sheltered marina provides. I loved it.

The following morning we pulled the boat away from the dock and headed back to New York. Bill was no rocket scientist and I don't think he had any idea how to evaluate weather. I certainly was no expert, but the western skies looked ominous. We motored out of the marina and into the open Atlantic and then it hit: a squall. Suddenly, the skies opened up, the rain came down in buckets, the calm seas turned into eight-foot waves, and we were right in the middle of it. Bill had a giant cat. Where was the cat? Suddenly the cat crawled up onto the windshield of the wheelhouse in the downpour, clinging to the window frame outside. Bill opened the side door of the trawler, grabbed the cat and pulled it inside, drenched and scared half to death. And then lightening struck the boat—and blew out all the electronics; the radio, the radar, everything. I really thought this was where my life was going to end. But like most squalls, it didn't last long and twenty minutes later it passed, and we continued limping into the New York harbor. Bill seemed totally non-pulsed by the whole affair; I was shaken but energized. It was frightening and thrilling, an adrenaline rush like I had never had.

I continued to try to turn Bill into a cultured man but it was no easy task. We sailed to London on the *QE2*. The ship was very formal so Bill had to buy a tuxedo. One night halfway through the crossing, we went to dinner in the Queen's Grill. At the end of the meal, Bill smoked a cigarette (you could still smoke in the restaurants on the *QE2,* as amazing as that might seem today). When he finished his cigarette, he put it out in the center of his plate. That was the point I realized this was too big of an Eliza Doolittle job for me. I knew it wasn't going to work; however I was not ready to let go of the limo and the boat just yet.

We returned to New York and I went on the road for my fall lecture tour. A few weeks later, I came back and called Bill and he said, "Dougie... how are you? Let's have lunch!" Lunch? Not dinner? I knew something was up. The following day he arrived in the battered limo. He had asked me where I wanted to go and I said, "The 21 Club." I figured I should get as much out of this as I could since it might be coming to an end. Over lunch, he told me that while I was away he had found a new boyfriend—a window dresser from Bloomingdales—and he had already moved him onto the boat. *Well!* It is true that I planned to end the relationship but I expected to do the dumping—not be the dumpee—and for a window dresser no less! I was incensed.

After lunch, I was driven back to my apartment in the limo, fuming. I opened the yellow pages (how dated is that) to find "boat brokers." I found the telephone number of the broker at the 79th Street boat basin. I called him up and told him I was in the market for a boat. He asked me what I had in mind. I said I was flexible; I only had one requirement: it had to be a least one foot longer than the *Stella Maris.* Men, boats, length, ego... it's such a guy thing. And thus began my journey into the world of those "holes in the water you throw money into" that are boats.

Years passed. Bill's relationship with the window dresser soured. The guy wanted a grander life and tried to get Bill to buy an apartment and move off of the boat. Bill, who always tried to please people, started shopping with him for an apartment but first he had to get the money together. He did this by launching a huge insurance fraud scheme. He collected premiums, wrote policies, but never paid the insurance companies. This went on for about two years until one day the FBI walked into his office and arrested him.

The window dresser was Bill's only connection on the outside and it was his job to raise bail, which he would fail miserably at. So who did he call? Me. I'm sorry, much as I liked Bill, I was not bailing him out of jail.

For God's sake, he had a boat! He would be sailing into some Caribbean offshore haven as fast is he could throw the lines.

Shortly before his arraignment, the window dresser boyfriend called and said Bill had asked if I would come visit him in jail. The Tombs is the legendary New York City prison that houses criminals after their initial arrest. It is a way station on the way to bigger lockups.

I went to the jail. I approached the desk and a very large, gruff woman asked me who I was there to see. I said, "Bill Less." She picked up the phone and in a gravely voice shouted, "Bill Less, get him up and bring him down!" Yikes. I was taken into the visiting room, I sat and waited, and a few minutes later Bill appeared in prison green. He sat down and smiled that smile that I was always a sucker for.

So how do you start a conversation with someone in jail? "Seen any good movies lately?" didn't seem appropriate. So I asked him how they were treating him, how his cell was, and did he have a cellmate? He told me they were treating him all right, his cell was OK, and yes he did have a cellmate and they were getting on very well. I asked him what the cellmate was in for and Bill said, "Murder." A chill went up my spine. "But it's OK," Bill said, "He's really nice. In fact we're planning to do some business together after we both get out." I asked the cellmates name and Bill said, "Andrew Crispo." I nearly fell off my metal stool. Andrew Crispo was a gay New York art dealer accused of murder in an S&M scene gone bad. It was one of the biggest and most salacious murder cases of the decade—and he was Bill's cellmate. How's that for six degrees of separation!

After my fifteen minutes were up I left. Bill was sent upstate to some prison and time passed. Then one day, Bill called again. He told me he had another cellmate upstate who was a Mafioso who, in the loneliness of a prison cell, just *had* to tell Bill the details of the murder he was accused of—and Bill had decided to relay this information to the state in exchange for witness protection and early release—and he was calling me on my home phone from some safe house in Manhattan where he was being kept before the trial! I told Bill the Mafia was going to do everything they could to stop his testimony and maybe calling me—at home!—wasn't the best idea for my own personal safety.

Bill did testify. The guy was sent to maximum security for life. Bill got out and went into the witness protection program. He got his boat back and sailed off to an island in the Caribbean I will not name. But he called up and wanted to see me one more time before he left. I agreed. This had been, after all, one of the more colorful people in my life. We met at a friend's apartment in Midtown. Bill had a new name. I won't reveal it. He seemed wistful but that shy grin was still there. Somehow, I knew he would be OK. Like his cat on the windshield of the *Stella Maris* in the squall on the Atlantic Ocean, he had nine lives and there were still a few left to go.

* * *

I just had to have a boat. A boat broker in Freeport, Long Island was showing me a large Chris-Craft that needed a lot of work. While I was mulling over the scale of the project he said, "Let me show you a boat I just listed." It was a 37-foot wood hull Egg Harbor. Its name was *Sea'scape*. It was really the perfect size; not as big as the *Stella Maris* but close enough. It had a forward berth with two V-bunks and an aft cabin with two nice sized berths. I knew wood boats required more maintenance than fiberglass boats, but they have a charm that the big fiberglass boats don't have. There is something about the sea hitting the wood hull that sounds more like how a boat should sound.

Not unlike going into the travelogue business when I had absolutely no knowledge of photography, the fact that I really knew nothing about boats—or God help me, the *sea*—did not deter. I plopped down the cashier's check and took possession.

I left Freeport for Patchogue, Long Island on a Saturday morning in a thick fog. I should have waited but I didn't. I had charts and I knew how shallow the bay was. You had to stay within channels marked by buoys. If you wandered outside the channel, even slightly, you would run aground. Which is exactly what I did. I had not had the boat one hour before I had it aground on the sandy bottom of the Great South Bay. Somehow I knew the procedure to rock the boat free using forward and reverse props and I managed to free her up and continue on. It was the first but not the last time *Sea'scape* would be run aground with me at the helm.

The Great South Bay is a large, very shallow bay that is formed by Fire Island, a thin sand dune that stretches along the Atlantic on the south side of Long Island. It has several communities including The Pines and Cherry Grove, which are popular LGBT summer resorts. The "Island," as it was called, attracted the wealthy. People built palatial homes on the ocean and watched them wash out to sea in hurricanes with shocking regularity. Periodically, the storms would hit, the whole of Fire Island would be washed away, and within a few years it was all built up again. I never understood how anybody got insurance. It is a foolhardy place to build, but its popularity never waned.

My typical summer routine was this: On Friday morning I took the subway to Pennsylvania Station. I would board the Long Island Railroad for Patchogue, changing trains in Babylon. At Patchogue, I took a taxi to the marina. I would power up *Sea'scape* and sail across the Great South Bay and tie up in a weekend slip at The Pines, and then head to "tea dance" at the Pavilion, the dockside dance club. Tea dance was a Fire Island invention, loosely based on the English idea of tea at four o'clock. At Fire Island, it meant that everyone gathered at four o'clock to drink, talk, dance and plan the weekend ahead. It was fun, raucous, and a time in my life when I had a large circle of friends. The Pines attracted the best and the brightest. The crowd was made up of people from theater, dance, and the fashion and financial trades.

People at The Pines had a curious disconnect about time. We would all go to tea dance at four o'clock. At seven we would go home (or in my case back to the boat) and make dinner. At ten o'clock you would take a "disco nap." At 1:00 a.m. you would get up and head to the Pavilion to dance until the sun came up. Thousands of people did this every single weekend. They would then head back to Manhattan on the Sunday night ferry and resume their normal nine to five jobs. It was hard on your internal clock, but we were all young and my years at Fire Island were before the AIDS crisis really erupted into a full-blown epidemic. By that time my Fire Island years were over.

In my second year at Fire Island, I managed to bribe my way into a summer slip. Once I had a permanent spot for my boat, my social life flourished. My boat became a gathering spot in the harbor for a whole group of people who were constantly stopping by and coming aboard. Early in the morning the ferry would arrive with *The New York Times*. I would get up and grab a copy and sit on the stern of my boat in a bathrobe reading the paper. They are among the happiest memories of my life, those summer mornings on *Sea'scape*, in the harbor at Fire Island Pines, reading *The New York Times* and watching the world go by.

* * *

I was single. One day a friend said he wanted to set me up on a blind date. He knew how passionate I was about the theater. He had a friend in the theater. Would I like to meet him? Yes, of course. The friend was Jerry Herman.

Jerry Herman was (and still is) one of the best-known Broadway musical composers in America. He wrote hits like *Hello, Dolly!* and *Mame*, and other great shows like *Mack and Mabel, Milk and Honey,* and *Dear World*. He was wildly successful. He had a stunning house on the Great South Bay in The Pines in addition to a five-story townhouse in Manhattan.

A date was set up. I was to arrive at his house at four o'clock for drinks on a Sunday afternoon. I got myself done up to look my best and went down the boardwalk. I found the house, rang the bell, and a young man named Damien met me at the door. Damien was Jerry's houseman and general guy Friday. Unbeknownst to me, they had a cue between them. If Jerry didn't like me, he would somehow signal Damien to get rid of me. The cue was not used. Jerry liked me and we started on a short but memorable romance.

Soon after our first meeting, Jerry invited me back to his house on Fire Island for the weekend. We drove from Manhattan to the ferry dock at Sayville. It was a weeknight and Jerry had chartered the ferry to take us over. It was just the two of us sitting on the top deck, looking up at the stars, watching the lights of the homes twinkling on the bay. It was romantic. I was young, handsome, and had life in the palm of my hand. Jerry and I walked down the boardwalk and went into his house, which had walls of glass looking out onto the bay. I looked out at the magical scene. Jerry sat down at the piano and started playing a song. I asked what it was and he said he had just written it. It was titled "Song on the Sand."

Jerry had not written a new Broadway show since the failure of *The Grand Tour* in 1979. He lived on royalties and had no financial need to go to the trouble of writing a new show. He grumbled, with some justification, about spending two years of his life creating a show and then having a critic from *The New York Times* come and trash his work on opening night. He looked at various projects but nothing appealed to him. Then, one day he went to see a small French film called *La Cage aux Folles*. It was about two men in Saint-Tropez who ran a drag club. George was the owner and master of ceremonies; Zaza was his partner and the star of the show. The movie was based on a 1973 French stage play.

Jerry watched the wild farce, but he also saw the tender side of the characters. Jerry at that point was not publicly out. He watched the film and was inspired. Acquiring the rights was complicated, but eventually he managed to get permission to musicalize the film. "Song on the Sand" was one of the first songs he wrote for the show.

I had the experience of dating Jerry during the time he wrote *La Cage aux Folles*. One night, Jerry and I went to see a new musical on Broadway where a friend was in the cast, *The Tap Dance Kid*. Afterward, we went to Ted Hook's, a Broadway hangout, to meet up with Arthur Laurents, the *La Cage aux Folles* director, and Harvey Fierstein who had just been hired to write the book. I had to pinch myself to make sure that I was actually there. The show opened on Broadway in 1983 to rave reviews. It has gone on to be Jerry's single most performed show, even surpassing *Hello, Dolly!*

One night during the creation of the show, Jerry hosted a dinner party at his townhouse. I was the new boyfriend being introduced to his friends. After dinner, we gathered in his living room and Jerry sat down at the piano. Jerry told us we were going to be the first people to hear a song he had just finished writing. He played five simple notes and sang the lyric "I Am What I Am." The song starts small and builds into an anthem of triumph and self-confidence. The song was a statement about the pride of being different. It would go on to become an anthem of the gay community through the difficult AIDS years that lay ahead. The song is still a stirring, emotional, shout of defiance to the world, and a proclamation that "we all are what we are"—individuals, unique, each possessing dignity and self-worth.

The song closed the first act. The show ran on Broadway at the Palace Theatre, one of the few Broadway houses to have a center aisle. On opening night when George Hearn, who played Zaza, finished the song, he ripped off his wig, and marched right up the

center aisle and out the front door onto Broadway. There was a sense of near pandemonium in the house. The moment was unforgettable.

Sadly, this era of Broadway shows has, for all practical purposes, come to an end. The age of show masters like Jerry Herman is over. When you left a Jerry Herman musical, you were humming the songs. Nobody ever went to see *La Cage aux Folles* without humming "The Best of Times" as they left the theater.

In 1984 I went to the Tony Awards. Jerry was still not out to the public so he took his friend Carol Dorian. When the final award was given for Best Musical, there was tension in the Gershwin Theater. It was a horse race between *La Cage aux Folles*, Jerry's show, and *Sunday in the Park with George*, Steven Sondheim's new musical. Both composers had rabid fans and supporters in the house. When the winner was announced, *"La Cage aux Folles"* the house went into an uproar. The man sitting next to me booed and we nearly got into a fistfight. Jerry went onto the stage and said, "There is a rumor that the old fashion show tune is dead. I'm here to tell you it is alive and well at the Palace Theater." That seems like a simple enough acceptance speech but you would not believe the havoc it caused. Steven Sondheim supporters felt it was a slap in Sondheim's face. Jerry has told me he was bewildered by the outrage over the remark. He claims that he never intended it to be a smear against Sondheim; it was just a simple statement of fact.

Jerry and I continued to see each other for about a year. Then he met Marty Finkelstein, and well, I got dumped. I was sort of crushed because I really liked Jerry. He is incredibly bright, funny, generous and a terrific conversationalist. But somehow, in the back of my mind, I knew it was not going to work out. I had my own career and it was challenging to be the boyfriend of a celebrity. People are nice to you, but you know that you don't really register with them. I was always "Jerry Herman's friend." To date a celebrity, you have to be willing to take second place. Mind you, Jerry was very gracious. He always introduced me; he always said something about my work. Jerry was not the problem; his fame was.

I didn't see Jerry for a decade. Then one day, I was boarding a plane in Los Angeles and I passed Jerry sitting in an aisle seat in first class. We had a quick but fun conversation. He gave me his number and told me to call him. In 1996, we tried to see if love was indeed better "the second time around." It was not. Jerry for all his success and fame was quite possessive and he dumped me (again) over a misunderstanding regarding an old ex that I was trying to help. He actually broke up with me by fax. I still have the fax, but it has faded. When I look at the dimly faded message with Jerry's flourishing signature, I see that the relationship just faded away like the fax.

I don't see Jerry much anymore. He lives in Miami Beach now. But for a time, Jerry Herman and the world of Broadway, enriched my life beyond words.

One last story somewhat related to Jerry.

I have a distinctive voice. It doesn't sound unusual to me but everyone who knows me says it's so. I have made my living with my voice but, as one friend said, "so has Carol Channing." Back in 1983, there was a revival of Jerry's musical *Mame* with Angela Lansbury. I went to the first preview with a group of friends. Afterward, we were having dinner and I made the comment that the only thing I didn't like about the musical adaptation of *Mame* was that the snobbish character of Gloria Upson had been pared down from the original stage play. Gloria Upson was the snotty Park Avenue debutante who spoke in Long Island lockjaw where every other word was drawn out—"so chaaaaarmed to meet you." I said I thought Gloria Upson was the single most hilarious, annoying, obnoxious character ever created for the Broadway stage. At that point my friends became very quiet. Jerry looked at Drew and said "Drew, do you want to tell him?" and Drew replied, "No Jerry, you tell him." Then Jerry Douglas, one of my best friends, looked me squarely in the face and said "Well, Doug, 'Gloria' is what we all call you behind your back."

Jerry Herman, composer and lyricist, and one-time boyfriend. Jerry wrote *Hello, Dolly!*, *Mame*, *Dear World*, *Mack and Mable*, and several other shows. I was seeing him during the time he created *La Cage aux Folles*, ultimately his most successful show. 1984.

CHAPTER TWENTY-THREE

OUT OF THE FRYING PAN AND INTO THE FIRE

G*reater Tuna*. I always blamed it on *Greater Tuna*.
Greater Tuna is a two-man show created by Jaston Williams and Joe Sears about the fictional third-smallest town in Texas. They played dozens of characters and the piece is a valentine to small town Texas life.

I was in San Francisco showing *The Hawaiian Adventure*. I went out with a friend, Brian Dubrow, to see *Greater Tuna* at the Marines Memorial Theater. During the intermission, Brian said he had a friend staying with him he thought I might like to meet. The next night, Steve Cline knocked on my door. I opened it, gazed into those deep violet eyes and, well, it might as well have been Satan himself smiling back.

No one person has ever brought more grief, craziness, exhilaration, anger, passion and total outright nuttiness to my life than Stevan Cline. He entered my life in 1984 and was in and out until 2002. He was as addicting as heroin, and frankly, I suspect heroin would have been easier to kick.

He was tall, rail thin, a classic swimmer's body, a striking face, but it was really the eyes. They were hypnotic, like two pools of lapis lazuli. And he was the very definition of manipulative.

We went out for dinner but, of course, ended up in bed—and that's where the trouble began. I was more than smitten; I was drugged by his aura. The red flags should have been obvious from the beginning. He had been married and had a daughter. He was unemployed. He had recently declared bankruptcy. He never paid child support. He had no money, no job, just the clothes on his back and a Cheshire Cat grin—so *naturally*, I asked him come back to New York City and move in. What was I thinking?

The problem was my "big brain" wasn't thinking. It was my "small brain" that was doing the thinking.

We left for San Francisco International Airport two nights later to take a red-eye. Stevan was an artist. As we passed through security, the screener took his bag of art supplies and removed the biggest pair of scissors I have ever seen. "These cannot go on the plane," said the security agent. If only they had kept Cline *and* the scissors, how much easier my life would have been.

We arrived in New York at 6:00 a.m. We went to my apartment and Steve immediately declared that he hated it. His entire *raison d'être* seemed to be built around figuring out how to make the person he was with give up what they loved most—and then dump them. From the moment we set foot in New York, he made it clear he hated the city and wanted to return to California. Why I fell for this I will never know. But I was young—well, not that young. I thought I was in love when, in actuality, I was in lust. I would, foolishly, do anything to please him.

He wanted to go to Hawaii, so off we went. But once in Hawaii, he wanted to go back home. Back in New York, he wanted to sail *Sea'scape* up the Hudson River to Lake Champlain and Canada. We went to Canada and he bitched the whole time about missing California. There was no way to please him. Well, there was one way... and that was what kept getting me into trouble.

The first time he walked out on me was shortly after he came to New York. He went into a rage. He wanted to go back to L.A. I bought him a ticket. He left. And twenty-four hours later, he called up and whined, "Poopers," (his horrible nickname for me that he took from Katherine Hepburn in *On Golden Pond*, who called Henry Fonda an 'old poop') "I want to come back." So I bought another ticket and back he came.

Over the nearly two decades he was in and out of my life, he established a pattern, which I finally figured out. He would come back into my life. I would always say yes. He would stay around for exactly six weeks—you could almost time it to the day—and then he would leave. He would be gone anywhere from two days to two years, but eventually the phone would ring and I would hear, "Hi Doug, it's Steve." And every time I heard that on the phone—how can I say this delicately—well I can't—I got hard. He had that power.

He left and returned several times between 1984 and 1988. But in 1988, he set out to accomplish his biggest disruption: he cajoled me into moving to California. He made it sound so wonderful: the two of us, a house with a pool, no winters, etc. He did it with great charm. And against every bone in my body screaming, "don't do it," I put my wonderful West End Avenue apartment up for sale.

Meanwhile, Steve and I went to California to look at houses. He hated almost everything, but eventually we settled on a Spanish Revival house built in the 1930s. It was on a hillside in the Los Feliz neighborhood east of Hollywood. I made an offer on the house—God knows Steve wasn't putting up any money. Before long, I had an offer on my New York City co-op. The wheels were set into motion. I couldn't stop the process even though I had an ominous feeling.

On an April afternoon in 1988, movers loaded the last of my possessions from my West End Avenue home into a truck. I stood in that empty apartment and thought of all the wonderful memories: the parties, the people, and my whole New York life. I was saying goodbye, but I was opening a new chapter in California. There would be new experiences and new people ahead.

I closed the door behind me and headed to JFK to catch the flight to L.A. Steve came to LAX to meet me. As we drove into the city he said, "You know, I am really sorry, Doug, but I've been thinking and... this just isn't going to work out."

What the….??!!! I had just sold my beloved New York apartment, *my furniture is still on the Pennsylvania Turnpike* and you have decided, "It just isn't going to work out!?" No jury in America would have convicted me if I had murdered him right on the spot.

You would think dumping me on my arrival in L.A. after tricking me into selling my New York apartment would be enough to turn me off of him for good. But you would be wrong. It continued for years. I got used to it. The phone would ring. He would be back. I would get six weeks of craziness and good sex, and then he would be gone again. It was this insanity that finally drove me to Beverly Hills. Beverly Hills is known for movie stars, money, swimming pools, wealth—and shrinks, and in Beverly Hills I found Larry Ryan.

Dr. Larry Ryan was a psychiatrist. I spent several years on his couch trying to figure myself out. Psychoanalysis can be life changing. To have the time, intelligence, and interest in exploring yourself is an experience that you cannot put a price tag on.

Larry helped me to look at my past, and in doing so I learned a lot about my actions and reactions. The main goal of the therapy was to get me un-addicted to Steve Cline. In that respect, the therapy failed miserably. However, it did allow me at least to accept the good parts of the crazy relationship and steer me through the bad parts.

Larry was not in a position to diagnose my wacko partner, but he hinted that he believed Cline had Borderline Personality Disorder. There is a book written on the subject that explains it by the title: *I Hate You, Please Don't Leave Me.* Borderline people are rapturously in love with you one minute, and suddenly they despise you with a passion the next. Of all psychological disorders, Larry said, it was one of the worst to deal with in the context of a relationship. I could vouch for that.

The number of times Cline was in and out of my life is lost in my memory, but I recall the last time very clearly. It was 2002 and I was finally in a stable relationship. Cline popped back up like a mole in the front yard trying to bring havoc to my stable coupling. He invited us over for dinner. Steve was a great cook. The meal was wonderful but I was looking none too good. I was quite ill by this time.

The following day, Cline called and said "Doug you look terrible, what's wrong?" I told him about my medical problems and Steve said, "So how does it feel to know you are going to die soon?" Charming. I told him it was emotional and stressful. Finally he said, "Well it was nice knowing you, bye."

And that was the last I ever heard from him.

I knew through a friend he had moved to Puerto Vallarta to paint. Out of curiosity, I googled him. Since his first name was oddly spelled Stevan, he was easy to find. His paintings were online with a Mexican gallery. I assumed I never heard from him again because he thought I was dead. I considered sending him an email but then I thought, no, sometimes it's better to be thought of as dead.

In the spring of 2015, a friend forwarded an obituary to me. Stevan Cline died June 16, 2013. It was unclear where he died or from what. It was a maddening, exhilarating, painful, crazy part of my life. But I had a wistful feeling learning that he was gone.

Stevan Cline. The most intense relationship of my life. It was the eyes; they were hypnotic. 1984.

CHAPTER TWENTY-FOUR

SAILING DOWN UNDER ON THE QE2

For better or worse, I was now a Californian. Don't get me wrong; my life in L.A. was pretty great. I may have missed my old New York apartment, but I did not miss the winters, the subway, or trying to get a cab in the rain.

One of the first things I did in California was buy a car. Living in New York there was no need for a car. I hadn't owned a car since I left Indianapolis in 1978. Did I buy something practical? Oh course not. I bought an old MG. Buying an MG is like adopting an injured animal that you know will never get completely well. You love it. You agree to care for it. But you know it will bring you endless trouble and grief. To me, that MG represented life in California. I never put the top up. I loved zipping around Los Angeles in that bright orange car. I had a perpetual tan. I still have the car and I still drive it regularly.

I settled into the house in the Los Feliz hills, but I did miss having a foothold in New York. A year after I moved to L.A., I went back to New York and bought a one-bedroom apartment on East 72nd Street. It was small, compact; a New York *pied-à-terre*. It was emblematic of what I have always said about New York City life: In New York you don't live in your apartment, you live in the city. I still spend about a third of each year in New York.

But L.A. is really my home. At times it seems like there is no urban planning. The traffic is a nightmare and parking is maddening. But the traffic is so terrible and the congestion so bad because so many people want to live there—and a few afternoons driving with the top down in January will make you understand why. Steve Cline continued to come in and out of my life. He was like an emotionally charged revolving door. Meanwhile, I got on with my career.

The Great World Cruise of the QE2 was my first big success. I had two hundred and thirteen showings of the program across the country the first season, and my audiences were consistently large. The film was successful enough that I decided I would make another travelogue on the *QE2* called *Queen Elizabeth 2 Sails New Zealand and Australia*. I had not been "down under" and I thought this would be a good opportunity to see both countries and spend more time on the *QE2*.

Steve Cline was scheduled to go with me. We were both comped onto the ship by the Cunard Line, which was pleased enough with the success of the world cruise film to let me have a shot with another title.

In Steve's typical style, he announced the day before sailing that he was not going to go. Who but Steve Cline would turn down 37 days on the *QE2* in the South Pacific? It was going to cost him nothing, he was not required to lift a finger, he was not working at the time, nor did he have any intention of working. And yet, less than twenty-four hours before the ship was to set sail, he decided to say no.

He knew I would be upset. Somehow this provided him with some satisfaction—a bizarre pleasure at ruining someone else's experience. By this time, I had learned to let these insane actions affect me less. I was blue sailing out of the harbor that night, but I put Cline behind me and got on with shipboard life.

I was taking a thirty-seven-day leg of the one hundred and ten-day 1985 World Cruise. We sailed first to Tahiti. Since I was not including Tahiti in the film, I was able to act like a tourist. I rented a moped and spent the day driving around the island. The next day, the *QE2* docked in Mo'orea, and the following day we anchored off the Cook Islands.

Finally, two weeks into the cruise, the *QE2* docked at Auckland, New Zealand. I got off the ship and was met by a government guide who took me to Rotorua to film the geysers and Maori cultural attractions. New Zealand sits above an active geothermal region similar to Yellowstone National Park.

From Auckland we sailed to Wellington and then Christchurch. Wellington is the capital, best known for the beehive-like parliament building, gingerbread Victorian homes, and a funicular that travels to a perch overlooking the city. Christchurch is quaint and very British in both architecture and attitude. New Zealanders are gracious, polite, and courteous. I found them different from the Australians who are brash, outgoing, and bold. The difference between New Zealand and Australia is a little like the difference between Canada and the United States—or New Hampshire and Texas.

From Christchurch, *QE2* sailed on to Australia. I went up onto the bridge the morning we pulled into Sydney Harbor. Captain Robert Arnott, master of the ship on that particular world cruise, was calling out the orders. He referred to the *QE2* as the "boat." "Turn the boat five degrees port," "Slow the boat," "Stop the boat." It seemed like a quaint phrase to use to navigate the world's most famous ocean liner. There were thousands of people on the shore. *QE2* made only one annual stop in Sydney and it was a big deal. We also had the M.S. *Sagafjord* arriving in front of us and the S.S. *Canberra*, P&O's flagship carrier, behind. And overhead, swooping down like a graceful gull, was the Concorde arriving from London with passengers for the *QE2*.

QE2 docked next to the Sydney Harbor Bridge and I got busy filming. Koalas, kangaroos, ferry boats, beaches, skyscrapers, they all made their way across the viewfinder of my camera in those three days.

We sailed on toward Adelaide, where I filmed the city, the Barossa Valley wine district, a sheep station, and sheep shearing. The sheep shearing was fast and furious as the shearers would peel the fleece off the sheep and send them back to their pens, denuded.

From Adelaide we continued on to Perth. We docked at Freemantle, Perth's port city. In 1985 Perth was considered the poor cousin to Sydney and Melbourne. It was Australia's western-most city, and it was just starting to grow into the dynamic city it has become.

From Perth, the *QE2* departed for Bali. It was the end of my time on the ship so I packed up and debarked. I filmed the ship sailing away at sunset and then went to my hotel. I spent several days filming Western Australia including the Pinnacles, an unusual area of limestone formations left behind by receding oceans millions of years ago.

Once off of the ship, I began backtracking to pick up all the shots that I missed during the brief time the ship docked in each port. I first flew from Perth to Alice Springs in the center of Australia. I filmed the School of the Air, where students from ranches (called stations in Australia) would call in on shortwave radio to participate in classes. It was essentially a correspondence school. The students were isolated, scattered over millions of square miles, and rarely saw or spoke with people their own age. The School of the Air helped them with social as well as educational skills. The School of the Air continues today, but the short wave radio is long gone. Satellite phones, the Internet, and other technologies have changed the operations of the school.

I filmed the Flying Doctors Service. This was a medical facility that dispensed medical advice over shortwave radio to station owners throughout the outback. People from a thousand miles away would call in with questions and ask for medical advice. And when it was necessary, a team of doctors would assemble and fly small planes to the outback stations, land on dirt strips, and provide emergency medical care. It was an effort by the Australian government to keep a highly isolated part of the population healthy.

And, of course, I filmed Ayres Rock. Ayres Rock, or Uluru as the aboriginals know it, is a huge sandstone monolith in the very center of Australia. It is sacred to the aboriginal people. Uluru changes color throughout the day, but is most stunning just before sunset and just after sunrise.

From Alice Springs I flew to Sydney and picked up the remaining material I needed before I flew back to Auckland. I spent three weeks alone with a car driving through New Zealand. I took a ski plane to Mount Cook and landed on a glacier. I filmed the Kingston Flyer steam railroad. I shot from the front of a Jet Boat on the Shotover River. I watched bungee jumping off the bridge where it was invented, and I drove through Fjordland National Park. Finally, I drove through the Homer Tunnel.

The Homer Tunnel is a mile long, single lane rough-hewn rock tunnel. It has no lights. For thirty minutes of each hour, traffic moves away from Milford Sound, the other thirty minutes the traffic goes toward Milford Sound. There is a red/green light at the entrance to the tunnel and you have to trust you will not meet anyone in the center. If you do, someone has to back all the way out. It is pitch black going down toward Milford Sound because there is a slight curve at the end—just enough to cut off the "light at the end of the tunnel." But when you emerge, you are in front of the fjords of New Zealand and Milford Sound, one of the most beautiful places of the world. The jagged mountains, the waterfalls, the shimmering water; it's hard to describe it if you have not seen it first hand. After a lifetime of travel, I regard New Zealand as the most beautiful country on earth.

Once I had wrapped up shooting New Zealand, I was ready to go home. Air New Zealand had given me a return ticket in exchange for a shot of one of their planes in my film. I flew from Auckland to Los Angeles by way of Honolulu, where I spent a few days before continuing on to California. It was Palm Sunday in Auckland. Early that evening, I headed to the airport and got on the plane. When we arrived the following morning in Honolulu, it was still Palm Sunday because we had crossed the International Date Line.

The best memory I have of returning from New Zealand was the fact that Air New Zealand flew me in first class. This was something I could never afford so the luxury was really appreciated. The cabin purser knew I was onboard as a guest of the airline and he asked me if I wanted to go up into the cockpit and meet the flight crew. Well of course! I was then taken up to the bubble and into the cockpit of the 747. What a display of instruments. I stayed for quite a while chatting with the crew (it was long before I became a pilot myself). Time passed and before you knew it we were approaching Honolulu. The captain said to sit in the jump seat and buckle up. So I sat in the cockpit of the 747 as it landed at Honolulu International Airport. What a rush, what a memory, what a very different time.

Noted travelogue presenter returns home to Kansas City,

By Stormy Wylie
News editor, Wyandotte West

The last time Doug Jones performed on the stage at Washington High School, he was in the school's production of "The Music Man." That was 21 years ago.

He was on the stage again recently, but this time as a popular speaker on the film lecture circuit.

Jones was at the school last month to present a film of his called "The Great World Cruise of the Queen Elizabeth II," a travelogue sponsored by the Kansas City, Kansas Kiwanis Club.

Jones is the son of Mr. and Mrs. Harold P. Jones, 38 N. 78th. He graduated from Washington in 1966.

He now lives in Los Angeles and is single.

Jones calls himself a "ham from the earliest age." He said he really began performing in his school days playing banjo in a Dixieland jazz band which toured throughout the Midwest.

Besides his career in film lecturing, he has also taught guitar, banjo and mandolin, has been a European tour guide, a radio announcer and an art gallery owner.

He said his interest in film lecturing began in 1967 when he was on his way to Austria and went to see a travelogue at the Plaza Theater, Kansas City, Mo.

"I was no dummy," he said. "I saw the box office draw and decided 'I can

Doug Jones

subjects as London, Venice, San Francisco, Egypt, Belgium, Austria, the Far East and the national parks system. Most of the films take from eight to 12 weeks to film.

The recent film on the Queen Elizabeth II is Jones' only documented trip. It took 80 days to complete the trip around the world and was "increasingly more expensive" than previous films, he said.

But traveling to 54 countries, presenting more than 4,000 film lectures to millions of people and being on the road about 230 days a year didn't help Jones overcome a nervousness about returning to his old high school.

"Last week I was at Constitution Hall in Washington, D.C., for a National Geographic Society lecture," he said. "I had to introduce the ambassadors from Austria and Belgium, but I told the audience I was more nervous about coming back here!"

More than 400 persons turned out to welcome Jones back to his alma mater.

Jones said people come to see travelogues for three reasons– to relive travel experiences, to see places they are planning to go to and to experiences places they will never go to.

For his part, Jones said he enjoys making films.

"It has been gr: not only provide it people a chance to experience."

Jones said he countries that are spots," although mi do films in these co working in several Th though.

"You do jt on the am regarded as a j one doing a touris don't distinguish bet

Jones said most the "red carpet" i wherever he goes, case.

"Sometimes the corrupt and you h: bribe," he said. "If find out who to bril get the shots anywa Much of his fil legally," he said– mission.

Jones' next film Far East." Most of and just needs to Also in the works is cities of Europe.

"I'll just keep p said. "I'll probably years from now."

A newspaper story written to coincide with an appearance I was making at my old high school—Washington High School—auditorium. Local boy makes good. 1987.

A newspaper ad for *Queen Elizabeth 2 Sails New Zealand and Australia* at Michigan State University in East Lansing, Michigan. 1987.

Filming atop a glacier on Mount Cook after arriving on the ski plane during the film shoot for *Queen Elizabeth 2 Sails New Zealand and Australia*. 1985.

CHAPTER TWENTY-FIVE

FILMING THE GREAT CITIES OF EUROPE

After I returned from Australia and New Zealand, I took a couple of years off before shooting my next film. I did release a travelogue in 1986 called *Portraits of the Great Far East*, but I made it from outtakes from *The Great World Cruise of the QE2*. I had shot so much footage for that film that there was enough left to produce a feature from shots that never made it into the first cut.

My lecture tour was at its peak. I had two hundred and thirty-seven shows during the 1985-1986 season. In looking back on forty years of presenting travelogues, I think the peak year was 1985. The audiences were large and I had more offers to do lecture dates than I had time available to accept.

I would be on the road for months averaging nine shows a week. By the mid-1980s I had been doing my work for close to twenty years and many people at that point in their career start taking things for granted. I was paid well, able to save money. I lived big and it did not occur to me that it would ever come to an end.

But there were ominous signs. In 1985, George Lourbis in San Francisco declared bankruptcy with Explorama—twenty-six auditorium shows in California—poof! Gone. The collapse of the fifteen thousand subscriber series at the Grand Rapids Civic Auditorium in one season—poof! Gone. The closure of Travelventure in Florida—eighteen shows—poof! Gone. They were not good omens.

And cable television, which had originally been created to provide a decent television image to farmers in rural areas, was starting to be used to offer more varied programming in cities. My Uncle Fred outside of Otis, Kansas had the first cable television hookup I ever saw. In New York City, I still had rabbit ears pointed toward the World Trade Center antennas. And then VHS videotape came along and everyone could play movies without commercials on their own TV. These groundbreaking ideas would impact many entertainment models that had once flourished.

By the late 1980s, I knew things were starting to head in the wrong direction, but I didn't want to stop making travelogues because I loved the work. I loved the domestic travel around America giving lectures as much as the overseas travel making the films. My travels in all fifty states gave me a sense of how Americans felt about things that I couldn't have known if I never left New York or L.A. I probably should have ditched the travelogue business in the 1980s, or at least moved into television production like Rick Steves, but I didn't want to give up my constant wandering. By the time the travelogue business was in severe decline in the late 1990s, I was older and establishing a new career or even making a lateral move into television would have been difficult.

But in the 1980s, everything was going strong. After not shooting films in 1986 and 1987, I started production on two films in the same year. I began making *The Great Alaska Cruise* in 1988 by accepting a press junket with Princess Tours that started in Deadhorse, Alaska on the Arctic Ocean, and took me all the way to Anchorage by way of the Dalton Highway and the Alaska Railroad. It was a ten-day trip and I got a lot of basic footage that would be cut into the finished film. The other film project that summer was *Great Cities of Europe*. After I returned from Alaska, I put that footage aside and concentrated on the European shoot.

Great Cities of Europe was a look at seven European cities: London, Amsterdam, Copenhagen, Berlin, Vienna, Rome, and Paris. I sailed from New York on the *QE2* to Southampton. I shot London and then continued on to the other cities using European trains and a Eurail pass.

By 1988, security at airports was getting much tighter, and it was particularly tight in Europe. Today's digital filmmakers have no idea what a panic it was to board an airplane during a film shoot. You could not check the undeveloped film. The baggage screeners used for checked baggage would destroy the latent film images. The screeners for carry-on luggage were not a lot better. I would beg for hand inspection of my film at every security checkpoint. It was difficult in the United States, but by the 1980s, it was becoming impossible in Europe. You sent your film through the X-ray machine or you didn't board the plane. I couldn't risk a summer's worth of work being destroyed in a flash by an incorrectly calibrated airport X-ray machine, so *Great Cities of Europe* was produced without ever getting on a plane.

The Houses of Parliament on the Thames. I shot them for *Royal London* and again for *Great Cities of Europe*. 1988.

I began my shoot in central London. I had been to London a dozen times by that point, so I knew the places to set up the tripod. Since each city sequence was only going to be about twelve minutes long, I didn't need to dig as deep for stories and footage. I shot the usual: Big Ben, Buckingham Palace, the Changing of the Guard, Piccadilly, the Tube, the Tower of

London, St. Paul's, Hyde Park, and the West End theater district at night; about 1,900 feet of film.

I did my London filming in six pleasant days. I had allotted seven days for each city, so when I finished early I could move on and keep ahead of the shooting schedule. I made *Great Cities of Europe* in September and October. I had beautiful blue skies for almost the entire seven-week shoot.

I left London on a train from Victoria Station to Dover where I boarded the ferry for Calais. At Calais, I boarded a waiting train for Paris. Once at the Gare du Nord, I got my equipment and film gathered up and off the train. As I was rolling my luggage along the platform, the French police came up and started shouting at me. They grabbed me and lead me into an interrogation room and looked through my papers, my film, my cameras, and all of my luggage.

Someone had clued the police in that somebody was getting off of the train from Calais carrying God-knows-what, and the French police had mistaken me for their perp. It was scary. I was alone. I didn't speak enough French to negotiate this. Many phone calls were made, my film, equipment, clothes, and personal effects were scattered everywhere. I was held two hours, but eventually I was told I could leave. I threw everything back into the suitcases as fast as I could and headed off to a hotel on the Left Bank. It was a tense and frightening experience and it would not be the last such experience of the trip.

Paris, the police aside, is still my favorite city in Europe. Spending the week shooting there was wonderful. I went back to places I had shot before in 1970. I shot the Eiffel Tower, the Champs-Élysées, a boat ride on the Seine, Montmartre, Notre-Dame, the Metro, Pompidou Centre, and the cafes of the Left Bank. I did not shoot the Arch of Triumph or the Louvre because both were undergoing renovation and covered in scaffolding. I can't bring myself to shoot famous landmarks covered in construction rigging. I've been criticized for not including certain things in films and scaffolding is usually the reason.

It was autumn, the leaves were turning colors, and Paris was just magical. I didn't want to leave. But I had all the material I needed so I went on to Amsterdam by train. I had been to Amsterdam before but I had not shot film there. I was given access to some unusual places including the pumping stations that keep the whole region, which is below sea level, dry. I filmed diamond cutters, Delft porcelain makers, and the cheese market at Alkmaar; Organ grinders, bicycles, yellow trams, boats on the narrow canals, houses that are tall and narrow, the Rijksmuseum, and Dam Square. Amsterdam is a charming city and easy to work in since everything is flat and public transportation is good. I hauled my camera and tripod around on the trams, getting off to shoot what I needed.

Things were going well. I was consistently running one day ahead of schedule, so I was able to board the train for Copenhagen earlier than planned. Copenhagen is on an island. They load the trains right onto ferry boats, stacking the coach cars, and then cross the water and couple the cars back together to continue the journey.

Copenhagen was lovely. I filmed the Little Mermaid, Tivoli Gardens, the castles in and around Copenhagen, the Danish crown jewels, the canals, and several churches and other attractions. I filmed at the Carlsberg Brewery and rode on a horse drawn cart to deliver the beer. I filmed at the Georg Jensen Silversmiths and the street entertainers which are everywhere in the city. I was again running ahead of schedule so I left early and made my way on to Berlin.

It was 1988 and the Berlin Wall was still up. It would be one more year before the wall fell and three before the USSR would come apart at the seams. But in the fall of 1988, to get from Copenhagen to West Berlin I had to pass through East Germany—the German Democratic Republic. The word "Democratic" was such a joke. The GDR was as undemocratic as you could get. I boarded the train in Copenhagen and headed south to the Baltic Sea. At the Baltic I boarded a ferry to Rostock. The East German government operated the ferry. I instantly started seeing what was wrong with the Soviet system. I had left Copenhagen, one of the friendliest, happiest places on earth, and the moment I set foot on the ferry, I was in a different world. I have rarely encountered such surly, miserable people. I had lunch at the restaurant onboard. The food was dreadful, but it was the attitude of the people that was so shocking. They were dismissive, disinterested, unhappy, and didn't have a clue (nor could have cared less) about customer service. Communism looked great on paper, but the reality was very different. The system provided no incentive. You had no control over your career, your future, or your life. The system bred generations of slothful, unhappy people. It was a glass half empty culure.

The train arrived at the border between East and West Berlin. It was late, about 11:00 p.m., and the East German police came into my compartment. I was the only person in the six-person compartment. They started hassling me, asking questions that made no sense. I could see this was trouble. In the middle of the interrogation, two police officers came in and took my suitcases off the train. I had to remain onboard. I started panicking about how easily they could plant cocaine in one of my suitcases and arrest me for transporting drugs. In the end, the suitcases were returned. The train powered up and in a few minutes we were over the border and inside the Zoo Bahnhof railway station in West Berlin. I breathed a deep sigh of relief to be back in a Western democracy—even if it was surrounded by a wall.

West Berlin in 1988 was like a party that wouldn't stop. There was this sense of live fast and live for today. It was one of the most peculiar places on earth. The city was a showcase of capitalism and consumerism. The Kurfürstendamm, or the Ku'Damm as it was better known, was filled with shops. The KaDeWe, the Kaufhaus Des Westens, the giant department store, couldn't sell luxury goods fast enough—and all of this commercial activity was surrounded by a high concrete wall. The wall was built in 1961 by the GDR to "protect its people." Suddenly, West Berliners were trapped; completely encircled. You could leave by air or on certain trains that went directly to West Germany. You could also go into East Germany through Checkpoint Charlie, the crossing point between the old American Zone and the GDR. I rented a car in West Berlin and drove through. It was nerve-racking, just like the train. The East German border guards put long sticks into my gas tank, as if I was hauling something in the fuel compartment. They ran mirrors under the car looking for contraband—and on the return trip to the West, they were looking for people being smuggled under the car. Some people in West Berlin said the East Germans did this just for show. Tourism was important to East Germany, and this was a part of Cold War tourism. The East Germans were paranoid and they happily showed that off to visiting tourists who wanted to see life on the other side.

Life on the other side was not unsafe, not dangerous, just drab. The new architecture was uninspired, the people poorly dressed, and there was a general sense of weariness. One thing that made the place so lifeless was the lack of advertising. In a communist country where all businesses are owned by the state, there is no reason to promote anything so there is no advertising. Returning to West Berlin and seeing the blazing neon signs and billboards, you appreciated how much advertising adds to the life of a city. Advertising brings more color and vividness to our lives than we realize.

I did my filming in East Germany in a single day. I was required to exchange some U.S. dollars for twenty-five East German marks. They could not be changed back in West Berlin, so I stopped at the renovated Grand Hotel for a late lunch to spend the money. It was lavish, intended only for foreign visitors. I went to pay with my twenty-five East German marks and the server said in a hostile tone, "No marks, only dollars." They built this lavish hotel, would not let East Germans even in the front door, and only took U.S. dollars.

There really wasn't much to film in East Berlin, but I did get a chance to see how people lived in the GDR during the final year before Germany was reunited.

The Berlin Wall. I shot this less than a year before the wall came down. The footage was for *Great Cities of Europe*. 1988.

One of the ironies of the wall coming down was that West Germany now had a new source of labor, which had always been in short supply. In fact, West Germans were given special incentives to move to West Berlin. The problem was the new labor pool of East Germans had no history of actually working. They would show up late, take two-hour lunches, smoke cigarettes, and waste massive amounts of time. It was a shock to both sides. The West German employers were not prepared for a work force with no idea how to *really* work, and the former East Germans didn't understand that in order to achieve success, they had to put in a long hours. In time, this changed. Visiting Germany today, it's hard to realize how divide the country once was. But I saw it firsthand and filmed it at the very end of the Cold War.

After seven days in Berlin, it was time to head to Vienna. Once there, I filmed the Schönbrunn Palace, the Belvedere, and the Hofburg Palace. Vienna is known for the Sacher Hotel and the chocolate *Sachertorte*, so I filmed one of the pastry shops. The Viennese love their pastries and making them is very visual. Vienna is also known for music, and I got the chance to film at the Bösendorfer Piano factory. Bösendorfer pianos are among the most expensive in the world, and are constructed with exacting detail. I filmed a violin and cello maker in his studio and I got to film at Wiener Sängerknaben, the Vienna Boys' Choir school. The Vienna Boys' Choir has been in existence since the Middle Ages, and has toured the world for close to a century. I remember hearing them at the Music Hall in Kansas City when I was growing up.

From Vienna, I boarded the Vienna-Rome Express for a long train ride through the Italian Alps. The scenery is magnificent, as you would expect, and the quality of food in the dining car was excellent. I arrived at Roma Termini Station, a chaotic madhouse of porters and taxi drivers all yelling and vying for your attention. If you can survive Termini Station, you can survive Rome.

Like each of the other cities I filmed, I had a contact with the local tourist authority. The Italian Government Tourist Board maintained offices near the Spanish Steps. I had an appointment to meet with the head of the office. He and I got on well and began discussing some of the problems involved in shooting film in Rome. He was very proud of his English and his use of American slang. His concept of how Americans spoke was to finish every sentence with the phrase "fucking bastards." I mentioned the difficulty of getting the guards at the Colosseum to accept my letter of introduction and he said, "Ah, yes, the guards at the Colosseum, fucking bastards, well you will need to…" I brought up the problem of dealing with the police over my tripod at the Spanish Steps, "Ah, yes, the police at the Spanish Steps, fucking bastards, well you will need to…" He was dignified, educated, and proud of his "American" English which he somehow believed included "fucking bastards" in every possible sentence.

I was staying in a hotel near the Vatican. My contact in the Vatican publicity department was a woman from the unlikely city of Milwaukee. I walked in and introduced myself. She was absorbed in something in her typewriter and acknowledged me in a somewhat detached manner. As I passed through Saint Peter's Square on my way to her office, I noticed all sorts of temporary barricades and other paraphernalia I was not expecting. I asked her what was happening and she said, "Oh, tomorrow we're having a big 'do'." The big "do" was the beatification ceremony of six figures of the Catholic faith on the final road to sainthood. She asked me offhandedly if I wanted to film it. "Yes, of course," and the following morning I was atop the Bernini columns with television crews from all over the world. I was given a position between CBS News and the local Los Angeles NBC outlet. One of the figures being beatified was Junípero Serra, a Spanish Franciscan who spent most of his life in California, so there was enough interest to send a crew from L.A. There I stood, alone, one camera on a tripod, surrounded by all this wattage.

The mass began with the longest procession of priests I have ever seen. Finally, Pope John Paul II arrived. He celebrated the mass and spoke of the six figures being beatified. I couldn't understand his homily since my Italian is almost non-existent, but the scene was majestic. Regardless of whatever your own religious beliefs might be, one really could not help but be moved by the pageantry of the Church in the heart of Rome that autumn morning.

I love Rome and I love the Italians. They can make you frazzeled, but I challenge you to find any other group of people in the world with more zest for life. They live in the moment and while their government is disorganized, their traffic appalling, their politics erratic, we can learn a lot from them about the basic art of living and enjoying the everyday moments of life.

From Rome I returned to London and boarded the westbound *QE2* for New York. I had 28,000 feet of undeveloped film and another travelogue to edit. The first show was in January for the National Geographic Society at Constitution Hall in Washington D.C. I had limited time to cut the picture, but I got it done and I showed the film for several years. And when it came time to move into the world of selling videotapes, it was one of the first films I released to the home entertainment market.

CHAPTER TWENTY-SIX

NORTH TO ALASKA

The 1988-1989 travelogue lecture season was packed, and by the end of the tour I was exhausted. I had just started showing *Great Cities of Europe* and since the film was new, I had plenty of bookings. I wrapped up the season in May and had to begin work immediately on *The Great Alaska Cruise*. My first scheduled showing of the Alaska film was for The Philadelphia Geographical Society in October, just five months away. I had to get to work fast.

Gordon Thorne, who did publicity for Princess Tours (the land division of Princess Cruises) approached me about making an Alaska film. He made a good offer, a ten-day overland press junket, and two seven-day Inside Passage cruises. Princess Cruises felt the promotional value of the film warranted the deal.

The previous summer in 1988, before I left to make *Great Cities of Europe*, I flew to, Alaska on the Arctic Ocean where I joined twelve journalists at Mile Zero of the Alaska pipeline. Deadhorse is a community of oil field workers living in barracks on the tundra doing strenuous, lonely work and it's as far north as you can go; gray, bleak, and filled with a sense of solitude.

I spent the night in Deadhorse in what was essentially a trailer. Luxurious it was not, but it was near the water. The Arctic Ocean was right in front of me; the next stop was the North Pole. I filmed the Mile Zero sign where the pipeline begins, and from there we boarded a motor coach that took us down the Dalton Highway, a 500-mile long gravel road. It's called the Haul Road and was built to move equipment and supplies to the starting point of the pipeline. We set out from Deadhorse; it would be one hundred and fifty miles before we would see a tree. The vastness of the tundra is impressive; a surface of seemingly lifeless land as far as you could see.

We spent the night in Coldfoot, the northernmost truck stop in the world. Every truck on the Haul Road stops here for fuel. Again, the motel was a mobile home affair, cobbled together to house truckers and the handful of visitors allowed to travel the Haul Road on small organized tours. That night in Coldfoot happened to be the summer solstice, the longest day of the year. That far north, the sun never sets in summer. It takes a few days to get used to going to bed in daylight. We arrived late and dinner was not served until ten o'clock. Afterward, I was talking with some locals, one of whom realized I was a cinematographer and he said, "Hey, wanna go up?" He was a pilot with a single engine Piper Cherokee. I quickly got my camera and off we went. We took off from a gravel strip and went soaring up over the Brooks Range. The mountains were still covered in snow and everything had a yellow glow. I looked at my watch—it was midnight—in the land of the midnight sun. I still remember how vast and thrilling Alaska was at that moment.

The following day, we made our way on to Fairbanks where we boarded the Midnight Sun Express. The Midnight Sun Express is made up of several double-decker train cars attached to the end of the Alaska Railroad passenger train. The train cars were refurbished by Princess Tours as a part of a marketing plan to take cruise ship passengers on overland journeys into the center of the state. We were headed for Denali.

At Denali we checked into the Harper Lodge. The next day we were up at dawn to go spot wildlife. Denali is a protected wilderness and you can't drive into the park without a permit. The goal is to disturb the wilderness as little as possible—a continuing challenge as more visitors arrive in Alaska each year. Transportation into the park consisted of old, uncomfortable school buses.

At the end of the day, I had an experience that changed my life. There had been no sign of Denali, Mt. McKinley, the Great One, the tallest mountain of North America. Most visitors to Denali never see the mountain. The constant layer of clouds makes it invisible. But as the day drew to a close, I boarded a single engine Cessna. We took off and in a few moments we came out above the clouds in the heart of the Alaska Range. The view was jaw dropping. The tallest, most jagged, dramatic, snow covered scenery

I had ever seen, and it seemed to go on forever. We circled the base of Mt. McKinley at about 12,000 feet, the mountain loaming above us. The pilot banked the plane so we could see the top of the peak. I didn't want the experience to end.

It is some of the most beautiful footage I ever shot, but I was more enthralled with the experience of the plane. This happened only days after I had gone up in the Piper over the Brooks Range. I wanted to sit in that left seat. I wanted to learn how to fly. A seed was planted that grew into the biggest experience of my life. My piloting years would soon begin.

From Denali, we headed back to the Harper Lodge and boarded the southbound train to Anchorage. It's a pleasant city; not a lot to see, but easy to navigate and quite livable.

Before I returned to Los Angeles, I boarded a coach to Portage. At Portage, the coach was loaded onto a flatbed car and the train went through a tunnel in the mountains to the sea. At Whittier, I went out on a small boat, the *Glacier Seas*, which took me to the face of the Columbia Glacier.

The Columbia Glacier is one of the largest tidewater glaciers of North America. As we approached the face of the glacier, the water was packed with icebergs. As the glacier recedes, ice calves into the sea, creating this stunning frozen panorama. Shots of ice falling into the sea are the current go-to shots to visually show global warming. I have sold my ice calving shots as stock footage clips many times. When I shot the footage, I thought it was dramatic but I didn't give much thought to whether or not an environmental factor was involved. It was before the world woke up to the reality of global warming.

I returned to Anchorage and took a plane back to Los Angeles. I was home only a week before I flew to New York then sailed to London to shoot *Great Cities of Europe*.

A year later in June of 1989, with *Great Cities of Europe* finished, I returned to *The Great Alaska Cruise* project. I flew to Vancouver to board the *Island Princess*. This was one of two ships (the other being the *Pacific Princess*) used in *The Love Boat* television series, which ran from 1977 to 1986. It was credited as being a big part of the public's new interest in cruises; the beginning of the modern cruise ship industry.

When I shot *The Great Alaska Cruise*, there were only two ships doing the journey each week during the summer. One was owned by Holland America, the other by Princess Cruises. The towns in the Inside Passage were simply overrun when these two 600-passenger ships would arrive. I have not been back to Alaska since I made the film, but I shudder at what it must be like today when there are four or five 3,000-passenger ships in these ports at the same time. I suspect any quaintness has been lost.

The *Island Princess* left Vancouver heading north. I made the seven-day journey through the Inside Passage, then spent two weeks working out of Anchorage picking up additional footage. Some of my films, like *Great Cities of Europe*, were shot in sequence, meaning I shot everything in roughly the same order it appears in the finished film. Other films, like *The Great Alaska Cruise,* were shot out of sequence. The finished film, with its logical movement from Vancouver, up the Inside Passage, and up through the interior of the state to the Arctic Ocean, was very different from the way it was shot.

The ship docked first in Ketchikan, a fishing port in the Inside Passage. Fish canneries are never my favorite things to film, but salmon is so important to Alaska that I included one in the film. I flew in a floatplane to the Misty Fjords. We landed on a lake and deplaned several fishermen. The plane returned late in the day to pick them (and hopefully their catch) up. Again, the experience was filled with the natural beauty of Alaska.

From Ketchikan, the next stop was Juneau, the capital. There are no roads going in or out; the city is accessible only by sea or air. The Mendenhall Glacier, just outside the town, glows with blue ice. I took a helicopter to the Juneau Icefield. Flying low over the crevasses of the glacier was dramatic; landing and filming on the glacier was even more so.

These shore excursions are a part of any Alaska cruise. Unfortunately, they have become one of the leading sources of income for the shipping lines. Cruises to Alaska are relatively inexpensive, but once you are onboard, you are at the mercy of the cruise line. When you leave the ship in these small ports, you have few options other than the planned shore excursions and *that* is where the cruise lines make much of their money. The helicopter ride to the Juneau Icefield is over three hundred dollars a person—nearly half the cost of the entire cruise. The cruise lines use the cruise almost as a loss leader to make money off the shore excursions. This stops many people from seeing the real pageant of Alaska because they can't afford the prices of these add-on experiences.

The next stop was Skagway, an old gold rush town. Remnants of the gold rush days are still there, although much of the town is a re-creation.

The prime attraction is the White Pass and Yukon Railroad. A steam locomotive pulls the narrow gauge train up the mountains right alongside the edge of the cliffs. The experience is chilling if you stand between the cars and see just how close to the edge the tracks really are.

Back in Skagway, the *Island Princess* sailed on to Glacier Bay. The National Parks Service oversees Glacier Bay and controls the number of ships going in. Not all ships traveling the Inside Passage are allowed access. This is where you are most likely to see icebergs calving off the face of a glacier.

The *Island Princess* in Glacier Bay, Alaska. The ship I sailed on to make *The Great Alaska Cruise*. 1989. Photo courtesy of Princess Cruises.

The ship then sailed across the Gulf of Alaska to College Fjord. This is a beautiful part of the state, and fortunately, it costs nothing to stand on the deck and take it all in. One of the great pleasures of the Alaska cruise is sitting in a deck chair as constantly beautiful scenery passes by. On most cruises, you see little once the ship leaves port.

At Whittier, I left the ship and took the train into Anchorage. I was on my own for two weeks to backtrack through the state and pick up additional material needed to fill out the film. I headed to Palmer to film the farms where cabbages grow to forty pounds in size. During my visit the Alaska State Fair was going on. It had a great small town feeling and provided me with some interesting footage. From Palmer, I drove on to Fairbanks, stopping in Denali to pick up additional material. I finally made my way back to Anchorage and took the train to Whittier to board the southbound *Island Princess* for the return trip to Vancouver.

Two nights into the south-bound cruise, I was watching a show in the theater. After it was over, the cruise director came onstage and told us we were in for a treat and all we had to do was to step outside onto the decks. The aurora borealis was on full display. It's the only time in my life I have seen the Northern Lights and it was something I will never forget. The experience was hallucinogenic. The whole night sky was filled with these colorful, swirling, curtains of light.

* * *

Later that summer, while I was cutting the film, Fran and Brooke Reidelberger, fellow travelogue makers, came to visit me in Los Angeles. Fran was busy at one of the Hollywood labs doing postproduction work. Brooke and I went to Marina del Rey to have lunch. We ate on the deck of a restaurant overlooking the marina. On the bulkhead, almost directly in front of me, was a beautiful motor yacht with a "for sale" sign. I called the yacht broker the next day. Once I had seen that boat I could not get it out of my mind. All of my memories of Fire Island and *Sea'scape* came flooding back. Within a couple weeks, the boat was mine. She was a 47-foot Pacemaker Motor Yacht made in New Jersey in 1968, a beautiful, classic wooden boat.

I started spending a lot of time at Marina del Rey on the boat. The boat was named the *Joie de Vivre*. I knew, of course, what the name meant. It is a common French phrase meaning "joy of life," a very appropriate name for a boat. But the boat broker and most of the people in the Marina had no idea what it meant, or how to pronounce it. It had been known for years as the "Joey da Vever."

The first year I owned the boat, I found that I had many more friends than I realized. Everybody wanted a weekend cruise. People who had not put me high on their list suddenly started calling. I didn't mind because

I loved being the captain. I would take people out for harbor cruises at night and three day jaunts up and down the coast to Long Beach, Santa Barbara, and Oxnard.

The second year I owned her, fewer people came out to the boat. By the third year, I had to drag people onboard. It was a case of "been there, done that." Within five years, I was spending my time on the boat alone. I would sail her down to Long Beach, tie up at the marina, and go to the Terrace Theater to see a Broadway show. I remember a particularly wonderful performance of Stephen Sondheim's musical *Company* with Patrick Cassidy playing Bobbie and Carol Burnett playing Joanne. I didn't really mind doing these things alone, but eventually I felt I had done everything I wanted to do with the boat so I put her up for sale.

As I signed the papers on the day of the closing, I realized that I had owned the *Joie de Vivre* exactly ten years to the day—and I sold it for exactly the same price, to the penny, I had paid for it. Not bad. But if I had put the money I spent on maintaining that boat into a mutual fund, I would be a rich man today. Owning a boat involves the two best days of your life: the day you buy it and the day you sell it.

Captain Doug atop the bridge, steering the *Joie de Vivre* into a slip at Marina del Rey, California. 1988.

I rarely went back to the marina after I sold the *Joie de Vivre*. I never really had much of a desire to own another powerboat, but I did develop an itch for something else.

One day, I was driving along Sherman Way past the Van Nuys Airport. On the side of a building was a sign: "Flying Lesson $25." My memories of flying in Alaska came back, as well as those of flying with Jim Metcalf in his Cessna 172 when I was just starting out in the business. I walked into Bud Walen Aviation and said I wanted a flying lesson. A kid, probably no more than twenty-two, was my flight instructor. I paid my $25 and we went out onto the ramp and got into a Piper Tomahawk. This was a training plane with a 112 horsepower engine. It was little more than a flying lawn mower.

The instructor had me sit in the pilot seat on the left hand side. The tower cleared us for takeoff, and with the instructor's hand on top of mine, I pushed the throttle forward. The propeller spun up and we started to roll down the runway. The instructor told me to pull back on the yoke and the plane lifted off into the sky.

The instructor might as well have been a heroin dealer. I was hooked. I was instantly addicted to the thrill of flying and it would become my newest and greatest passion.

CHAPTER TWENTY-SEVEN

LEARNING TO FLY

I was forty years old when I decided to learn to fly. It was the single most complex skill I ever mastered. It takes concentration, coordination, and daring to trust your ability to take an airplane into the sky and bring it back down in one piece. Becoming a pilot makes you feel special. And trust me, all pilots, whether they admit it or not, feel special. Flying would become the biggest experience of my life. But there would be a few bumps along the way.

I was totally hooked after my first flying lesson and I signed up for training at the Van Nuys Airport. The young instructor who had taken me up on my first flight was none too patient with his slow, middle-aged student. Learning to fly requires a good connection between student and teacher. Like relationships and marriages, you sometimes have to go through more than one before you get it right.

Much as I loved flying, this kid was not going to get me ready to face the FAA flight examiner. I drove to the Burbank airport and wandered into the Pilot's Co-op, a flight school operated by a man named Dan Tompkins. His small lobby was filled with young CFI's, Certified Flight Instructors, each eager to pick up a new student. They were like aviation ambulance chasers.

In order to fly for major carriers, a pilot has to accumulate hours. Since most young pilots don't have the money to just go up and "drill holes in the sky", they usually acquire those hours by teaching. All of them want to get to the magic number of fifteen hundred hours. At that point, the major carriers will hire them—though they are worked to death flying short routes for appallingly low pay, not unlike an intern in a hospital.

I spoke to the operator of the school and explained what my problems had been with the previous instructor. I asked him to recommend someone who would be patient with me. He introduced me to Paul Fancett. Paul had a quick wit, he was funny, and he taught me how to fly. He made the process fun, and over time, I learned the skills necessary to handle the Piper Warrior we were using.

Normally people solo after about fifteen to twenty hours of training. It took me thirty-seven hours. You don't learn as fast when you're forty years old. When Paul was convinced I could take the plane up alone, he turned me loose, (I'm sure he crossed his fingers) and waited for my return.

I learned how to fly at Burbank. It was one of the most valuable aspects of my training. I learned in the most complex, busy airspace in the country. If you learn to fly in the Los Angeles Basin, you can fly anywhere. I never had any hesitancy to go into New York airspace, San Francisco, Boston, Miami, or Atlanta. I learned to fly with Boeing 737's bearing down on my tail. It was an invaluable experience.

For my first solo flight, I was to take off from Burbank and fly to Van Nuys six miles away, land on Runway 16, come to a full stop, taxi back, takeoff, and return to Burbank, landing on Runway 8. It was all pretty clear and straightforward. (Runways are numbered by the compass heading less zero—Runway 16 is 160 degrees, south-southeast, Runway 8 is 80 degrees almost due east.)

I took off from Burbank and turned west toward Van Nuys. I was in communication with the Burbank Tower. They handed me off to Van Nuys Tower and I was cleared to land on Runway 16. I put down a pretty decent landing; the plane was at least in one piece. I taxied back for takeoff. The Van Nuys Tower cleared me. I took off and changed over to the Burbank Tower radio frequency and suddenly I was getting no responses to my transmissions. I had complete radio failure. In reality, I don't really know what happened. I probably pushed the wrong button. The radios were probably fine, but I was only six miles from the end of the runway at Burbank and a Southwest jet was getting ready to land behind me. I did what I had learned: I squawked 7600 on my transponder. The transponder is the piece of equipment in the cockpit that sends out a signal to the radar that identifies you. Normally, you are given a specific four number "squawk" to identify yourself on the control tower radar screens. When you change from your assigned number and squawk 7600, it means you have radio failure.

This set in motion a series of events—including diverting a Southwest jet. They brought out the light gun that they flash from the tower. The solid green light means you are cleared to land. I got the green light, the Southwest jet turned to do a go-around, I made my approach, and I put the Piper Warrior down on Runway 8 and taxied back to the hangar. My instructor Paul was standing there dumbfounded. How could I have radio failure on my first solo flight!?

You would think this might have scared me away from the whole flying thing, but it did not. It did, however, make me obsessive about my radios. Later on, I always had two separate handheld radios, fully charged, ready to use in the event that both of the onboard radios failed. Over the years, I have had various radio failures. It's usually not the radios themselves but the intercom system of microphones and headsets. I have used those hand held radios on more than one occasion. That first solo experience established a strong awareness of the need for communication in the air.

I continued with my training. I did my first cross-country flight to Palm Springs. I passed my ground school test of basic aeronautical knowledge. It was then time for my check ride with the FAA. I had 57 hours of flying time in my logbook. I made arrangements with an FAA examiner that operated out of El Monte Airport. We met at on the tarmac at El Monte; she had a stern and unfriendly demeanor and made me nervous from the get-go. After grilling me on basic aviation knowledge, it was time to fly. We went up. I don't recall the exact instructions—something about flying over the brewery that was to the east. In any event, I made enough mistakes that when we landed, she flunked me. This was very disheartening, but I hung in there. I spent more time in the air with my instructor, swallowed my pride, and went back to her. Fortunately, I only had to repeat the specific things I had failed—not the entire check ride. I satisfied her enough that when we landed the second time, she handed me my private pilot certificate. I was a licensed pilot!

The whole idea from the beginning was I would learn to fly, buy a small Cessna or Piper, and take friends to lunch in Santa Barbara now and then. It never occurred to me that I would use my own plane to fly to lecture dates. I considered it to be undependable. There were too many weather variables to make it practical—or so I thought initially. But as I continued to fly, I learned more about weather. I improved my skills and

I started to realize that with careful planning I could, maybe, actually fly to do my shows.

So I set out to buy a plane. What led me to Long Beach Airport to look at a Piper 235 I don't recall. Today shopping for an airplane is done online and you have inventory to choose from scattered all over the country. But this was 1990. It wasn't so easy back then. Somehow I found this plane in Long Beach. The broker was a tall, strikingly handsome woman, who, when she got in the plane to take me up for a test flight, kicked off her high heels. She told me not to worry, that she always flew shoeless. We took off from Long Beach and flew out over the ocean. I liked the plane, I thought I could learn how to fly it, so I bought it.

I needed additional training to fly the Piper 235. I had been flying a Piper Warrior with a 180 horsepower engine, which I rented at Burbank. This plane had a 235 horsepower engine and a variable speed propeller. After about five hours of training with Paul Fancett, I was ready to fly my own plane by myself. I made my first trip to Las Vegas. I landed at McCarran International just as the sun was setting and the lights on the Las Vegas Strip were coming on. The final approach to McCarran for small planes is alongside the strip. I had my eyes glued to the runway ahead and I was watching my descent, but I couldn't help but take in the extravaganza that is the Las Vegas Strip at night. I put down a good landing. I parked the plane and spent the night at the Tropicana Hotel, which was almost walking distance from McCarran. I had a great dinner, went to see a show, and I felt like the world was mine.

The following morning I took off and headed back to Burbank. I quickly became immersed in the world of flying and soon I was ready for the big trip: New York, coast-to-coast, transcontinental, by myself, solo. I carefully planned the journey. I checked out the current and forecasted weather for the entire route. I had the navigation points all written down on a legal pad, and all the VFR (visual flight rules) charts onboard. There is an enormous system of "highways" in the sky that connect navigational aids. I planned a route using the Victor Airways. I would leave Burbank heading to Palmdale where I would join Victor 12. It begins in Palmdale, California and runs all the way to Pottstown, Pennsylvania outside of Philadelphia. It's like the Interstate 70 of the air. My destination was Westchester County Airport, just outside of New York City.

My first transcontinental flight was done in August of 1991. I took Paul Fancett with me as far as Colorado Springs. I wanted a little extra reassurance on my first trip over the Rocky Mountains. We left Burbank early in the morning and headed up into the California High Desert toward Palmdale. The route took us out over the Arizona Desert where I skirted the edge of the Grand Canyon for the first time. Flying at 11,500 feet above the Grand Canyon for the first time was a shock. Waves of warm air flow out of the canyon, which causes severe turbulence as you fly around the rim. I am always very cautious about the turbulence of the canyon. You slow the plane to maneuvering speed, which allows the plane to maneuver through turbulence and remain intact. Flying too fast in strong turbulence can cause airframe failure, which is a euphemistic way of saying you crash and die.

I continued east past Tuba City, and then on to Farmington, New Mexico at Four Corners, where Arizona, New Mexico, Colorado, and Utah meet. I landed for fuel. Paul and I grabbed a quick lunch at the airport cafe, then got back in the plane and headed toward the Rocky Mountains. I crested the range east of Alamosa. At 13,500 feet, crossing the continental divide, I looked east and everything was flat and featureless as far as I could see.

My first airplane. A single-engine Piper 235. On the field at Burbank before I left on my first trans-continental flight. 1991.

I landed at Colorado Springs and let Paul out. He took a commercial flight back to Burbank. He worked for US Airways so he was able to deadhead home without buying a ticket. I refueled and flew east out over Colorado, headed for Kansas City. I had called my parents from Colorado Springs to let them know what time I would be landing. Four hours later, I approached the Downtown Municipal Airport in Kansas City, flying in over the Missouri River. My life had come full circle. It was out of this airport that I flew the TWA jets to the far corners of the globe and here I was, returning to where all my world travel began.

I landed on Runway 1 and taxied to the executive terminal where my parents were waiting. I don't think I ever saw a bigger smile on my father's face than that day when he saw his son get out of his own airplane on the tarmac at MKC.

I spent a few days with my parents then I was ready for the final leg to New York. I took off into clear blue skies, but as the afternoon wore on, thunderstorms began to build in Indiana and I had my first major experience trying to weave through the towering cumulonimbus clouds which, while beautiful to look at, can kill you. I landed in Columbus, Ohio for fuel and continued on to New York. The Allegany Mountains were beautiful from the air, a canopy of green. The scenery improved after the long haul across the plains of the Midwest. I was flying VFR, which means visual flight rules, but I utilized what is called Flight Following for the whole route. I was in contact with Air Traffic Control from the moment I left Burbank to the final landing at Westchester County Airport.

The Air Traffic Control system (ATC) operated by the FAA is an unseen wonder of the American government. Controllers at any given moment are coordinating, guiding, and assisting as many as 5,000 planes in the skies over the United States. They are the first bastions of air safety in the US air system, which is the safest in the world. While it was not required to be in contact with ATC when flying VFR, I never flew without their assistance. ATC controllers have guided me through bad weather and helped me find altitudes with smooth rides when turbulence was shaking me apart. They have stayed with me through ice encounters, pouring rain, and moments when it was downright frightening to be in the cockpit alone. Almost all of my flying has been done solo and it was the calming voice of an ATC controller that often helped me focus on the task at hand.

Finally after crossing the whole country, I was eventually handed off to New York Approach. Boy was that a shock! From California to Pennsylvania, the ATC controllers were calm and measured, sometimes casually relaxed. But when I called in and said "New York Center, Piper November 16322 with you level at seven thousand five hundred," the response was fast, quick, brisk, tense, and no nonsense. They spoke and responded with an intensity that is so quintessentially New York.

I was handed off to Westchester County Airport within the hour. It was about 11:30 at night and the tower had closed at 11:00 o'clock. When the tower is closed, you self-announce and state your intentions to whoever is in the area listening on the same radio frequency. I called the common frequency and said "Piper November 16322 is ten miles south of Westchester County making left traffic for Runway 34." In response I heard "United Flight 1745 is twelve miles north making right traffic for Runway 34." Yikes! A commercial jet was landing and the tower was closed. I responded, and between the United pilot and myself it was decided they would go in first and I would circle and land second. I thought afterward how amazed the passengers would be to learn that the tower was closed and the landing sequence was negotiated in the air between a four-seater Piper and a regional passenger jet.

By midnight, I was on the ground. I had completed my first solo transcontinental flight. What a rush. I would fly solo coast-to-coast nearly sixty times over the next twenty-five years, but nothing came close to the sense of accomplishment that night on the ground at Westchester County Airport. I took a cab to my apartment in Manhattan and settled in for a good night's sleep.

Autumn arrived soon enough, meaning it was time to start my fall lecture tour. I decided to fly my plane to my shows. My first dates were in New England, and I landed at airports all over the Northeast. Finally, I left Boston on a very long flight to Seattle to show one of my films at the Seattle Opera House. I allowed five days to make the trip in case of bad weather along the way. As it turned out, I had beautiful weather for the entire trip. I stopped for fuel in Lansing, Michigan, and then flew on to Bismarck, North Dakota where I spent the night. The following morning, I began the flight over the Northern Rockies, then the Cascades, and into Puget Sound. I landed at Boeing King County Field in downtown Seattle. After my second transcontinental flight, I was starting to feel like a pro. But over the years there were moments when it was dicey. The weather would close in and I would have to land and wait it out. I never missed a show, but I had to land early and rent a car and drive several times.

Eighteen months after getting my pilots license and buying my first plane, I had a hundred and twenty-five hours of flight time in my logbook. It became clear that if I wanted to continue to fly to my shows, I was going to need an instrument rating. An instrument rating permits you to fly into the clouds, through weather, and often climb above the weather into clear skies. The rating involves complex training. I signed up with a company called Professional Instrument Courses, PIC, for a ten-day intensive instrument-training program. The instructor arrived at my house in the Hollywood Hills and set up a simulator. For ten days, I practiced on the simulator for four hours a day, then went to Burbank airport to fly for another three hours. I can tell you it's a lot easier to fly an airplane than a flight simulator. The simulator gives you no margin of error; the airplane itself is more forgiving.

I was absolutely exhausted by the end of the ten-day course. The check ride with the FAA was set up for the following day, so I went out with the instructor to do my last training flight before the test. We flew to various airports all over the Los Angeles Basin shooting instrument approaches. The last approach I did was the VOR approach at Santa Monica Airport. After I landed, the instructor looked at me and said "Good job, you're ready the FAA check ride." I taxied back for takeoff and the short flight over the Santa Monica Mountains to Burbank.

In front of me waiting for takeoff was a single engine Mooney. The Santa Monica tower cleared the Mooney for takeoff and it went rolling down the runway and lifted into the sky. The Santa Monica tower then said "Piper November 16322 into position and hold." The instruction "into position and hold" means taxi onto the runway and wait until the tower clears you for takeoff. This is to allow the aircraft in front of you sufficient time to distance itself from the field. I taxied onto the end of the runway and I was lined up for my departure. Moments later came a tense, quick call from the tower "Piper November 16322 exit the runway *immediately*." I quickly turned the plane around and hightailed it back onto the taxiway. I looked up and saw the Mooney had turned around and was trying to make it back to the field. Its engine had failed.

The Santa Monica Airport is on a plateau. At the southwest end there is a steep drop off. The area is surrounded by a dense residential neighborhood. I looked at my instructor and saw his face go white. The plane did not make the end of the field. We saw it disappear below the plateau, and moments later the explosion, the fire, the billowing smoke. The pilot and his three passengers all died instantly. It was sobering. It is the only time I have ever witnessed a crash and it was the last day of my instrument training. The tower was silent. The ground frequency was silent. There was a long passage of time. Eventually, the tower cleared me to take off and as we lifted off from the field, I looked down at the smoldering wreckage. It's something I'll never forget.

The following day, I took my check ride with an FAA examiner at Van Nuys Airport and passed. It is the only one of my three piloting certificates (private, instrument, multi-engine) that I got on the first try.

I left the very next day on a winter lecture tour. My first stop was Bakersfield, California. It was January and a condition known as a Tule Fog was hanging over the Central Valley. The ceiling at Bakersfield was about 300 feet. Fresh off my check ride, I shot the approach, landed the plane, did my shows and got back in the plane that night and flew on to Phoenix. I was headed to Florida, but this time I had the backup of an instrument rating. It made flying easier and much safer.

I flew the rest of the 1992-1993 season in my Piper and continued to fly the following year. I planned to fly to Nashville for the annual December travelogue industry convention. I was coming from Florida. I got a weather briefing and felt the forecast was acceptable. I left Sarasota on a lovely morning, flying up the west coast of Florida. I landed in Dalton, Georgia for fuel and called the Aviation Weather Service once more to verify the forecast into Nashville. Some weather was expected to move in but the "tops" (the top layer of clouds, above which everything is clear) were to be 6,000 feet. I would be flying at 8,000 feet, well above the weather, but I would have to descend through it to land in Nashville.

I left Dalton, Georgia at 3:30 p.m. My plane climbed out, entered the clouds, and eventually came out above the cloud layer. It was clear on top, but I could see the cloud layer below me was solid and stretched as far as I could see. The sun was starting to set, so I would be doing the rest of this trip in the dark. Additionally, the cloud layer ahead was rising. I had to climb to 10,000 feet to stay on top. I looked at the clouds and I realized

I was going to have to descend through a much thicker layer than I had expected. And I knew what was in those winter clouds. Ice.

My intention was to delay my descent into Nashville until the last possible moment, then descend through the clouds quickly, hopefully picking up as little ice as possible. Ice on the wings and propeller is serious stuff. It disrupts the flow of air over the wings and your speed slows. If your airspeed is too slow, you stall, you lose lift, and you fall out of the sky and crash. Not good. In crisis moments, it's amazing how focused you become. You always keep in the back of your mind the cardinal rule of aviation: "fly the airplane." That may sound obvious, but when lots of things are happening, it's easy to forget that simple rule.

I was flying along at 10,000 feet, about a hundred miles from Nashville. The sun had fallen below the horizon, and the last glow of daylight shimmered over the tops of the ice filled clouds. I was handed off from one controller at Memphis Center to another. The new controller said "Piper November 16322 descend and maintain 4,000, cross the Shelbyville VOR (this was a navigate point) at 4,000."

What I should have said was simply "unable." As a pilot you have the right to refuse an instruction if you feel you are unable to accept the instruction safely. But I did not. I was fairly new as an instrument pilot and I did not have the confidence to challenge the controller. I replied in some half aviation, half normal conversation about how I was concerned about ice and I wanted to wait until I was closer to Nashville to descend.

In a lifetime of flying and conversations with literally thousands of ATC controllers, I have never run into a bad apple—except for this one time. The controller snapped back "I don't care if you drill circles in the sky, descend now to 4,000 and cross the Shelbyville VOR." I was nervous. Another pilot in another plane spoke up and said they had just made the descent and the ice was "not too bad."

I began the descent about eighty miles out and things quickly turned south. The wings were icing up fast. I had a flashlight I could shine out the window and watch how much ice was accumulating. "Fly the plane, fly the plane," I kept repeating to myself. I was handed off to another controller. I told him I was in trouble. I had a lot of ice on the wings and I needed to descend further. If I could get to a lower altitude, the temperature would be slightly above freezing and the plane would shed the ice. I was at 4,000 feet and the temperature was right at 32 degrees. If I could descend to

3,000 feet I could probably lose the ice. I asked for permission to descend to 3,000 and the controller said "unable, terrain." I was flying over the low mountains south of Nashville. If I went any lower I would "hit the rocks."

In this moment of tense piloting, I had a flashback to 1963.

My parents were not big country music fans, nor was I, but I loved all forms of entertainment and I had seen an ad in *The Kanas City Star* that major figures of the Grand Ole Opry were coming to town for a benefit concert to raise money for the family of a popular disk jockey who had died in a car accident. I nagged my parents into going. It was at the Memorial Hall in Kansas City, Kansas, not a particularly glamorous place. The last act on the bill was Patsy Cline. She came out and sang several of her hits, including the Willy Nelson song "Crazy." The following morning, I got up for school and my mother was sitting at the kitchen table looking serious. It had just come over the radio that Patsy Cline, along with Hawkshaw Hawkins, Cowboy Copas, and her manager Randy Hughes had died in a plane crash. They were flying in a single engine Piper Comanche. Hughes, the pilot did not have an instrument rating. They crashed in bad weather in the low mountains west of Nashville. I had seen her very last performance. And now, here I was in a single engine Piper, covered with ice, the airspeed down to 67 knots, and close to the same place where Patsy Cline died.

As these thoughts dashed through my mind, the controller came back on and said "Piper November 16322 descend and maintain 3,000 report Nashville Airport in sight." I had cleared the terrain and I could go down. I nudged the yoke forward and pushed the nose down to begin the descent. I kept looking at the outside air temperature indicator hoping to see it go up slightly. Right before I leveled off at 3,000 feet, only eight miles from the field, the ice broke free. It went flying off the wings, but the most shocking thing was how much ice had built up on the propeller. The ice came flying into the windshield like someone had just thrown a truckload of gravel at the plane. The windshield was covered with ice and I could not see out, but I was using the airport's Instrument Landing System. I had the plane on the runway centerline and the descent on the glideslope—if I just held those two needles on that one instrument in the center, I would land on the runway. Finally, the ice melted off of the windshield and I saw the "ball of fire," the pulsing sequence of lights at the end of the runway that guide you in for final approach. I slowed the plane, and pulled the nose up slightly to flare, and landed smoothly at Nashville International Airport. I taxied to the parking area and got out of the plane drained.

I went on to the convention, I saw friends, I did some business, and I went to the Grand Ole Opry. I left four days later for California and made the trip home in one day with two fuel stops. All the way back to California, I kept thinking, it's time to get a twin. I needed a plane with de-icing boots and heated propellers and two engines to avoid this happening again. The twin, a Cessna 310Q, with a tail number of N9924F would come into my life the following summer—and that's when flying really got fun.

CHAPTER TWENTY-EIGHT

THE CANADIAN TRANSCONTINENTAL TRAIN RIDE

Sometime back in the 1980s, I applied for membership in the Society of American Travel Writers. They did not admit applicants freely; I had to prove my professional stature and be sponsored by a current member. I submitted pages of press clippings and show programs. After some time I was approved to join the organization. Membership in SATW gave me credibility and opened doors when I went to government tourist offices.

One day in early 1990, a cardboard roll arrived at my door. Inside were two large wall posters, one in English, the other in French, sent by the press representative of VIA Rail, the Canadian passenger rail service, to all SATW members. The posters depicted the newly restored *Canadian* and announced the relaunch of the streamliner train.

The *Canadian* is Canada's long-haul transcontinental passenger train. Launched in 1955, it has a fabled history as important as the *Super Chief* or the *California Zephyr*. The train was initially a great success. It was fast and luxurious, and passed through some of the most beautiful scenery in the world. But in 1959, the jet plane arrived and Canadians could travel to the west coast in only a few hours. Ridership started falling off fast and by the 1970s the train was limping along.

In 1989, the last *Canadian* ran on the Canadian Pacific route; from Vancouver to Toronto by way of Calgary and Winnipeg. Everyone assumed it was the end of Canadian passenger train service. But the Canadian government had a change of heart and invested two hundred million dollars into restoring the train. When the restoration was finished, it was once again a great luxury train offering a leisurely three-day journey through the heart of the Canadian Rockies.

But on the day those posters arrived, I knew none of this. All I did know was that the idea of traveling across Canada in a streamliner train evoked images of mountain scenery, rolling prairies, and leisurely travel. The success or failure of a new film was based on whether or not the title would draw a crowd. I imaged the title as *The Great Canadian Train Ride*. I felt the title would create mental images of beautiful scenery and entice people to see the film.

My interest in the project went back to my college days. Even though I was able to travel on TWA free of charge, I loved trains. Kansas City was a railroad town. Union Station remains one of the city's most prominent architectural landmarks. Both the Santa Fe and the Union Pacific ran their long haul trains through Kansas City. The *El Capitan*, the *City of Saint Louis*, the *San Francisco Chief*, the *City of Los Angeles*; they all pulled into Kansas City each day.

My first train ride was on the Santa Fe *El Capitan* to Chicago. It was 1966 and riding on the train was actually a dress up affair. The coaches were two stories high and the seats were remarkably comfortable. It was the very end of the golden age of streamliner rail travel. Like so many things that I caught at the very end of their time (burlesque, New York nightclubs, the travelogue industry itself), I feel fortunate to have had the experience of seeing what great American trains were once like. The highlight was always "dinner in the diner." The diners had white linen tablecloths and flowers. You shared a table with other passengers so everyone onboard could be served. Conversation was required and most of the time I found people interesting, if for no other reasons than the fact that we all probably loved traveling on the train.

I loved Chicago (and I still do). The trip from Kansas City to Dearborn Station in the South Loop was about eight hours, a nice amount of time to be on a train. I never had a sleeper until much later when I started making cross-country train films. Coming back from Chicago, the *San Francisco Chief* would leave at 4:00 p.m. and much of the trip would be after dark. I have memories of sitting in the observation dome car alone late at night, looking up at the moon and stars, watching the towns roll by. It was travel with peaceful solitude, something the airlines could never provide.

So when the idea came to make *The Great Canadian Train Ride*, I thought it would be an opportunity to relive travel memories from long ago. I didn't make the film because I thought it would become my most successful travelogue, but in time, it would be.

I had been making travelogues for twenty-two years and I was well established. The sponsoring organizations and show promoters wanted films that were new and, because of my track record, they were usually willing to book my films before I made them. I announced in early 1990 I was making *The Great Canadian Train Ride* and it would be available for the 1990-1991 season. The bookings came in, and soon I had almost two hundred shows scheduled for a program I had not shot a foot of film for. I am amazed I had the gumption to do this year after year, but I did. And I always delivered the finished program on time.

I thought the film would be popular, but I could never have imagined how successful it would become. My first hint of this was in Fort Wayne, Indiana. I was showing *The Great World Cruise of the QE2* at the Embassy Theater in April of 1990. The man who introduced me announced the new shows for the coming season as I stood in the wings getting ready to go on. After he went through the list, he finished by saying, "And tonight's speaker, Doug Jones, is going to be back with us again next season with a new film called *The Great Canadian Train Ride*." There was this very audible murmur in the theater. That was the moment I realized I was going to have a good run with the film. I showed the *The Great Canadian Train Ride* to nearly full houses all across America for the next five years. Additionally, the film ultimately sold over a million copies on videotape and DVD. A film like that really only comes along once in a lifetime. I never duplicated the success of that film again.

Shortly after I received the poster in the mail, I contacted the *Canadian* press representative, a man named Paul Raynor. VIA Rail was willing to give me a cross-Canada ticket on the *Canadian*. At the time, few Americans had done this trip. VIA Rail gave me complete run of the train. I was allowed in the galley, the sleepers, and the locomotive. I was given every courtesy possible and making the film was one of the easiest shooting experiences of my life.

I started in Montreal in June of 1990. I went there to film the restoration of the streamliner passenger cars. Several consists ("consist" is the term for a fully assembled train, the locomotives, baggage cars, lounge cars, sleepers, and coaches) were already completed and making the three day run to Vancouver. VIA Rail still had another fifty cars to finish for the eastern service to Halifax. VIA Rail could have just bought new cars (which is what Amtrak did), but being mindful of the history of this train, VIA Rail decided to restore the original rolling stock.

After filming the railcar restoration process, I made my way to Toronto. The *Canadian* originally started in Montreal, but the newly restored train was going to originate in Toronto. When I arrived in Toronto, I set out to film the sights of Canada's largest city. I stayed at the Royal York Hotel. It was, at the time, Canada's largest hotel. It was built in 1929 by the Canadian Pacific Railway. Both of Canada's large railway companies, the Canadian Pacific and the Canadian National, built grand château-like hotels across the country. From the Frontenac in Quebec City all the way to the Empress in Victoria, Canada is covered with impressive railway hotels, which still operate today.

The *Canadian* left Toronto on a Tuesday morning at 11:45 a.m. I needed to get a shot of the train pulling out of Union Station. I spoke with the conductor and the engineer, and they agreed to let me shoot from the very front end of the platform as the train pulled out. At exactly 11:45, the engineer powered up both F40 General Motors diesel electric locomotives, blew the whistle, and slowly, the *Canadian* pulled out of Union Station. I had just a few moments to get three great shots, the locomotives leaving and the cars rolling by, a quick low shot of the rolling wheels and a great upshot of the silver streamliner cars rolling west, with the CN Tower looming above. Once the train had "left the station," the engineer stopped the train, backed it up, and I got on board.

The *Canadian* boasted a special feature: the Park Car. The last car on the train, it had a bullet-shaped lounge with a large observation dome on top and great views from the back of the car with the tracks retreating at eighty miles an hour. The Park Car quickly filled with passengers and attendants served drinks and passing hors d'oeuvres and canapés. We were on our way, the beginning of a 2800-mile journey, and people were settling into the quiet, relaxed, and leisurely pace of traveling on a train.

I filmed my sleeping car attendant making up my berth and afterward settled in for a night of sleep. The following morning, we were traveling out over the Canadian Shield, a 700-mile wide slab of granite that connects the Great Lakes with Hudson Bay. At eleven o'clock in the morning, we pulled into Sioux Lookout, one of the service stops for the train. At Sioux Lookout, diesel fuel was added to both locomotives and other employees watered the cars. The cars, coaches, sleepers, and galleys, all have tanks holding hundreds of gallons of water. The water is quickly used up and must be replenished throughout the trip. From Sioux Lookout, the train continued west, passing onto the prairies as we approached Winnipeg.

I knew Winnipeg from my many travelogue showings at the Centennial Concert Hall. I filmed in and around Winnipeg for several days. I also scouted trackside locations out of town so I could film the train passing by. These are called passing shots. I would shoot three or four of these in each of the places the train stopped. People would ask "How did you shoot out of the window and then shoot the train passing by outside?" It wasn't magic, it just required some planning. While the film is presented as one train traveling across Canada, the exterior passing shots are of many different trains. Fortunately, they all look alike, but if you look closely at my film, you see there are different identification numbers on the locomotives passing by. Not many people catch that subtlety.

In Winnipeg, I boarded the front locomotive as the train pulled out toward Saskatoon. There were two engineers who took turns driving the train. They had their eyes glued to the tracks ahead and constantly monitored the speed, the air brakes, and the electrical output. Train locomotives burn diesel fuel in electric generators. The electricity then operates traction motors. It's the most efficient way to pull a train. This technology has been used by the railroads since the 1950s after the end of the age of steam. It took decades for the same technology to be adapted to cars. Today's automotive hybrids use technology that railroads have used for over half a century.

In Saskatoon, I got off and checked into the Bessborough Hotel. I filmed around the city and the surrounding farms. Saskatoon is a part of the Great Plains. In June the wheat nears harvest and the fields surrounding Saskatoon are particularly beautiful. The region also has a rich history of nomadic, native North American people who wandered the plains.

The next stop was Edmonton, the capital of Alberta; an oil town, dynamic, and moneyed. The Grand Trunk Railway built the MacDonald Hotel on a bluff overlooking the North Saskatchewan River. It was completely restored a year before I arrived.

From Edmonton, the real beauty of the trip began as the *Canadian* headed west toward the Rocky Mountains. The observation dome car filled with passengers, everyone taking in the expanding scenery of the mountains as we headed toward the Yellowhead Pass. I got off at Jasper, rented a car and spent a week exploring the Canadian Rockies. I stayed in one of the cabins at the Jasper Park Lodge. The morning after I checked in, I ordered breakfast. A few minutes later, my breakfast arrived by bicycle. The bellmen all use bicycles to deliver room service throughout the lodge.

I filmed white water rafting, the Jasper tramway, and the Icefield Parkway, one of the most beautiful stretches of road in the world. It is a hundred and forty miles long, connecting Jasper with Lake Louise and Banff. It passes through two national parks, Jasper National Park and Banff National Park. Along the way, I rode a snowcoach out onto the Athabasca Glacier and stopped at Lake Louise to film both the lake and the Château Lake Louise. This large railway property started out as a humble affair. In the 1890s, it was a one-room cabin for passengers traveling west on the train. But the Canadian Pacific Railway saw the commercial possibilities and built one of the great hotels of North America on the shores of Lake Louise. Nearby is Banff, best known for the Banff Springs Hotel, a giant brick pile, and the first of the railway hotels. In front is a statue of William Cornelius Van Horn, who was the chairman of the Canadian Pacific Railway at the time the hotel and the railway were completed. It's inscribed with his quote, "Since we can't export the scenery, we shall have to import the tourists."

From Banff, I drove back up the Icefield Parkway to Jasper and re-boarded the *Canadian* heading west toward the Yellowhead Pass. The Yellowhead Pass is fairly low and was easy to survey by the Great Northern and the Grand Trunk Railways. These two railways went into competition with the Canadian Pacific shortly after the first transcontinental track was completed in 1885. By the early part of the 20th century, both competitor railways were bankrupt. The Canadian government took over both and renamed the operation the Canadian National.

Canadian Pacific laid the first transcontinental track through Kicking Horse Pass to the south. It was high and required steep, dangerous grades. To crest the pass, they had to build spiral tunnels. The tunnels are famous because you can watch a train enter the tunnel, then emerge at the bottom while the rest of the train is still entering the entrance high above.

The question arises, why did the Canadian Pacific use this difficult pass when the easy Yellowhead Pass was available? The answer is—the Americans. America was in an expansionistic mood and Canadians feared Americans would simply walk across the border and declare the land their own. The Canadian government insisted on using the Kicking Horse Pass so the tracks would be closer to the US border, the land would be settled more quickly, and that would hopefully keep the Americans away.

From Jasper, the train continued west on the most beautiful part of the journey. Finally, we came out of the mountains past Mount Robson to the north, and the train headed into the central highlands of British Columbia. I got off at Kamloops, a railway town where all three transcontinental tracks converge. I worked in and around Kamloops, then went down to the Lake District and filmed around Kelowna. Then back on the train for the final leg through the Frasier River Canyon and on to Vancouver.

In Vancouver, I took the ferry to Victoria, which feels more British than Canadian. The Canadian Pacific originally intended to bring the train to Victoria by putting the train onto ferryboats but the plan was never carried out. Anticipating this, the Canadian Pacific built the Empress Hotel. The train never came to Victoria, but the hotel was an instant success. Tea in the lobby of the hotel is one of the great travel experiences of Canada, though today it is somewhat overwhelmed by tour groups.

With 26,000 feet of film, I returned to Los Angeles. The film was processed at Fotokem in Burbank. The footage looked good and I got to work editing the picture. The first show at Orchestra Hall in Chicago for the Chicago Geographic Society was fast approaching. I finished the film just in time and headed out on the road with my new travelogue.

Making *The Great Canadian Train Ride* was one of my happiest filmmaking journeys, and it proved to be my most successful project ever. If you have never traveled west on the *Canadian,* I urge you to consider it. It is one of the world's great travel experiences.

The *Canadian* with Mount Robson in the background. *The Great Canadian Train Ride* was my most successful film. 1990. Photo courtesy of VIA Rail.

It was time for a new headshot for the release of *The Great Canadian Train Ride*. A Hollywood photographer on Gower Street, whose name I cannot, recall shot it. 1990.

CHAPTER TWENTY-NINE

NEW TECHNOLOGY THAT WOULD CHANGE THE WORLD

Sometime around 1980, I was sitting in my apartment on West End Avenue reading *The New York Times* and I saw an ad from Crazy Eddie (the long defunct electronics store) for a "home video tape recorder." This seemed like magic: a machine in your own house that you could record television shows on and then play back when you wanted. The machine was a Magnavox that weighed about twenty-five pounds and cost $400. I went out that afternoon and bought one. Little did I know how much those machines would change my life, my career, and the way entertainment was delivered to the public. All I knew was I could now record my favorite TV shows and fast forward through the commercials. A godsend.

When the first VHS machines came out, there was a rumor that Hollywood would start releasing their old movies on videotape. Initially, this was done only for rental stores. In the early days of home video, you couldn't purchase the films. The video rental stores bought them for, in some cases, several hundred dollars apiece, and would rent them to you. Eventually, the prices came down on videotapes and people could buy their own. It was assumed this would only be for Hollywood movies. No one thought there would ever be a market for "special interest" titles. The first breakthrough was in fitness. Home fitness videos took off like gangbusters with people all across America suddenly popping in VHS tapes of Jane Fonda and getting fit, or at least trying to, in their living rooms. If exercise videotapes could find an audience, maybe there was an audience for travel videos as well.

Dennis Burkhart of Portland, Oregon was a friend in the travelogue business. In the 1980s, Dennis decided to try to sell travel videotapes. He had material of his own but he wanted two of my titles to add to the initial collection of videotapes he was offering. I licensed him the rights to my films *The Hawaiian Adventure* and *Portraits of America—The National Parks*. Our agreement was very simple, probably no more than a page. I would receive a royalty of twenty-five percent of gross sales. Dennis edited the films to make them suitable for video distribution, added soundtracks, and set out to market his videotapes. His initial operation was so simple that he was printing the box covers on a Xerox machine in black and white and using double stick tape to affix a color photograph of the Grand Canyon on my National Parks video and a hula dancer on my Hawaiian video.

He moved very small numbers and my quarterly royalty statements were, as you would expect, very low: twenty dollars one time, maybe fifty dollars the next quarter. After a year or two of this, Dennis approached me and suggested that rather than pay out such small amounts, perhaps he could buy the video rights from me for a lump sum. I asked him what he thought was fair and he suggested an amount. It seemed reasonable and I signed a letter assigning him the video rights to both films for three thousand dollars. Big mistake.

We now travel back to a travelogue convention in Chicago in the early 1980's. A man named Albert Nadar made a presentation to the travelogue filmmakers about a travel television show he was going to produce. Albert was (and still is) a P.T. Barnum type—a huckster and a born salesman. These were the early days of cable television and Albert envisioned getting his program on a cable network and he needed product. He wanted the travelogue producers to sign agreements giving him the exclusive broadcast rights to our programs in exchange for no upfront money but promises of riches down the road. Most of us signed with him. He had a magnetic way of convincing us this was going to be our ticket to wealth.

Albert went to work trying to sell the television series but made little progress. Each December, he would show up at the travelogue convention promising us it was just a matter of time before the program would be on the air and we would be getting checks.

After about three years of this, the travelogue producers were getting antsy. When was this going to happen? Other opportunities were popping up in broadcast and none of us could pursue them because of our contracts with Albert.

In 1985 the travelogue convention was held on the *Queen Mary* in Long Beach, California. The filmmakers group met privately before the convention to discuss what to do about this. We all knew Albert was going to tell us everything was just around the corner. The group decided we needed to confront him. Someone suggested that I be the one to do it and I stupidly agreed.

The INTRAFILM convention on the *Queen Mary* in Long Beach. It was here that I challenged Albert Nadar of Questar Communications. Left to right: Top row; Jerry Neff, Fran Reidelberger, Steve Gonser, Sheri Yeakey, Sandy Weir, Doug Jones. Front row; Cecil Houghton, Bunny Kamen Longe, Joan Lark, Carolyn Lutz. 1985.

The first night of the convention there was a cocktail party in the dome that held the *Spruce Goose*. The *Spruce Goose* was the behemoth balsa wood airplane built by Howard Hughes that only flew once. It was huge, bigger than a 747, the largest airplane ever built, and it was on display next to the *Queen Mary*. Albert called all of us together under the left wing of the *Spruce Goose*, the silent, monstrous engines directly overhead. He started in with the litany we had heard before and I stopped Albert. I can't remember what I said. I was probably not diplomatic but it was something to the effect of, "Where's the beef?" Later, an associate of Albert's told me, that he had never seen Albert speechless. I represented the whole group of filmmakers but I would be the one to pay for challenging him.

Back to Dennis Burkhart and his videotape business. I took my three thousand dollars for the video rights buyout and didn't give it much thought. Two years later, the travelogue convention was held in San Diego. I ran into Dennis and asked him "How's your video business going?" Dennis smiled and said, "Pretty good." I said "How good?" and Dennis grinned and said that The National Parks film was in the first *Reader's Digest* video catalogue and the first mailing had produced 60,000 videotape orders. My jaw dropped. I did some math. Videotapes, in those days, were selling for $39.95 apiece. Forty times sixty thousand?—jeeze, the gross take had been $2,500,000! And I had sold the rights for three thousand dollars! And the sales were just getting started.

I have no idea how many copies were ultimately sold worldwide or how much money Dennis made off of my title, but I did smell a rat. Dennis was just too nice a guy. Somehow I knew Albert Nadar was involved. He had abandoned the television show idea and contacted a relative that worked for *Reader's Digest*. They were the kings of direct marketing at the time. Their first videotape catalogue was a huge success and my National Parks film (which had been retitled) was one of the biggest sellers out of the gate. I do not know for a fact that Albert suggested to Dennis to buy me out. Possibly Dennis thought of this before he and Albert went into business together—but I find it doubtful.

Dennis was bothered enough by the whole incident that he sent me a check, unsolicited, for ten thousand dollars; a great and kind gesture on his part. He did not have to do it and I know it came out of his own pocket. It was a business decision to take the buyout. I made a mistake. But they were the early days of video, and there was no way I could have foreseen the potential of the film in video. But I'm practical in business matters and as irked as I was, I wanted a piece of the action myself, so I went to Albert and asked if he would release some of my other titles. I believed that *The Great World Cruise of the QE2* and *Great Cities of Europe* would do well in video. Albert said yes, and he then set about releasing every other travelogue filmmaker's titles and let mine sit on the shelf. His company, Questar

Communications, was becoming big. He was the king of travel video. And he was letting me dangle on a string.

After several years, I decided if my titles were going to be released, I was going to have to do it myself. But first I had to convert my 16mm films to videotape and put sound on them. Remember these were silent pictures that I narrated live. They had to be post-produced for video.

The first step was converting the 16mm film to a video image. This was done before digital technology came along, so the early films were converted to analog images on one-inch videotape using a machine called the Rank Cintel. An operator would stare at the video monitor while the film ran in another room. He could make adjustments to the colors and fix a lot of problems that were unfixable on film. The film-to-video transfers were expensive.

Once this was done, I had a one-inch video master with no sound. I was given the name of an audio facility in Burbank called Juniper Studios. I would later learn that Scientologists owned it. I won't digress into that subject, but they were all nut cases. None of the Scientology audio engineers were available to do my project, so I was assigned the one non-Scientologist audio engineer on staff, a guy named Steve Sharp. I would narrate in a sound booth as the videotape ran on a monitor. After the voice track was complete, we sat together and added music, sound effects, and eventually the whole twenty-four-track audiotape was mixed. The mixing process was extremely important and hard to get just right. Balancing all of these elements, voice, music, sound effects, into a listenable soundtrack is an art.

Steve was great at his job, and also tons of fun. In the process of laying in music tracks for one of the shows, he casually mentioned that he had just had a birthday. I said, "Me too." I asked him when his birthday was, he said June 25th and I said, "Me too!" Then I asked the year he was born—1948. "Me too!!" The time? He was born on the east coast in a different time zone, but we realized the two of us had been born in the *same hour*. It was uncanny. Even more uncanny, we became best friends. He is the most comfortable straight man around gay people that I have ever known; totally cool, self-confident, sure of himself. Before he married his wife Leslie, he had a string of crazy girlfriends and I had a string of crazy boyfriends (I was unattached during my early "Steve Sharp years"). The two of us would prowl all over L.A. doing goofy things like seeing *Bevis and Butthead* at the Chinese Theater, flying in my airplane, drinking too much, laughing at our own jokes. It was one of the happiest times of my life. He was the best friend I ever had. He eventually moved back to his hometown of Portland, Oregon and I still miss him. I was the best man at his wedding and later he was mine. You don't get a lot closer than that.

Steve and I worked through the summer to complete the audio on five of my films. I was then ready to try to sell my travel videos myself. To hell with Albert Nadar. I got the name of the video buyer at *Reader's Digest*, a woman named Wendy Maples. I went to their offices in New York and made a presentation to Wendy and her associate, Chuck Chesnut. I had flashy packaging and they liked the titles. We made a deal. I would get 40% of the retail price, which was now down to $19.95, a price point that would hold for many years. I would be paid $7.86 for each unit, (my manufacturing cost was $2.25 per tape). They would pay for the shipping from my video duplication house in Los Angeles to their warehouse in New York.

I went back to my apartment in New York very satisfied with the meeting. A few days later I returned to Los Angeles. In those days, fax machines were used to conduct business. I was sitting in my office when the high pitched screech of the fax machine started and out came an order from *Reader's Digest* for 5,000 copies of *The Great World Cruise of the QE2* and 5,000 copies of *Great Cities of Europe*. Holy Cow! It was a $70,000 order.

This was not a licensing deal, this was a hard goods transaction. I had to get the videotapes made myself. Video duplication houses were sprouting up like mushrooms in L.A. I settled on a company called Dubs, Inc. in Hollywood. The process of duplicating videotapes couldn't have been more rudimentary. The duplication house was filled with hundreds of videotape machines that were exactly like the machines the consumers had in their homes. They were all linked to a master machine that ran the one-inch videotape and sent the signal to the hundreds of VHS machines. Once the film played out, worker bees would go along and rewind the tapes, pop them out, put in new blank tapes and start the whole process over again. There were countless glitches in the machines and quality control was a horrible problem.

Once the tapes had been duplicated, they had to be put into a clamshell case. The artwork was printed and slipped into a clear sleeve on the packaging. The tape went into the box, then the box went through the shrink-wrap machine and voila! You had videotape ready to ship.

I got a call that the order was ready to ship to New York. I went over to the duplication house to inspect the shipment. It was huge. Ten thousand videotapes, fifty to a box, two hundred big boxes. I opened a box and pulled out a couple tapes. They looked fine on the front, but when you turned them over, the backs of the tape boxes were completely melted. The shrink-wrap operator had the heat set too high and the backs melted as each box went through the machine. I called the owner of the dubbing house to the loading dock and told him this was not acceptable. He sighed but agreed, and all ten thousand tapes had to have the shrink wrap, printed sleeve, and video tape removed, and get re-boxed and shrink-wrapped at a lower temperature. It took days to do this. Finally, the shipment went out and I got my first big check from *Reader's Digest* and I was off and running.

The videotape business was very good to me in the early years. I initially released five titles, *The Great World Cruise of the QE2*, *Portraits of the Great Far East*, *QE2 Sails New Zealand and Australia*, *Great Cities of Europe*, and *Portraits of America–The National Parks*. Dennis Burkhart owned the rights to the National Parks film, which Albert was selling through *Readers Digest*, but they were not exclusive rights, so I had the legal right to release the film under the original title.

The next year, I shot *The Great Alaska Cruise* and quickly released it on video. *Reader's Digest* carried this title as well, but it was in 1990 when I made *The Great Canadian Train Ride* that I would reap the big benefits. *Reader's Digest* put *The Great Canadian Train Ride* in their Christmas gift catalogue and it did stunning business.

Meanwhile, I was going to the big video trade show in Las Vegas every year. VSDA—Video Software Dealers Association. It was a huge event. The Hollywood studios put up massive exhibits and movie stars from new releases would be on the convention floor. I had a small booth on the far north wall of the Las Vegas Convention Center. To say I was small was an understatement. But I put up my display with my videotape boxes, passed out flyers, and talked to buyers who wandered by. Trade shows are exhausting because you have to be on your feet for hours talking with hundreds of people, most of whom owned mom and pop video stores that might buy one or two copies for rental. But you had to be nice to everyone because you never knew when someone important was going to pass by.

I had an odd location in the convention hall in 1992. A large part of the video show was devoted to "Adult" which, of course, meant porn. To get to the Adult section, you had to pass down a long aisle that ran right in front of my booth. The Adult section, like the big studios, had their stars on hand to sign autographs and have pictures taken with their fans. I spent the convention watching the most amazing assortment of porn actresses pass in front of my booth. One I remember particularly well was Wendy Whoopers and I don't need to say more. How she walked and balanced herself on those spiked heels was a feat of physics. Jaws dropped as she passed. There were dozens of sightings like this throughout the week. It was an experience.

In the middle of all of this, a woman named Lynn Hamlin stopped by my booth. She picked up *The Great Canadian Train Ride* and said, "This looks interesting. Can I have a copy?" I handed her the videotape and she gave me her card. She was with a company called National Syndications, Inc. Several weeks later, she called and said their staff watched the video and wanted to "test" it. What I learned was that National Syndications, Inc., NSI, bought the remnant advertising space in *Parade Magazine*. *Parade Magazine* was (and is) the insert magazine stuffed into almost every Sunday newspaper in America. Their circulation at the time was a staggering twenty-four million.

They ran a test ad for *The Great Canadian Train Ride* in *The Atlanta Constitution* and *The Denver Post*. The response was good and after a couple of weeks they decided to do a full rollout. This was a licensing deal. I received fifteen percent of the revenues generated. Videotapes were still selling for $19.95, so I was going to get about three dollars for each tape sold. I loved this. I didn't have to worry about manufacturing, shipping, packing, or handling complaints. All of that was now was in someone else's hands. All I had to do was go to the mailbox and cash the checks.

I went to a newsstand in Los Angeles late on Saturday night before the first national rollout to buy the Sunday edition of *The Los Angeles Times*. I quickly pulled out *Parade Magazine* right on the street and there on page five was a full page, full color ad for my video. The first national rollout produced 92,000 orders. The tapes sold and sold and sold. They rolled it out again a year later and lowered the price to $9.95 and sold more. Finally, years into selling the video, NSI rolled it out a final time at $4.95 and sold even more. NSI, in spite of its successes, eventually crashed and declared bankruptcy. I was owed some money at the end but I had made so much from them over a five year period that I wasn't going to dwell on being shorted a small amount in the bankruptcy.

The title is still available in DVD and continues to sell remarkable well twenty-six years after it was released. I used to keep track of the total volume, but once it passed a million copies, I quit counting. Frankly, I have no idea what the total number is now. but for a long time *The Great Canadian Train Ride* paid my bills. I was able to save, which would come in handy in the years ahead as the travelogue business faded away. And Albert Nadar could have had all of this business if he had not kept me dangling on a string.

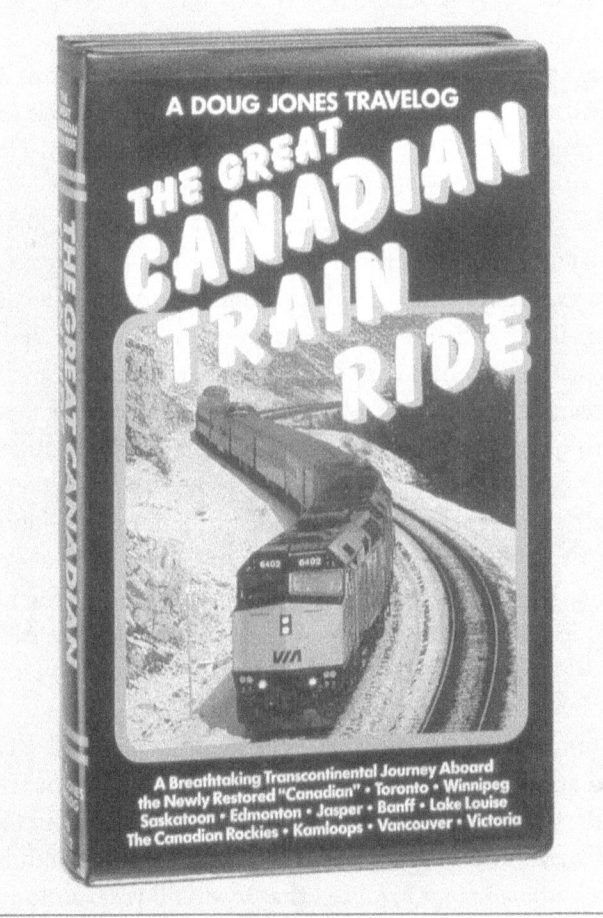

A videotape of *The Great Canadian Train Ride*. The home entertainment market was good to me. The video and subsequent DVD have sold over one million copies. 1990.

I made other deals with different companies for licensing my film titles. In 2004, I released *Sailing Down to Rio on the Queen Mary 2*. By this time NSI had folded, *Reader's Digest* had quit selling videos, and the whole DVD market was headed south. For all the people who came and went in the home entertainment specialty title business, Albert Nadar was about the only one left. I put aside past differences and offered him the Rio title. He released it, but by this time not much of a market remained. He also released *Cruising the Orient on the QE2* and again, not much business was left. The peak years were long gone. Finally, in 2011 I released a film memoir of my forty years of shooting travelogues called *Around the World–One Man's Journey*. Again, Albert took it on and released it but with limited success.

I was passing through Chicago doing lectures in the fall of 2011 and I contacted Albert wanting to see if we could have dinner. I wanted to make a business proposal to him but I wanted to do it in person. He hesitated making a commitment. His assistant kept telling me maybe yes, maybe no. I was told to keep my phone close and Albert would call me if he could see me. Fran and Brooke Reidelberger were also in Chicago, and following the adage of "a bird in hand…" I made arrangements to have dinner with them. Then Albert called and told me to meet him at an Italian restaurant on Halsted. I told him that I had made arrangements with Fran and Brooke. Albert, knowing them, said to bring them along. I went into the restaurant thinking that finally I was going to normalize my relationship with him; let bygones be bygones. It was a group of five; Albert's wife was along; Albert and his wife sat on one side of the long table and the three of us on the other. Albert proceeded to talk to Fran and Brooke and ignore me as though I wasn't there. Fran tried desperately to get me included in the conversation, but Albert persisted in ignoring me. Slowly, Albert moved his chair away from me so he would be opposite Fran and I was verbally and physically excluded from the conversation.

After a long dinner and me seething, Albert finally at the end of the evening looked at me and said, "You know Dennis Burkhart has made three million dollars from my company." I said "Well, that's nice for Dennis." Albert then went onto a jag about how great Dennis was and how much money they had made and I realized that it was 30 years almost to the day from that fateful night under the wing of the *Spruce Goose* in Long Beach and he was still mad at me. I left the restaurant feeling sucker punched.

CHAPTER THIRTY

ANOTHER RELATIONSHIP, TWO FILMS, AND THREE FLOPS

Life was going pretty well as I, and the rest of the world, entered the last decade of the millennium. My videotape business was humming along, the checks were coming in, and I still had strong travelogue lecture tours. I was also starting to shoot footage specifically for my stock footage library. I sold footage from my decades of filmmaking and throughout the 1990s it would provide another stream of income (that would later come to a crashing halt with the development of high definition television). I had shots popping up in prime time television shows. *MacGyver* was shot on a Hollywood back lot, but they needed an opening establishing shot for an episode that took place in Bangkok, so they called me. The sitcom *The Nannie* needed a shot of the Eiffel Tower for an episode in which the Nannie went to Paris, so I sold them one of mine. *The Tonight Show*, *The Colbert Report*, and *The Daily Show* used my shots well into the 2000s, until Hollywood studios decided to open their vaults and make their footage more readily available. I also had a lot of national commercials, ranging from Red Lobster (my Columbia Glacier footage from Alaska) to Fancy Feast Cat Food (they used a shot of Venice) to Trans World Airlines (The Eiffel Tower elevator ascending in Paris).

It was a thriving decade. I felt good. My health was great, I had a successful business, and I was single. After the on again, off again relationship with Steve Cline, I was happy, living a peripatetic life between New York and Los Angeles. I wasn't looking for someone new, but a friend, David Griffiths, offered to set me up on a blind date with a friend who he thought I would like.

Robert Smith came to my apartment on East 72nd Street. The doorman buzzed me on the intercom to announce my visitor. Robert rode the elevator up, knocked on the door, and when I opened, he didn't look at me but rather peered inside the apartment. It was curious and maybe a sign of what was to come. I made him a drink. I asked him what he did for a living and he told me he was a travel agent. I asked him where he worked and he said a small boutique agency in Rockefeller Center and that I wouldn't know it. "Is it Mercury Travel?" I asked. He looked shocked and said yes.

Mercury Travel had been my travel agency for years. I started doing business with them in 1982 when I met one of the daughters of the owner on a cruise to Bermuda on the old M.S. *Vollendam*, a Holland America ship. Her name was Mary Lou Parkinson and she solicited my business. I did my travel bookings through her until one day when I was standing in O'Hare Airport trying to make a flight to get to a lecture date and something went wrong. I have forgotten what actually happened—a poorly timed plane connection probably—but I did "go off" over the telephone.

A trait I possess, which I am not proud of, is that I can "go off" when I am upset. I can move from zero to sixty in a flash, and while I see it as being firm, other people see it as aggressive and nasty. (I have fortunately lost most of this trait as I have aged.) Whatever happened that day in Chicago on the phone with Mary Lou was enough that the agency called me and told me to take my business elsewhere. I must have been a complete jerk.

Back to Robert: When he told me he worked for Mercury Travel and I told him I had been a client. We started comparing notes and we had a lot in common and, of course, we both loved to travel. The evening went well and soon we began doing other things together, and slowly we started a relationship of sorts.

At some point, Robert told his boss, one of the Parkinson daughters, that he was dating me and her shocked response was, "He was a good client but he was so obnoxious!" No one likes to hear this about themselves but it was probably true.

Robert came to California several times. He loved to fly in my airplane. As a travel agent, he was an expert at making travel arrangements, and he put together some great trips. We did a trip in my airplane to Monument Valley and Las Vegas. On another trip, we flew the airplane to Miami and then out to the Bahamas. Another time, we traveled through the South to North Carolina and Georgia. But the best trip we ever took was to Yellowstone National Park in January to go snowmobiling. We flew from Los Angeles non-stop. In looking back on my flying history, I sometimes wonder if I would have the courage to do these things today. But I was younger, in my early forties, and my confidence in my flying skills was high.

Robert Smith, Central Park, New York, 1993.

We left Burbank and flew to Jackson Hole, Wyoming. By the time we arrived, weather had set in. The ceiling was low and I was put into a holding pattern. In 3,000 hours of flying, it was the only time I was ever put in a holding pattern, and it was a bit creepy. The outside air temperature was about ten below zero. The heater in the plane was working overtime to keep the cabin warm, and while I wasn't extremely low on fuel, we had done the trip without a fuel stop and I was not in a position to fly a holding pattern for a long time. And I was in the clouds, socked in just southeast of the Grand Tetons. A few goofs would have put me into the side of the mountains. Fortunately, I was taken out of the holding pattern and cleared for the approach in about twenty minutes. I flew down under a low cloud layer, landing at Jackson Hole under a 700-foot ceiling on Runway 19.

We rented a car and spent the night at a hotel in Jackson Hole. The following morning we drove to the snowmobile company on the border between Grand Tetons National Park and Yellowstone National Park. They gave us full-length winterized suits to wear that were lightweight and kept all the body temperature inside. We were given our snowmobiles, helmets, and some basic instructions, and off we went into Yellowstone.

Snowmobiling in Yellowstone has been under attack by environmentalists for years. I suspect I would agree with some of the concerns today, but in 1993, the negative effects of snowmobiling in Yellowstone were not being brought up and I remember the day as one of the most memorable experiences of my life.

We headed into the park on the main highway before intersecting the Loop Road. If you think of Yellowstone as a giant square then draw a large circle in the middle, that is the Loop Road. The entrance to the park is twenty-six miles south of the six o'clock position, Old Faithful is at the eight o'clock position. We turned left and went straight to Old Faithful, thirty-nine miles from where we picked up the snowmobiles. It was bitterly cold, but the sun was out and there wasn't a cloud in the sky. We were comfortable inside our astronaut-like suits. The helmets had face shields on them and I remember being warm the whole day.

After watching Old Faithful erupt, we headed back to our snowmobiles. Most snowmobilers turn around at Old Faithful and head back to the base camp by turning left out of the Old Faithful turnoff. If you turn right, there is no going back. You are committed to making the complete one hundred and one mile loop around the park. Doing that in the dead of winter on a snowmobile takes nerve. But Robert was always one to go for broke, so we turned right and started out around the entire Loop Road. We were doing a steady sixty-five miles an hour on the snowmobiles. We saw almost no one else. The road was packed with hard snow and the ride was fast and rough. We didn't have time to dally anywhere because the sun would set by 4:00 o'clock.

Late in the day, we stopped at Yellowstone Falls and watched the waterfall, nearly frozen but still flowing out of the Yellowstone River. We took some snapshots and hurriedly got back on the road. We did not want to be in the park once the sun went down because the temperature would drop dramatically—and not unlike the airplane—our fuel was running low. We drove at nearly seventy miles an hour for the final leg, and pulled into the snowmobile camp just as twilight was fading into dark. We drove back to Jackson Hole, had a drink at the Wort Hotel's Silver Dollar Bar, ate a hearty meal, and I went into one of the soundest sleeps I can ever remember. It was a great day of travel and adventure.

The following day, we returned to the Jackson Hole airport. I had the engines preheated in a hangar so they would not be damaged when I started them. We taxied to the end of the runway and took off climbing north alongside the Grand Teton range. I went to raise the landing gear and nothing happened. The gear was stuck. It would not come up. The landing gear creates drag and I couldn't fly to Los Angeles with the gear down. It would be too slow and there would definitely not be enough fuel, so I told the tower I was heading back to the field. The plane was hauled into a hangar and inspected. The squat switch was frozen shut. The squat switch is a switch on the left main landing gear that opens up when you take off. If the switch doesn't open the gear won't go up. It's a safety measure to prevent the pilot from accidently raising the landing gear when the plane is on the ground. The mechanic finally got the switch unthawed and dried out and two long hours later we were back in the air headed to Los Angeles. It was a very long day.

Robert and I continued to go to the theater and travel, our two favorite activities. In the summer of 1993, I booked us on the M.V. *Horizon*, a Celebrity Cruise Line ship that made the seven-day New York to Bermuda journey. Robert had never been on a ship. I had done the Bermuda cruise in the past. In fact, it was where I met Robert's coworker, Mary Lou Parkinson. It's an easy travel experiences. The ships leave New York on Saturday or Sunday and return one week later. There is one day at sea each way, and the rest of the time the ship is docked in Bermuda. On Front Street in Hamilton, the capital, Robert and I rented motor scooters and drove all over the forty mile long coral reef archipelago looking for coves and bays to swim and snorkel in. Bermuda is charming and a great place to visit IF—and it's a big IF—you are comfortable driving a motor scooter. There are no rental cars on the island. There is too much traffic in such a small place already; families are limited to one car. There is a bus system, but it's slow and cumbersome. With a motor scooter there is a sense of freedom. Without one, you feel stuck on Front Street with nothing to do but shop. You must drive on the left (it's still a British Overseas Territory) and there are dozens of roundabouts, but traffic moves pretty slowly and if you're careful it's safe.

Robert made no apology about the fact that he liked spending my money. He rarely paid for anything. I was affluent (or sucker) enough to pick up the tabs. Once we were riding a bus on Fifth Avenue, Robert was getting out at the next stop, I was continuing on. We were talking and I asked him rhetorically if he would stay with me if I didn't have any money and Robert, who was a gym rat with a body that showed it, said, "Would you stay with me if I didn't have my muscles?" In fact, I would have because his muscles didn't mean that much to me, but his reply was shockingly honest and woke me up to the fact that I was dating a gold digger.

This relationship continued steadily for about three years. There were never any fights because if any contentious issue came up, Robert's response was simply, "I don't want to talk about it." I had my doubts about the relationship from the beginning. His previous partner had died a couple years earlier from AIDS. His name was Anthony, and ultimately I knew I was competing with a dead man. Robert remained close to Anthony's family in Queens and one night he took me to dinner there. I was on display to the former in-laws and being evaluated as to whether or not I was worthy to take Anthony's place in Robert's life. I tried hard to be charming but felt I was being interrogated. Ultimately, I knew Robert was not ready to let go of the memory of his life with his late partner.

One weekend in the spring of 1994, we had an amazing time. We saw *Passion*, the new Stephen Sondheim musical, we went to the Metropolitan Opera and saw *Falstaff*, we had dinner at the Four Seasons Restaurant, and we finished the weekend on Sunday night at a small cafe in Chelsea called Eighteenth and Eighth. As I sat blissfully remembering all the wonderful things we had just done over the past three days, Robert went into a conversation that I sensed was not going to turn out well. That summer, the Gay Games (Olympic like competitions) were being held in New York and there were going to be, in addition to the games themselves, lots of big dance parties and thousands of people in town for the events. Robert asked me if I was planning to be in New York during the Games and I said yes. And—after a weekend in which I had dropped a thousand dollars on things to amuse and entertain him—he said he did not want me to come. He wanted me to stay in Los Angeles so he could go to the games, events, and dance parties with other friends. Robert ran with a "fun" crowd (party people) and he did not consider me to be "fun." I was hurt. It went to the core of my childhood insecurities of being the one always left out. And I did what I usually do when I feel hurt. I stopped talking. We left the restaurant and I got in a cab and headed uptown (we were not living together). And that was the last time I ever saw him. I was hurt and did not understand why I was being treated badly. He decided to end the relationship and he did so by leaving a message on my answering machine the following day. It devastated me. I had no closure, no explanation, no chance to right a wrong. It was just over; like a cleaver chopping off my hand.

Robert on a moped in front of the M.V. *Horizon* on Front Street in Hamilton, Bermuda. It was the year before I shot *Cruising to Bermuda*. 1993.

It fit with his personality; not wanting to talk about anything that might be upsetting. But this breakup hurt a lot because I had been really happy with him. The breakup sent me into a fit of despair, which led me back to my shrink in Beverly Hills, Larry Ryan. Because I traveled, I would have occasional consults on the phone. I was in New York talking to Larry and pouring out my sadness over the loss of my relationship with Robert. Larry said, "Doug. No one is every going to love you the way you want to be loved." That was hard to hear. And he said it to me while I was in a fit of deep depression, standing in front of my knee-to-ceiling plate glass windows—which opened—on the 34th floor of 353 East 72nd Street. I looked down at the sidewalk, the depression flooded over me, and for a moment the thought was there. Months later, I went and saw Larry in his office in Beverly Hills and yelled at him to NEVER say something like that to someone in a fit of depression—over the phone—who is on the 34th floor of a New York City apartment building—alone!

Well I didn't jump, and I did, in time, get over Robert. I have no idea what ever happened to him. I wish him well. It began a long period of bachelorhood. I did not enter another relationship for eight years. I decided it was time to learn to be happy with myself, and during those eight years, I did. And when I was finally happy with myself, someone did come along who really would love me—but I am getting ahead of myself.

I was still riding the success of the *The Great Canadian Train Ride*, but it was time to make a new film. Thinking that I would take Robert along, I decided during our Bermuda cruise that the subject of Bermuda would make a good film, so I announced and started taking bookings for a new program called *Cruising to Bermuda*. By the time I actually started to shoot the film, Robert was long gone. I did two back-to-back cruises on the M.V. *Horizon* and got enough film footage to edit a ninety-minute show.

Cruising to Bermuda was my least successful film ever. When I showed it in large auditoriums, I was lucky if the ushers showed up. While the film came out pretty good, it's an example of how critical the title is. No one could see the title as interesting and so almost nobody came. Video sales were dismal. It was a bona fide flop on the heels of my biggest success. Life sometimes has a way of putting you in your place.

A year later, I felt that I needed to get another hit, so I decided to make a sequel to *The Great Canadian Train Ride* and call it *The Great Trans-American Train Ride*. It would be a cross-country train trip on three trains, the *Broadway Limited* from New York to Chicago, the *California Zephyr* from Chicago to Salt Lake City, and the *Desert Wind* from Salt Lake City to Los Angeles. Along the way, I would get off and film in Philadelphia, Lancaster, Pittsburgh,

Chicago, Omaha, Denver, Salt Lake City, Arches, Zion, and Bryce National Parks, and Las Vegas.

When I made *The Great Canadian Train Ride*, VIA Rail was very cooperative, and I expected the same from Amtrak. I was wrong. VIA Rail had credited my film as a reason for the spike in train travel on the *Canadian*, so I thought Amtrak would be eager for some positive publicity. They were completely disinterested and, in fact, suggested that I pay them a royalty for the privilege of making the film. I received no assistance. I paid for my tickets and sleepers all the way. I was really down to only one request: a letter of introduction. Without this I would get nothing done on the trains. I needed a letter from Amtrak to show to the conductors that I was authorized to be shooting in the dining car, the galley, the locomotive, etc. At the last minute Amtrak produced this letter of reference:

May 23, 1995

TO ALL STATION AND TRAIN PERONNEL:

> *The bearer of this letter, Douglas Jones, is the owner and producer of International Travel Films. He will be traveling on Amtrak with the full knowledge and concurrence of Amtrak's Public Affairs Department*
>
> *Please accord him all possible courtesies and assistance needed for interviewing and photographing throughout the trains and in the stations.*
>
> *This letter does <u>not</u> authorize access to the locomotive cab or any operating facility where the public would normally be denied access.*
>
> *Should any questions arise please contact me in Public Affairs.*
>
> *Sincerely,*
>
> *Patricia Kelley, Manager*
> *Travel Industry Communications*
> *Amtrak Public Affairs*

Well, hello?? How the hell was I suppose to make the film if I had no more access than a regular passenger? It's the behind-the-scenes material that is essential to any film. I was leaving New York on the *Broadway Limited* in three days. What to do? The answer was simple: white out. White out is so last century, but we all used it when we had typewriters. I simply made a copy of the letter, cut it up with scissors, whited out certain sentences, made another copy, touched up the copy, and after a little more doctoring, I had a letter of introduction that basically said I was allowed to go anywhere I wanted on the train.

Was it dishonest, yes; illegal, perhaps, but these were the types of things I had to do to get a film done. With the letter in hand, I filmed in the galleys, dining cars, lounge cars, and most importantly, I used the letter to talk my way into the cab of the front locomotive of the *California Zephyr* as it left Denver to climb the front range of the Rockies. I stayed in the cab all the way to Grand Junction, Colorado. The footage was spectacular. The *California Zephyr* passes through thirty tunnels on its climb to the Continental Divide. The scenes of the tracks rushing ahead, the engineer's eyes glued to the gauges and pressing the dead man's switch every 30-seconds (a safety feature in case the engineer passes out or is incapacitated), made this some of the best material I ever shot. A lot of footage I have shot over the years was done without permission, sometimes using out right lies. This was one such case and I have no regrets. Viewers can experience the vicarious thrill of being in the locomotive of the *California Zephyr* as it travels through the Rocky Mountain range. I'm really proud of the film.

In September of 1995, I started showing the film on the travelogue circuit and I released the film on video at the same time. Hopefully, I would have another hit like *The Great Canadian Train Ride*. Wrong again. While not quite as bad as *Cruising to Bermuda*, it was darn close. Again, it was the title. Americans looked at *The Great Canadian Train Ride* title and they envisioned romantic images of beautiful trains and spectacular scenery. They looked at the title *The Great Trans-American Train Ride* and they envisioned Amtrak, delayed trains, surly staff, and bad food. Amtrak has a terrible image. It isn't totally fair (though some of it is), but the public looked at the title and decided to stay home. It did lousy auditorium business and video sales were anemic.

I made two film flops in a row, and I had another failed relationship. Well you can't win them all.

The *Desert Wind* with a new Amtrak Genius locomotive moving through Utah. 1995.
Photo courtesy of Amtrak.

CHAPTER THIRTY-ONE

FLYING THE CESSNA 310

The incident at Nashville, where I nearly crashed my single engine plane because of ice, caused me to look seriously at my flying and my airplane. Most of my flying was done in the fall, spring, and dead of winter. I needed to get to my travelogue lectures without killing myself.

So I decided it was time to upgrade to a twin-engine plane. The plane would need to have oxygen so I could fly high above the weather, and an instrument called a Stormscope to "see" the thunderstorms ahead. And the plane would need to have inflatable rubber de-icing boots. De-icing boots operate with a simple principal. Once you have ice on the leading edge of the wing, you hit a switch. The boots inflate, the ice breaks and flies off of the wings. Additionally, the plane would need to have heated props. These are electric heating elements in the root of the prop blades. Even though the propellers are spinning at 2,400 rotations per minute, ice will build up on the base of the blades.

I decided to buy a twin for safety. Most pilots will tell you that is the reason they bought their twin. But underlying the decision is a simple fact: There is just something magical, testosterone driven, about flying a twin. Sitting at the end of a runway and pushing both throttles forward to the firewall, feeling 600 horse power of engines spin up and starting to roll—it's exciting, pure and simple. It's a monster of a machine, and as the pilot you tame it and control it. In nearly sixty coast-to-coast flights, I never tired of the thrill.

I decided to buy a Cessna 310. The Cessna 310 was introduced in 1954. It was the plane Sky King flew on the Saturday morning television series of the 1950s. It was manufactured until 1980 and changed very little in design over the years. It has a stylish design with large fuel tanks on the tips of the wings. It is one of the most beautiful planes ever designed and anyone who has flown one will tell you the experience is unmatched.

I found a Cessna 310 at a company called Colemill Enterprises in, of all places, Nashville, where I had my wake up call to move up to a twin. I purchased the plane based on photographs mailed to me and, of course, the specs. The specifications on an airplane are the determining factor of its value; the number of hours the plane has flown, the number of hours of flying time on the engines (the engines are replaced and/or overhauled throughout the life of the airframe), the electronics (avionics) in the panel, plus cosmetic conditions such as the paint and interior.

The majority of private planes flying in the United States are between thirty and sixty years old. There are almost no new piston engine planes manufactured. For pilots and mechanics, keeping this aging propeller fleet flying means constant vigilance. The FAA requires planes to undergo annual inspections and every repair must be recorded. If anything is wrong it must be fixed, otherwise the plane is not legal to fly.

The plane I purchased was a 1973 model Q Cessna 310. It had brand new engines, a fresh paint job, a nice upgraded interior, and a set of radios and avionics that, at the time, were up to date. Its "N number" (registration number—American planes always begin with N) was N9924F, and after wiring the money to Nashville, it was mine.

The only problem was I didn't know how to fly it and I didn't have a twin rating for my pilot's license. I decided to hire a local Nashville instructor to teach me to fly the plane and prepare me for my multi-engine rating. I would then take the FAA check ride in Nashville, have my multi-engine rating endorsement, and fly off to California. I assumed the multi-engine rating would be easy to get. How naïve.

I flew to Nashville on a one-way ticket since I intended to fly my new plane back to L.A. I met the instructor the following morning and we hated each other immediately. He was a strident military type. Things did not get off to a good start. After some ground instruction, we got into the plane and started to fly. His primary teaching method involved yelling. It was classic old-school military training. Since I had not been in the military, and since I was now forty-two years old, this was not an effective way to teach me. The louder he got, the more nervous I became. This continued for several days and each session got worse. He just couldn't understand how I could be so thick and stupid. He didn't use those exact words, but that was what he implied.

Multi-engine training is all about what you do if an engine fails. It's all about surprises. You're flying along and the instructor pulls the throttle of an engine back to idle and it's your job to stabilize the plane and land with one engine. It's tricky, particularly in a crosswind.

Right after my Cessna 310Q N9924F arrived at Burbank. 1994.

Over lunch one day, I mentioned to the instructor the irony of the Patsy Cline story; how I had seen her last performance and how I had made my decision to buy the twin after an experience in similar conditions to what killed her. The instructor leaned back and started reminiscing. It turned out that he had been the instructor who taught Randy Hughes, Patsy Cline's manager and pilot, how to fly. He tried to teach him how to fly on instruments but, "God damn it, he just didn't get it…" So here I was, sitting with the instructor who taught the pilot who killed Patsy Cline—and he was badmouthing him the same way he was badmouthing me. This did not elevate my confidence in the student-instructor relationship.

Toward the end of the following day, I was being prepped for the FAA check ride. I made a mistake or two and he went off in the cockpit. "I do *not* understand how you can make such *stupid* mistakes after all this time! I don't think you'll ever get it right." At that point I radioed the tower and said "November 9924 Foxtrot is returning to the field." The instructor looked over at me and did not say a word. I turned the plane back toward the airport. I landed, taxied up to the parking ramp, got out and said, "Thank you for your time but we are done."

I went in and told the owner of Colemill Enterprises, a nice man named Ernest Colbert, that I could not work with this instructor and I was flying back to Los Angeles on a commercial flight and I would need a pilot to fly the plane I had purchased to Burbank. Mr. Colbert shook his head in dismay but arranged for a pilot and a few days later my new airplane was at Burbank—and I still couldn't fly it.

I called my trusty instructor Paul Fancett. Paul had hoped for a career flying with the commercial carriers, but after years of trying to get an airline job, he gave up and took a job driving locomotives for the Union Pacific Railroad. He was not teaching anymore, but he made time to get me up to speed on the Cessna 310 and ready for my multi-engine check ride. The people who conduct check rides are not employees of the FAA. They are individuals licensed to conduct the exams. I went back to the crusty old guy at Van Nuys who had done my instrument check ride. He was nasty and difficult, but he had passed me on the instrument exam so I thought I would be OK with him for the multi-engine endorsement. Wrong. He barked at me in the air, I made a couple of goofs and he said to land the plane. Back to Van Nuys we went and he flunked me.

So, back to Paul for more training. After another five hours in the air, I decided to try to pass the check ride again. I found an FAA examiner in the high desert in Apple Valley. I explained my saga on the phone and he agreed to do my check ride. I flew the Cessna out to Apple Valley. (It was legal to fly solo to my check ride even though I didn't have the multi-engine endorsement). I landed and went into the airport office. The examiner was an older guy, very soft spoken, and he set me at ease right away. He did the required ground test of multi-engine knowledge and then we got in the plane to fly.

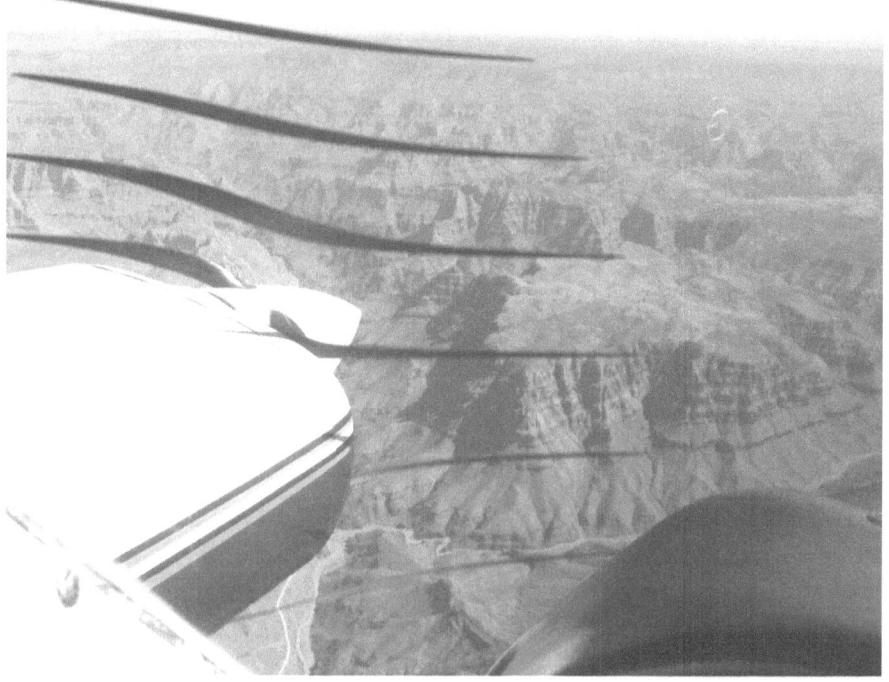

Out over the Grand Canyon at 15,000 feet, heading east. The black streaks are the propeller blades, a photographic anomaly. 1998.

One of the skills you have to demonstrate is your ability to abort a flight during the takeoff roll if an engine fails. Since we were going to make several takeoffs and landings, I assumed this would come later in the check ride. It did not. As I pushed the throttles forward and started down the runway, just before liftoff, the examiner yanked the throttle back on the right engine and I had to immediately react, pull the left engine throttle back and stop the plane while keeping control of the aircraft. It took me by surprise (which is the whole purpose of the test). I did get the left engine pulled back to idle, but I somehow lost control and ran it off the runway into the sand.

I hung my head down. I assumed this automatically flunked me. But the examiner decided that since I still had the left wing landing gear on the runway and only the right landing gear and nose wheel in the sand, this qualified as properly aborted takeoff. It was a real stretch in the evaluation of my skills. We got out of the plane and a tug came and pulled the plane out of the sand and back onto the runway. I restarted the engines, took off, and went through the rest of the check ride and did pretty well. The exam involves shooting multiple approaches on one engine. As you can imagine, a twin flies very differently on one engine. You fly at an angle because of the asymmetrical thrust and you have to straighten the plane out just as you touch down. Fortunately, the 310 had a lot of power and flew well on one engine.

I satisfied the examiner enough that he signed me off as a multi-engine rated pilot. Within a week I was ready to make my first trip to New York in the twin. The plane was fast and it had long-range fuel tanks. I could make New York City on one fuel stop, which I usually made in Kansas City.

I flew N9924F for twenty years. I made fifty-eight coast-to-coast flights in the plane, most of them alone. I landed at two hundred and eighteen different airports in the United States and Canada. I logged 2,975 hours of flying time in the airplane, roughly 600,000 miles. That's equivalent of flying around the equator twenty-four times. I had 568 hours in instrument conditions, meaning no visibility; flying by the electronics on the panel. I made 1,578 landings and 468 instrument approaches, some of them at the bare minimum of a 200-foot ceiling. Most of the flying was uneventful, but you couldn't fly that much year-round without some occasionally harrowing moments. As careful as I was, there were some moments of high drama.

One Sunday morning in April 1994, I left Lansing, Michigan after appearing at Michigan State University to show *The Great Alaska Cruise*. I was flying to Sandusky, Ohio for a matinee. I had a weather briefing before taking off and I knew the ceiling at Sandusky was low. I made three attempts to land but the ceiling was too low and the fog was too thick; I could not see the runway.

After the third try, I aborted the landing and told ATC I was heading to Cleveland Hopkins Airport about fifty miles to the east. I landed at Cleveland using the Instrument Landing System and quickly got out of the plane, rented a car, and sped off to Sandusky, arriving at the State

Theater just before show time at two o'clock. After the show, I drove back to Cleveland. I was planning to fly on to New York City. It was a classic case of what pilots call "get home-itis." I had been on the road for a long time and I wanted to get home.

I filed my flight plan from Cleveland Hopkins to Teterboro, New Jersey. I got in my plane and radioed ground control that I was ready for taxi. As I got on the taxiway, I was surrounded by passenger jets. It was Sunday night, a busy time at any commercial airport. I had a large Continental jet in front of me and another behind. It was so foggy that the tower could not see the end of the runways. All of the landings and takeoffs were being done on instruments.

Cleveland has parallel runways, a right runway and a left runway. They were alternating between both runways for takeoffs and landings. A plane would takeoff from Runway 6 Left while another plane was landing at the same time on Runway 6 Right, then they would use Runway 6 Right to takeoff the next plane while landing another plane on Runway 6 Left. All of this was being done using radio instructions. No one in the control tower could actually see what was going on. They gave instructions and pilots were expected to follow.

Finally, I got up to the head of the line. I switched radio frequencies from ground control to the tower. The person handling the ground frequency controls your movement on the taxiways, then hands you off to the tower controller who clears you for takeoff. The tower controller said to the commercial jet pilot in front of me on the taxiway, "Continental 1569 cross Runway 6 Right, into position and hold, Runway 6 Left." Then he continued, "November 9924 Foxtrot (me) taxi to Runway 6 Right, hold short."

Let me translate this for you: The tower controller was telling the Continental jet in front of me to cross over the first runway, line up on the second runway, and wait for his clearance to takeoff. I was told to taxi to the first runway and stop. I was not supposed to go onto the runway and line up for my takeoff.

It was harried. No one could see anyone and the radio commands were fast and quick. A lot was going on. And I was tired. It had been a long day.

When you, as a pilot, are given an instruction, you "read back" the instruction. This is done so that if you have heard something incorrectly, the controller can catch it.

After the Continental pilot had read back his instructions, I read back mine. "November 9924 Foxtrot taxiing to Runway 6 Right into position and hold."

This was a BIG mistake. My instruction had been to taxi to Runway 6 Right and "hold short," (stay off the runway). I said I was taxiing to Runway 6 Right "into position and hold," meaning I was going onto the runway and holding (stopping) in takeoff position awaiting my takeoff clearance. I had heard the instructions given to the Continental pilot ahead of me and I mistakenly read back his instructions, not mine.

If the tower could have physically seen the end of the runways they would have caught the mistake, but they could not. And the tower controller missed the fact that my "read back" was incorrect.

So there I was, sitting pretty on the end of Runway 6 Right getting ready for the tower to clear me for takeoff, when suddenly, there was this huge "Wuuuush!!!!" I look up and a Continental jet on final approach to Runway 6 Right came out of the clouds at 200 feet, saw me on the end of the runway, and flew back up into the clouds.

Pandemonium broke loose. The tower said something to the effect of, "What the Hell!?—November 9924 Foxtrot are you on the end of the runway!?"

Shaking, I replied, "Affirmative." After a few seconds they came back, "November 9924 Foxtrot cleared for *immediate* takeoff." They needed to get me off that runway fast and the only way to do it was to get me in the air. So off I went into the sky, the Continental jet circling around for another approach.

Once I was out of the Cleveland airspace and settled onto my heading for Teterboro, ATC came on the radio and said, "November 9924 Foxtrot I have a telephone number for you, ready to copy?" I said yes. I knew what this meant. Once I landed, I was to call the FAA—and I knew this meant trouble.

I got out of the plane at Teterboro. I did not call immediately (this was before cellphones). I took a cab into Manhattan and settled down for a few minutes before I made the call. I dialed the number and got the Cleveland Hopkins tower. The tower manager reviewed what had happened and the radio recordings of the whole episode. There was plenty of blame to go around. Yes, I had made a terrible mistake—but the tower controller was equally to blame for not catching my incorrect read back. The manager said the system worked as it was supposed to. The other pilot did his go-around and there was no immediate danger of collision (not exactly true). The whole ordeal stopped with that one phone call. I never heard another word about it. There is no record of the incident.

Another time, in March of 1996, things did not turn out as smoothly.

I left Daytona Beach, Florida on a beautiful day to fly non-stop to Teterboro. I was heading home after finishing a long Florida lecture tour. There was no weather en route up the Atlantic coast, but there was a fast moving late winter snowstorm moving over the New York area when I took off. The storm would be long gone and out to sea by the time I arrived. I flew the whole trip on autopilot making adjustments for navigation as I passed the various navigational aids.

As I passed over Philadelphia, I was handed off to New York Approach. I was listening to the ATIS (Automated Terminal Information Service) at Teterboro to get the current weather conditions. The storm had passed, but behind the storm were strong gusty winds and the runway was icy and partly covered in snow. I was vectored (directed) to the ILS approach for Runway 6, which means I would be landing to the northeast. The winds were coming out of the north so I was going to have a quartering crosswind, a fairly manageable condition, though the winds were gusty—varying from 18 to 25 knots (20-29 mph). As I got closer, the winds shifted around and started coming out of the west. I was now landing with a quartering tailwind—not good. I struggled to maintain control of the airplane in the strong winds. I flared the plane and dropped the main wheels down on the runway. I knew the runway was icy and braking was going to be limited. Then in a flash, a gust of wind from the southwest came up and hit my tail fin. The Cessna 310 has a particularly large tail fin and wind gusts are more dangerous with a 310 than planes with smaller tail surfaces. The wind whipped the plane around, I tried to regain control but the ice on the runway won and I ended up slammed into a snow bank. I was not hurt but the plane's nose wheel suffered major damage and it was over a month before the plane was flyable again.

There I was, stuck in a snow bank. My little "incident"—it was not classified as an accident, a much more serious term with the FAA—caused the closure of Teterboro Airport for almost an hour while they dug me out and towed me off the field. Teterboro is the business jet center for New York City. By the time they had me off the field, there were eighteen corporate jets lined up for departure, all of them filled, no doubt, with disgruntled CEOs. I have no idea how many planes were in the sky in holding patterns waiting to land. Suffice to say, I turned Teterboro into a mess that day.

This episode did not go unnoticed by the FAA. I was called on the carpet and had to go in for a hearing. It was decided that the tower shared equal blame. The runway should have been changed when the winds shifted. I should not have been cleared to land on an icy runway with a tailwind. The runway was not changed because the north end of the runway had not been plowed and was covered in snow. Changing runways means reversing the flow using the other end of the runway, which, in the case of Runway 6 at Teterboro, is Runway 24—same runway, different direction. The FAA said the tower should have changed runways, and if they couldn't use the appropriate runway because of snow cover, they should have closed the airport. I got a slap on the wrist and no suspension of my license, but I can tell you sitting in front of an FAA panel trying to explain your goof ups is not a pleasant experience.

I have dozens of "hangar stories." That's the term pilot's use when they sit around hangars regaling each other with tales of their flying adventures. I will spare you a long list. I'll add only one more.

I was working hard to make my videotape business a success. Lynn Hamlin was the person at National Syndications Inc. who put *The Great Canadian Train Ride* in *Parade Magazine* and changed my life. As I mentioned earlier, National Syndications Inc. did a test in *Parade Magazine*. It was successful, but there was a time lag before they made the decision to do the full national rollout.

While NSI was mulling over whether or not they would do the full *Parade Magazine* blitz, I had lunch with Lynn. Any successful business enterprise involves doing things that have nothing to do with the business transaction itself, but curry you favor with the client. I took her to the Four Seasons which is where I took anyone I was trying to caress into a large-scale business deal. During lunch, it came up that I was a pilot. Lynn said that her husband Bob was dying to learn how to fly but had never been up in a plane. Sensing a way to get a business edge, I offered to take her and her husband up flying. A date was picked two Saturdays away. I was going to fly them from Westchester County Airport out to Nantucket Island for lunch. Lynn was excited and her husband was apparently thrilled.

I got up the morning of the planned lunch jaunt and checked the weather. Everything was beautiful and lovely. The flight to Nantucket would be clear, no turbulence—a perfect flying day. But late that afternoon, weather was coming in from the west and if I didn't get them back on the ground at Westchester before three o'clock, there would be heavy weather to contend with.

I met them at the airport. I showed Lynn's husband how I pre-flighted the plane. We boarded and I had Lynn sit in the back and her husband in the co-pilot seat. We took off from Westchester heading along the Connecticut coast and then on to Martha's Vineyard as we made our way to Nantucket Island. As we neared Nantucket, I turned in for the final approach. It was a beautiful sight, the water was filled with sailboats; it was a lovely summer day.

We took a cab into town and went to lunch at some forgettable restaurant. Food was not the purpose of the trip. During lunch, Lynn indicated to me that NSI was planning to go ahead with the full rollout but she was leaving the company the next week and a man named Jess Joseph would be taking over my account. I thought, damn, what a waste of time. I've gone to all this trouble and the person I'm doing it for is leaving the company. Still, it was a nice day and they were lovely people.

Before we returned to the airport, I called aviation weather for a briefing. Things were not good. The storm over central New York was moving faster than expected. I was not going to be able to beat it in. I explained to Lynn and Bob that we were likely to encounter some weather on the return flight. They didn't seem bothered by this and we got back in the plane. We took off from Nantucket and all was fine on the front end of the flight, but by the time we got to Groton, Connecticut, the weather had closed in. We were in the clouds. Zero visibility. I was flying on instruments, and my passengers started looking nervous.

The showers began, gently at first, then the turbulence started and the plane was getting beat up pretty badly. Then the showers turned into pouring rain. We were in a full-scale squall with 80 miles still to go. My passengers were visibly concerned. While I was confident in my ability to get the plane on the ground, I did not have time to be holding their hands and reassuring them. I had to concentrate on flying the plane as conditions continued to deteriorate. Updrafts and downdrafts were pulling the plane in every direction. By now I was seeing little blimps on my Stormscope, which identifies electrical strikes—which means lightning.

I flew the approach into Westchester County Airport, but Air Traffic Control sent me far to the north because they were trying to land several other planes at the same time. The visibility was zip. The rain was torrential, the noise in the cabin was deafening. As ATC turned me onto the final approach course, I had the plane in a steep bank to intercept the localizer, the radio signal that indicates the centerline of the runway. Then in a flash, the left wing lit up! We had been hit by lightning. The plane is designed to drain off the electrical charge and a lightning strike is not that dangerous, but it's frightening to passengers and unnerving to the pilot. My passengers' faces were ashen. Finally, I had the ILS needles lined up; I was on the centerline of the runway and the other needle, the glideslope, showed me on a correct, steady descent. If I could keep both needles centered we would be on the end of the runway when we came out of the clouds.

I watched as the altimeter spun down. We were getting closer and closer to the ground and still no visibility. The field is at 439 feet above sea level, meaning the minimum safe descent altitude is 639 feet—200 feet off the ground. If I could not see the field at 639 feet, I would have to fly back up into this mess and try again. But at about 700 feet there it was—the ball of fire, the pulsing strobe lights at the end of the runway. I checked that the landing gear was down, slowed the plane, pulled the nose up, set her down with a nice smooth landing, and let out a sigh of relief.

I taxied up to the parking area, shut down, and escorted my pale and shaken passengers to their car. We exchanged pleasantries but I knew this experience was not going to help me close my big business deal. I just accepted the fact that I had blown it. Lynn would go into the National Syndications office on Monday morning and say nix to the big rollout since I had scared her and her husband half to death. She would likely take some action as payback for a flight that, in her mind, nearly killed them both. Or so I assumed.

I sent her an email afterward and apologized for the experience. On her last day at National Syndications, she called me and said, "Congratulations, NSI is going to do the full national rollout in *Parade Magazine*." I said, "Wow, thanks!" Once again I apologized for the frightening flight and she said, "Apologize? That was the most exciting thing my husband and I ever did. We haven't stopped talking about it. You're an amazing pilot and my husband is going to start flying lessons!"

Sometimes, the things you think are your biggest mistakes end up being your best decisions. The flight to Nantucket sealed my biggest business deal—lightning strike and all.

A fresh blue, gold, black, and white paint job for the Cessna. 1998.

My happy place. In the left seat. 1999.

CHAPTER THIRTY-TWO

LIVING IN THE WILD IN THE HOLLYWOOD HILLS

I first settled in Los Angeles in 1984 during the beginning of the Steve Cline years. I bought a small condominium in West Hollywood at 1411 North Hayworth Avenue. I sold that condo in 1988 and bought the Spanish house at 3628 Cadman Drive in the hills of Los Feliz, east of Hollywood. Built on a hillside in 1938, it had a large living room and an arched window that looked out onto the undeveloped land of Griffith Park and the Verdugo Mountains. The pool was in front of the house. It was completely private. At night I would sit in the Jacuzzi (with or without Steve Cline, depending on whether he was in or out of my life) and stare up at the stars. It was what I dreamed life in L.A. would be like.

What I did not expect when I bought the house was that it would be like moving to the Serengeti. The amount of wildlife that thrives in L.A. is astonishing. My house faced a large undeveloped lot that bordered Griffith Park, the largest urban park in the country, most of which is natural chaparral. I got my first taste of what it was going to be like on Cadman Drive when I woke up after my first night in the house and saw two deer drinking out of my pool. It was a particularly dry year and the deer claimed my pool as their summer watering hole.

But the deer were the least of the problems. Next came the bees. I was sitting by the pool one day on a chaise lounge reading the Sunday paper when I looked up and the entire front of the house was covered with bees—tens of thousands of them. I soon learned the house had hives in the walls that had been there for years, maybe even decades, and each season the bees would come back, place queens in the hives and get to work. Dealing with this was next to impossible. There were two large colonies; one in a turret next to my den that was forty feet off of the ground and very difficult to access, the other next to the my bedroom. You could hear the bees buzzing in the walls.

I am ashamed to say I called an exterminator. I would *never* do it today, knowing how important honeybees are to the environment and how endangered many bee colonies are, but I was fresh out of New York, and I didn't know what to do. Bees would get into the house and I was stung repeatedly. I had to do something.

The way it should have been done would have been to tear out the walls on the outside of the house and remove the hives but the physical location on the hillside made this next to impossible. The exterminator, a Theravada Buddhist from Thailand named Woody, was very unhappy about this. I asked him, "Woody, if you're a Buddhist, you believe in reincarnation, right?" He said yes and I said, "Then why are you an exterminator?" He shook his head and said, "Yeah, I gotta get another job."

In spite of several attempts, the bees came back to the hives every year. Eventually, I just learned to live with them and considered the buzzing in the walls to be white noise.

One evening, I walked up the stairs to my front door and at the top, as if it was waiting for me to come home, was a skunk. I slowly opened the door. The skunk just sat there. I closed the door and prayed it would just leave. And there were coyotes. Griffith Park is filled with coyotes. In the middle of the night, a pack would capture some poor critter and the howling would be deafening. It would wake up the entire neighborhood. And there were gophers. I planted a flowerbed in front of the house and watched as the marigolds literally vanished in front of my eyes. They would just go "pop" and disappear as the gophers pulled them down.

But it was my sleep that was most disrupted. And it was because of the goings-on in the attic. Why are so many animals nocturnal? I had a menagerie in the attic. I had rats, which sounded like the pitter-pat of tiny feet, possums which had a slower, plodding sound, and raccoons, that were loud and ran around like crazy when they came back at four in the morning. I tossed mothballs up there (at the suggestion of my Beverly Hills shrink), but they did no good.

I borrowed traps from the animal shelter and placed them outside. The traps were very good at getting the possums, which were slow, and none too smart. I probably caught ten possums during the time I lived in that house. I would haul them off to the animal shelter where I was assured they would be taken into the Angeles National Forest and released.

But the raccoons were more difficult. They were wily and smart as a whip. And they were noisy. They would go out at dusk and return about 4:00 a.m. and have a party in the attic. I eventually got serious about solving this problem. I discovered they were getting in and out of the attic through an unfinished gap in the roof where two different angles overlapped. I watched one night as the mother, followed by four little baby raccoons, came out of the attic and went onto the roof where they were able to climb into a tree (that I had failed to trim), giving them access to the hillside and their nightly escapades.

The next day, I rented a tall ladder and bought a roll of chicken wire at the hardware store. I came home and I wrangled the ladder into place. Then I waited. The sun went down and my raccoon family came out of the attic and went trotting off for the night. I grabbed a flashlight, the chicken wire, and some other tools, and climbed up the ladder and started to work. Within twenty minutes, I had the hole covered. They would not be able to get back in. I took the ladder down and went to sleep with a smile on my face. I had outfoxed the raccoons. I was half-sleeping, waiting for four o'clock when they would return to find their home sealed off.

Suddenly, I woke up from my half-sleep, the house was shaking, and my immediate thought was, "My God, those raccoons are mad!" It took a few seconds for the reality to settle in. It was the Northridge Earthquake—magnitude 6.7 on January 17, 1994 at 4:31 a.m. I don't know what happened to the raccoons, but the city of Los Angeles was brought to its knees. I suspect the raccoons fared better, but they had to find another home and it wasn't going to be mine.

I loved the Cadman Drive house. I would have stayed in it forever except for one problem: the neighbors. New neighbors bought the house on the corner. Opposite my house, and next to theirs, was a large undeveloped lot that I could have bought when I purchased the house. I didn't buy it. It would only have been to protect my view. Big mistake. Soon the lot was sold to the new neighbors who proudly announced to everyone on the street, they were building—and these were their exact words—"A Las Vegas-style show palace!" Their "show palace" took seven years to complete. The quiet Spanish Revival flavor of the neighborhood changed. I hated to leave but the decision was ultimately wise. L.A. has zoning codes but no laws concerning aesthetics, which is why Los Angeles is such an architectural mish-mash, old Tudors next to Italian villas, next to gold-columned faux marble palaces, next to Spanish haciendas, next to Mid-Century moderns. There is no consistency.

Meanwhile, I stumbled onto another house by accident. I was driving through Hancock Park on a Sunday afternoon and saw an "Open House" sign in front of a 1920s English Tudor. I walked inside and fell in love with the house. It was the bottom of a bad real estate market and the house was reasonably priced, given its size and location. It was on one of Los Angeles' best streets, Rossmore Avenue. The Cadman Drive house sold and I bought 224 North Rossmore Avenue.

Hancock Park is one of Los Angeles' beautiful, old neighborhoods. When it was originally developed in the 1920s, it was built for bankers, attorneys, and financial people who worked downtown. Hancock Park was home to people like the Ahmanson banking family, the Chandlers who owned *The Los Angeles Times*, J. Paul Getty, Howard Hughes, and Harry Warner of Warner Brothers.

One of the selling features of Hancock Park when it was subdivided in the 1920s was that it was "exclusive." The developers made no apologies about outright, open, discrimination. In fact, the original deed I had on the Rossmore house stated in clear and emphatic terms that no one could purchase or live on the property of "Negroid, or Chinese descent" unless they were employed as household staff. Several other ethnic groups were also listed as "forbidden." Curiously, there was no mention of Mexicans or Hispanics. In the 1920s, Mexicans were still part of the aristocracy of Los Angeles. They owned the ranchos and were among the moneyed people of L.A.

In 1948, Hancock Park was thrown into turmoil. Nat King Cole bought a house on Muirfield Road and it caused uproar in the neighborhood. The homeowners association actually sent him a letter stating there were to be no "undesirables" in the neighborhood and asked him to move. Nat King Cole responded that he too wanted no undesirables in the neighborhood, and if he saw any he would be happy to report them. Nat King Cole bravely stayed. He raised his family in the house and lived there until he died.

On New Year's Eve of 2000, I hosted a party at the Rossmore house. I threw the party with several friends; Sam Paul, a television producer; Mat Plendl, the world champion Hula Hooper; Tim Toohey, my attorney; and Robert Jones, the music librarian for the L.A. Opera. Each of us invited our friends. It was black-tie and nearly two hundred people showed up; it was a memorable night.

After the last guests left and the caterers packed up and went home, I sat in the house and felt very alone. I had adjusted to being single, but on that last night of the millennium, I felt sad to have no one special to share it with. Unbeknownst to me, it would be the last New Year's Eve I would spend alone. Someone new was about to come into my life.

The house on Rossmore Avenue in Los Angeles. I lived in this home in Hancock Park for sixteen years. 1995.

CHAPTER THIRTY-THREE

SHOOTING STOCK FOOTAGE ON THREE CONTINENTS

During the 1990s, my stock footage business became an important part of my income. I had been shooting film for decades and had shots of almost every major iconic sight of the world. I was located in Hollywood, making it easy to deliver the 3/4" sample viewing tapes to production offices. When original film negative was needed, I could pull it out of the film vault on San Vicente Boulevard, bring it back to my office, find the requested scenes, and deliver the film elements to the film-to-tape transfer houses where the shots would be prepped for broadcast.

Most sales were for episodic television and it was always surprising how close to the wire the post-production people would run. I would get a call at four o'clock in the afternoon, the production company—and this could be anyone from a small time player to Paramount Pictures—would call and say, "We need footage from your film *The Magic of Venice* and we need it from time code 01:14:10:00 to 1:15:25:00."

Time code was embedded on the master tape and the viewing copies had what was called visible time code—the time stamp would run in the lower part of the screen. This allowed the purchaser to tell you exactly what scenes they wanted. The finished product, which could be anything from a DigiBeta tape to an inter-negative piece of film, had the time code removed.

"And we need it by noon tomorrow because it has to be in post-production by one o'clock so they can cut the shots into the show—and oh, by the way, the program is airing nationally tomorrow night at 9:00 p.m. Eastern, so the feed goes out of Los Angeles at six o'clock."

This actually happened in 2005 on the first telecast of a popular prime time drama on NBC called *Medium*. I got the shots delivered in time and sat down that night to watch the program. My shots played a key element in the storyline at the very end of the episode. Why did they wait until the last minute to call me for the footage? Who knows, but things like this happened a lot.

Stock footage became the primary focus of my location filming. By adding footage to my collection, I was securing my retirement. I believed that stock footage sales would be my annuity and they would yield income to the end of my life. The idea was reasonable. What I couldn't see coming was high definition television, which would blow a hole in my business model. My stock footage business never recovered. But before the high-def revolution, I was going on film shoots to shoot footage just for my stock library. It was so much easier than shooting a feature film. I didn't have to worry about a story line and shots I absolutely had to have. If I made a feature-length travelogue film on Moscow, I had to have Saint Basil's Cathedral. If I went to Moscow to shoot stock footage and Saint Basil's Cathedral was in scaffolding (which happened to me), I just moved on and shot other things.

One of my first big stock footage shoots was in the U.S. In 1997, I flew my airplane across the country stopping in thirty different places to pick up shots. I went to Sacramento and shot the California State Capitol; I flew on to Reno to film the "Biggest Little City in the World" sign, I flew to Rapid City, South Dakota and filmed Mount Rushmore, I landed in Chicago and picked up new shots of the Windy City, I made my way on to New York to get more up-to-date footage, I landed in Washington D.C. at Reagan National Airport (one of the last times I landed there since that airport was closed to general aviation traffic after 9/11). I filmed all the Washington D.C. monuments. Then I flew back across the country filming in Indianapolis, St. Louis, Kansas City, and at the Albuquerque Balloon Festival. The final stop was Palm Springs.

In 1998, I decided to do a South American stock footage shoot. I had not traveled much in South America and there was a shortage of footage from the region, so I thought it would be a good investment. It was the first (and last) time I went on an organized tour. I chose a thirty-day tour that was quite inexpensive. It was the most cost-effective way to cover the airfare and hotel rooms for ten destinations. My intention was to only use the tour to get me around South America and put a roof over my head. I didn't intend to take the organized day excursions. I made my own arrangements for guides and drivers. In the end, I did a combination of things and went with the group at times.

Filming Iguazu Falls on the Argentine-Brazilian border. 1998.

The trip started at the Miami Airport where we gathered for the flight to Manaus, Brazil. There were twenty-five people on the tour. The tour director, a somewhat tired, aging hippie who had done this tour way too many times, met us and passed out our boarding passes. After we arrived in Manaus, we went to the hotel and had a brief meeting where the ground rules were laid out. "Be on time!" was emphasized over and over—no stragglers or you would be left behind. I told the tour director I was going to be going off on my own. He wasn't bothered, or particularly interested in what I was doing.

In Manaus I filmed the Theater of the Amazon, an elegant opera house that was built in the rainforest during the 19th century rubber boom, and is about the only thing of note in the city. Then we boarded a boat to go up the Amazon River. At a certain point, we transferred to small flat-bottom boats and I perched myself on the bow to shoot the Amazon jungle in the heart of Brazil. It is peaceful and belies the fact that it is disappearing at an alarming rate through deforestation, which endangers the entire world.

From Manaus we flew to Rio de Janeiro. I had a guide and driver and I didn't see the other tour people during the four days in Rio. I had been there in 1982 and reshot the classic sights, Sugar Loaf Mountain and the cable car ride, Corcovado and the Christ the Redeemer Statue, and the beautiful people on Copacabana Beach. Rio has the most attractive people on earth. It also has the highest per capita number of plastic surgeons on earth. I went into the favelas, the slums of Rio, and shot footage (some of which ended up being used at Epcot Center in Orlando, of all places). I filmed at Plataforma, the renowned nightclub where swirling samba revues happen each night. I was busy and got a lot of good, salable footage.

From Rio de Janeiro we flew to Iguazu Falls, one of the most spectacular natural attractions of the world, it is actually a system of 275 different waterfalls. It lies in a dense tropical rainforest on a bend of the Iguazu River on the border of Argentina and Brazil.

Next: Buenos Aires. I filmed the Plaza de la República with its massive white obelisk; Buenos Aires' most iconic sight. I filmed Eva Peron's tomb and the Casa Rosada balcony where she and Juan Peron delivered their rousing speeches. I had arrived in Buenos Aires during an odd moment. The movie musical *Evita* starring Madonna had just been completed. It had been released in the United States a few weeks earlier and was opening in Buenos Aires at the Atlas Cinema, a large 1967 movie palace, during the time I was there. I went to see the film. It was interesting to see the reaction of the Argentinians to a film that dealt with someone who still remains lionized. Audience response was subdued though not hostile. The next night, I filmed tango dancers and the following day I filmed the Colón Opera House, the Capital Building, cafes, and nightlife. Buenos Aires is very European and feels like Paris.

SHOOTING STOCK FOOTAGE ON THREE CONTINENTS

Machu Picchu, the Lost City of the Incas; part of a South American stock footage shoot. 1998.

From Buenos Aires the group flew to Bariloche, a mountain skiing resort. I rented a car and drove myself around, leaving the group behind. The scenery is a vista of beautiful lakes and alpine mountains. The next day we began a fascinating trip; a crossing of the Andes Mountain range. We boarded a boat outside of Bariloche and began by crossing a wide lake. The complete trip crossing of the mountains took two days and involved several different boats. Each boat would take us across a different lake, and on the far side a motor coach would carry us to the next lake. Midway in the Andes crossing, we spent the night in a hotel, and the following day we continued on passing jaw-dropping scenery and active volcanoes in Chile. The journey ended in Puerto Montt on the Pacific Coast.

From Southern Chile we flew to Santiago, a bustling city, though with few major attractions. Next was Lima, Peru. In 1998, Lima was a colorful but somewhat foreboding city. It's one of the few places where I felt somewhat unsafe on my own with my cameras and equipment. From Lima we flew to Cusco high in the Andes, and the following morning we boarded a narrow gauge railroad that would take us down from eleven thousand feet to eight thousand feet where we piled into a small van that took us up a series of switchbacks to the Lost City of the Incas, Machu Picchu. It's one of those "bucket list" places that a serious traveler should see. From Cusco, we flew back to Lima and then returned to Miami.

I had mixed emotions about the organized tour experience. It was cost effective, but the tradeoff was I did a lot of waiting. Bags had to be outside your door at 4:00 a.m. People had to be at the coach at 5:00 a.m. Checking everyone and their bags in and out at each airport, dealing with passport control, baggage retrieval, and moving twenty-five people in and out of different hotels—there is a lot of time wasted while the tour director tries to herd the group. Group tours are cost effective, but if you go on one, be prepared to spend a lot of time waiting. And be prepared for at least one member of the group who will drive you crazy.

In 1999, I decided to take a trip to the Far East on the *QE2* to pick up various Asian destinations for my stock footage library. I still had connections at Cunard and I was able to get space on the *QE2* from Sydney to Singapore. It was a forty-seven-day leg of the one hundred and two day World Cruise.

World cruises have made a comeback in popularity in recent years because of a new generation of travelers; baby boomers, who have the time and the money to go on extended trips. Today, a dozen ships make complete circumnavigations each winter and most of them are full, but in 1999, the *QE2* was the only ship doing world cruises and interest was low so it was fairly easy to get Cunard to comp me on. When we sailed out of Tokyo, there were only three hundred people onboard out of a capacity of eighteen hundred.

At the beginning of the trip I flew from Los Angeles to Sydney. I stayed at the Regent Hotel on the waterfront and arrived six days in advance of the ship so I could film around Sydney. I had filmed there in 1985 when I was making *QE2 Sails New Zealand and Australia*. It had changed a lot. There was a new monorail (which has since been demolished), high rises, and luxury apartments. It is one of the great modern cities of the world. I reshot the things I had shot before, the Opera House, the Harbor Bridge, koalas, kangaroos, Manly Beach, and Bondi Beach. The reason I kept reshooting things all over the world was that film stocks kept improving and the images kept getting better. Stock footage buyers insisted on the latest, most up-to-date, images with the best quality.

Finally, the *QE2* arrived. She had been sailing from New York for twenty-four days, traveling through the Panama Canal, up to Los Angeles, down to Tahiti, then stopping in New Zealand before docking in Sydney next to the Harbor Bridge.

We sailed from Sydney late the next night. The ship headed to Melbourne, then Perth. I had a great cabin, but I was assigned to a strange table in the dining room. It was where the "problem" passengers were placed. As the cruise progressed, an ever-stranger array of women came and went (world cruises attract far more women than men). Seated next to me was a woman named Pat who had been a waitress at a Denny's in West Covina, California. She had, only two years before, married a well-to-do older man, he died and she decided to go around the world on the *QE2*. She and I became friends and suffered the strange people who came and went. Aside Pat was a nearly deaf woman from Milwaukee named Madeline. Pat would look at Madeleine and in her loudest voice say, "How is your fish, Madeline?" and Madeline would look back and say, "Yes, I hear it's cold in Chicago too." Two strange women from Maryland, horsey types, were seated with us but decamped for another table after two nights. They felt superior to the riff-raff at our table. This left two spots that the maître d' could use for people who were being thrown off of other tables where passengers were fed up. One night, the maître d' seated an obnoxious woman next to me. She had boarded in New York and was already on her third table. She was a namedropper. She had been friends with Barry Goldwater and could not stop talking about how wonderful Barry Goldwater was. I was a guest of the Cunard Line and I had to be polite. The real problem was she was a drunk. She arrived at the table each night soused and proceeded to drink more as the evening went on. "Bourbon, neat," that was her call and the bar waiter kept three fingers of bourbon in her glass until she was nearly falling off her chair. One night in a drunken state she, for some reason I can't recall, started talking about the "homos." "They should round 'em all up and put 'em in a camp like we did with the Japs." That did it. I and the other six tablemates had had enough. A catfight broke out with all of us telling her off. We caused a horrible commotion in the Columbia Dining Room. The maître d', Jimmy Murray, arrived and tried to stop the shouting but to little avail. The woman was moved to yet another table the next night. It was maddening to have to deal with people like this but there were always a few "certifiables" on the world cruise.

Ships have moved away from fixed seating and operate more like restaurants where you come and go as you please, sitting wherever you like. It solves the dilemma of what to do when seated at a table with a drunk or a troublemaker. Still, those fixed tables gave me a chance to really get to know people and I have more good memories than bad.

From Perth we sailed to Bali, which was as beautiful as you would imagine, then Brunei. Brunei is one of the more remote places I've been. It's a sovereign nation on the north coast of Borneo. The Sultan of Brunei is one of the richest people in the world. The money comes from oil. There are spectacular mosques of marble and gold.

Next was Manila, with its crazy crush of traffic, horse carts, pedicabs, and the wildly painted jeepneys, which are half jeep and half bus. The stop in Manila was important to the crew since Filipinos made up the largest portion of staff on the ship.

On to Hong Kong. It was my third visit and it was now a true world-class city with stunning architecture, great wealth, and prosperity. I left the ship and flew to Xian to film the Terracotta Warriors. From Xian I flew on to Beijing to film the Forbidden City, the Summer Palace, the Temple of Heaven, and the Great Wall of China. By 1999, China had been fully opened up to western travelers and the Chinese were very aggressive in trying to sell anything and everything to their visitors. "One dollar one dollar!" was the cry you heard everywhere. Mao would have rolled over in his grave if he could see this.

I knew I would never get permission to enter China as a cinematographer so I went in on a tourist visa. I was very nervous as the customs inspectors looked at my film and my 16mm camera. I just pleaded, "Not professional, only amateur." I did not bring a tripod, so everything I shot was handheld. The footage looks good. I got adept at leaning against walls and using railings to steady a shot.

I flew to Qingdao and re-boarded the *QE2* and we sailed on to Japan. I got off the ship at Yokohama and made my way into Tokyo on the train. I got most of what I wanted to shoot but Japan can be a challenge for Americans. English is not widely spoken and the written language is impossible to decipher. When you are trying to read a map or a street sign you have no way to match things up. You don't need to know French to be able to read a street sign in France and match it up on a map. In Japan none of that works.

From Yokohama, the *QE2* sailed to Ho Chi Minh City. I loved Vietnam. I was impressed with how they had brought their country back—and with no assistance from the United States. I found the people friendly, though their museums, like the War Crimes Museum, reflected their version of the conflict.

Next we arrived in Pattaya and I headed into Bangkok. It was my third trip to Bangkok. The first time was in 1967 via TWA, the second in 1982 on the *QE2* World Cruise. It was as crazy and noisy and traffic clogged as ever. I filmed many things I had filmed before but the images were for stock footage so I composed and shot the scenes differently.

The following day, my driver was taking me back to the ship at Pattaya and I became aware of something. The Thais all learn English by listening to American music. The driver was singing away to disco songs blaring from the radio. Between songs the disc jockey would come on with fractured commentary like, "Get ready, dance wet, we have males coming with water from sky!" He was introducing "It's Raining Men" by the Weather Girls. The driver broke into song and knew every lyric even if he didn't know what any of it meant.

Finally, we docked in Singapore. Singapore always makes me crazy because, as I mentioned earlier, it is essentially a dictatorship, a one party political system, but one that operates so well that it's hard to criticize. Singapore had exploded since my first visit in 1982. There were fears that when China took over Hong Kong they would nationalize the banks, so in the mid-1990s, a lot of money and banking moved out of Hong Kong and into Singapore. Today Singapore is the primary banking capital of Southeast Asia.

At Singapore, I left the ship and the *QE2* sailed on toward India. I stayed in Singapore for several days and got to really appreciate what an exceptional place it is. I flew home on Northwest Airlines. It was the only time in my life that I have seen the sun rise twice on the same flight. We left Singapore in the predawn hours and I watched the sun come up as we flew into the skies of Southeast Asia. We were flying east and gained a day when we crossed the international dateline. Morning turned into afternoon and then into night. As we approached Los Angeles the sun was coming up again. It had been a productive trip. I shot 22,000 feet of film. While I never intended to make it into a feature, I ultimately edited the material into a film titled *Cruising the Orient on the QE2*, which I took out on the travelogue lecture circuit.

I had a major stock footage library. The footage all originated on motion picture film, which was still the preferred format as late as 2000. But by the early 2000s, high-definition television arrived and all of the clients that had purchased footage from me for years now only wanted high definition shots. Forty years of work, a half a million feet of motion picture film, all of it became nearly worthless in a span of about two years. I could have gone back to the vault, brought all of my film reels out and retransferred everything to high-definition, but the cost would have been astronomical. The potential income never justified the six-figure expense of retransferring everything to high-def.

And the business model had changed. Now clients want to see the shots immediately online, and if they want a shot, they expect to be able to download it instantly. My travelogue friend, Rick Ray, saw this early on and built the first downloadable stock footage website DVarchive.com. Before the digital revolution, if someone wanted a shot of the Taj Mahal, they came to me and paid me a decent amount of money because I had gone to India, shot the footage, processed the film, and owned the images. Today, some kid in Agra, India can buy a perfectly fine high definition camera for two hundred dollars, shoot the Taj Mahal at every hour of the day for a month, and upload all of the footage to a site like Pond5.com. Instead of several hundred dollars, he sells the shot for twenty-five dollars and is elated. The kid makes money; the client gets a great shot, and the cost has gone down to almost nothing.

The digital revolution has leveled the playing field. Now anyone with a high definition camera, anywhere in the world, can upload their material and sell it alongside established cinematographers. It gives everyone an equal chance to make money but it makes for a really big playing field. I compete with cinematographers from literally all over the globe for sales in the stock footage marketplace. Shots that I once got anywhere from $250 to $2000 for, depending on the usage, are all available now for $49.95, immediately downloadable with unrestricted use. I do sell my shots worldwide now. Someone in Moscow will download a clip of something I shot in Argentina, but I have to make a lot of sales and produce a lot of volume to make up for the steep price decline. And the volume of clips available online grows exponentially. When I first started selling my clips on Pond5.com I uploaded 8,000 shots. At the time they had a total of 125,000 clips online for purchase. When I last looked, they had over eight *million*—and by the time you read this, who knows how many clips will be on that one site alone. Today most of my stock footage sales are for archival use. It is my oldest footage that is most likely to sell; footage I shot in another time that no one can duplicate today.

The stock footage business did not turn out to be my great annuity. I do make steady sales but the income is nothing like it was in the 1990s. To quote a common phrase of our times: "It is what it is."

CHAPTER THIRTY-FOUR

FINDING HAPPINESS

When people ask me about my romantic life, I say that if I had one more boyfriend I would be in a tie with Elizabeth Taylor. I had quite a string of casual boyfriends, serious relationships, and committed partners, but nothing ever worked out. After Robert Smith, I decided to try bachelorhood for a while. I enjoyed making my own decisions and living without consulting anyone. But after seven years, I tired of being alone and yearned to have someone to share my life with.

So I decided to use a matchmaking service. This was a few years before the Internet revolutionized dating. I thought if I used a matchmaking service, I would meet higher quality people. The service was expensive so I was somewhat assured the people I would meet would at least have jobs. I went in for a consultation at their office in L.A. I filled out all sorts of questionnaires. Supposedly, the information was fed into a computer that would spit out the perfect match. It all sounded so scientific.

The first date was a high-end, Bentley driving, "I know the Maître d' at Morton's" type, who was rather charming but clearly had not the slightest bit interested in me. The second date was nice enough but there was no chemistry. He was interested in football; I was interested in show business. He said, "I've been to the opera. I went to see *Phantom of the Opera.*" Next came a nut case who spent the entire dinner date peering over his shoulder to see who else was in the restaurant. Then a complete psychotic who was loath to even shake hands because he was obsessed about not catching AIDS. By the end of the fourth date I was ready to bag the whole thing. I had bought five dates; I had one left. It was dinner with a guy in Silverlake. I was going to cancel but thought, what the hell, it's just dinner. I was flying to Palm Springs that night so I decided to meet him early at a restaurant called Chamois on Hyperion Boulevard.

I walked into the small restaurant and my date was sitting in the back in a corner. It was early. The restaurant was empty. He was guarded. He had a goatee and looked a bit like Burton Holmes. He had two earrings. Edgy. I am colorblind but I was fairly certain that the color of his hair was not God-given (I was told later it was purple). He was wary because, like me, he had been through several disastrous dates from this service. Part of our conversation included comparing notes on who had had the most horrible date. His name was John Sanger. After a while he relaxed and we began to exchange information. He was the Chief Financial Officer of a fashion eyewear firm called l.a.Eyeworks. I knew of the company because of a large national ad campaign that featured celebrities modeling their glasses with the phrase "A face is like a work of art…It deserves a great frame." He had a good job. He traveled to France four times a year to oversee their European operations. He had a subscription to the Los Angeles Opera. He was a theater enthusiast. He was knowledgeable about world affairs, and he liked to travel, and he loved New York. So far, so good.

It was December 15, 2000. During those years (and I suppose even now), gay men often exchanged information about their health status early in a relationship. He mentioned that he had Hepatitis C and at one point had been considered for a liver transplant. I was taken aback but mentioned that I had a case of Hepatitis B and I had recovered and I was just fine. My thought when he said he had been considered for a liver transplant was, "How insane, this man looks way too healthy, to be considered for something like that." This was a passing thought that would come to haunt me.

He looked healthy. I realized there might be some medical problems down the road but I thought I could deal with things. I decided to see him again. I said goodnight, walked to my car, and headed to Burbank to fly my plane to Palm Springs.

A week later, I returned from the desert and we went to a Coen Brothers movie *O Brother, Where Art Thou?* It was a funny film, quirky and ironic, and during the movie John reached over and held my hand.

In all the years that passed since that night, I never sat in a theater with him where we didn't hold hands. It was one of those quiet things that nobody sees, but is part of the fabric of a relationship. What I could not see at the time was how turbulent the years ahead would be. We were just getting started. It all seemed so perfect and right at the time.

We saw each other through the holidays and I decided to invite him to Palm Springs for New Year's Eve. I showed up at his place; he owned a charming house on Tracy Street in Silverlake. I drove him to the Burbank airport. We got into the Cessna, along with his dog, a crusty old pug named Pearls who could snore louder than any human I have ever known, and off we went to the desert. We met two of his friends, Steve Reinstein and Randy Hooczko, and we all went to a big dance party downtown. I think that was the weekend I realized this might work.

And then Steve Cline decided to come back into the picture. He was back in L.A. from Mexico and wanted to see me. It had been about ten years since the last time he wrecked havoc in my life. I told John I was going over to see him—but just for drinks. John was suspicious. Well, drinks turned into several drinks. I didn't hop in the sack with him, but I was late in coming back to John—by about two hours. John was furious and I was accused of doing the deed with Cline when I had, in fact, done nothing. Though, in fairness, he had a right to assume the worst given my history with Steve Cline.

We managed to get through that episode and soon I had to hit the road once again. I was traveling the East Coast during my spring tour, operating out of New York. I had time off at Easter and asked John if he wanted to come to the city. He said yes and a week later he showed up at my front door. He walked into the apartment, gazed out at the Manhattan skyline, we looked at each other, and that was it. We didn't leave the apartment for two days. Once we got out, we got busy doing what we both loved. We saw six Broadway shows, *Bells Are Ringing*, a revival of *Follies*, *One Flew Over the Cuckoo's Nest*, *The Full Monty*, *Invention of Love*, and the best treat of all, the last preview before the opening night of Mel Brooks' *The Producers*, one of the biggest hits in Broadway history. There was a sense of electricity in the air, the St. James Theater was packed, and everybody knew they were seeing a mega-hit. It still stands as one of the best nights of theater in my life.

It was a great ten days. Then it was time for John to leave. I went down in the elevator with him to send him off to JFK and in the elevator he just looked at me and smiled a big, wide grin. It was the beginning of something wonderful that would ultimately test our inner strength over events to come that neither of us could foresee.

John returned to Los Angeles. I came back a few weeks later. John was busy with his job at l.a.Eyeworks and I was planning another film shoot.

I was going to Russia for a stock footage shoot in August of 2001. I wanted John to come with me but he couldn't take more time off from work, so I went alone. But I felt lousy on the trip. I was tired—a lot—much more than normal. I wondered if I was OK. I returned from Russia and got busy transferring the processed film to digital videotape.

Then, a week later, at 6:00 a.m. the phone rang. It was my mother. She said, "Turn on your television, someone has flown a plane into the World Trade Center." I hung up. I turned on the TV just as the first tower started to fall. John and I watched in horror. The mood in America over the next few days was indescribable. It was similar to the Kennedy assassination, which happened when I was fifteen. It appeared that we were at war. But with whom? In looking back, it was a simple enterprise, carried out with little more than hardware store box cutters and nineteen zealots willing to sacrifice their lives for a cause that no one understood.

The more innocent world I had spent my life filming ended that day. Being allowed alone with the King Tut treasures, going to the top of Big Ben, riding in the locomotive of the *Canadian*, all of those things would either become impossible or require immense effort from 9/11 on. I didn't feel the full impact of the moment until several days later when I sat down and broke into sobs. It took some time for the depth of the human tragedy to sink in.

John and I had planned our first trip abroad for November 2001. We had booked a Mediterranean cruise. Travel immediately after 9/11 was strange and fraught with fears and concerns but we decide to go ahead with the trip. I booked a cruise from Istanbul to Barcelona. John had accumulated airline miles with British Airways so he provided business class tickets. From L.A. we flew to London, then on to Istanbul. Once we arrived at our Taksim Square hotel, we were exhausted and slept soundly before setting out to see the city the next day.

I was working, shooting for my stock footage collection. John was on holiday. Once I got a shot, I was ready to move on; I had more to film. John wanted to linger. I realized the first day John was not going to be much help. So we agreed to sightsee separately. He took his time moving through museums, palaces, and mosques. I roared along at a hundred miles an hour shooting everything I could.

We had a busy time in Istanbul and saw a lot; the Hagia Sophia, the Blue Mosque, the Süleymaniye Mosque, Topkapi Palace, the underground cistern; we even went to the oldest Turkish steam bath in the world and had pounding massages on an ancient marble slab. After four days in Istanbul, we boarded the *Norwegian Sun*. It was older, a bit down-at-the-heels, but we had a balcony cabin and dining was open seating so we had no tablemate problems.

From Istanbul we sailed west toward the Dardanelles, then on to Athens. John and I took a cab to the Acropolis. The Greeks were fussy about photography so I had to work without a tripod, and the Parthenon was partially covered in scaffolding which made shooting more difficult. John and I wandered down the hill and meandered through Athens, finally arriving at Syntagma Square where the Parliament Building stands. I filmed the Greek version of the Changing of the Guard, the soldiers wearing tights, pleated skirts, and shoes with pom-poms. John and I took a train back to the port and returned to the ship.

Next was Dubrovnik. It was gray and dreary the day we arrived. The overcast fit the mood of the ancient walled city. I had a conversation with an older man who said, "You Americans. You forget everything, you move on. Here we never forget, we hold onto the past." It was a simple statement but it highlights a problem in many parts of the world. Grudges, blood feuds, ethnic hatreds that date back centuries, people and cultures that simply cannot forget and move on. America can and does move on. It's one our best traits. We make many mistakes, but we are pragmatic. We look to the future. Germany and Japan are two of our greatest allies. Who would have imagined that in 1945?

From Dubrovnik the ship sailed to Venice. I was looking forward to showing John around Venice. But it was November and there had been heavy rains; the water level was up and the city was flooded. We spent the night docked in Venice and the ship was to sail the next day at noon. Early the following morning, we took a launch from the ship's dock to Saint Mark's Square. John went off to see things and I continued filming, slowly making my way back to the railway station which was adjacent to the dock. I walked the whole distance, shooting film along the way. I made it back onboard at about 11:30. John was not there.

At noon the gangway was pulled onboard. I leaned over the rails to see if john was anywhere in sight. The horn sounded and the ship slowly moved away from the dock. Still no John. Then, when the ship was about a hundred feet off the pier, I saw someone running wildly down the quay. It was John. He was not onboard. He had missed the ship. I would learn later that he had gotten caught behind a group of tourists in the Doge's Palace and couldn't get out. Once out of the Palace, he boarded a vaporetto. He should have taken a water taxi but it cost fifty dollars and he was trying to save money. The vaporetto should have gotten him back to the railway station and the dock in plenty of time, but the city was flooded and the vaporettos had to go at a snail's pace so they wouldn't throw a wake and make the flooded squares and streets and hotel lobbies even worse. Once off the vaporetto, John went running to the pier only to see the ship slowly slipping away. This was my first experience understanding that John Sanger was habitually late.

I knew the ship had almost an hour of slow cruising along the Dorsoduro before it would leave the lagoon. The pilot would not leave the ship until this point and I hoped John would be able to board the boat going out to pick up the pilot and get back onto the ship. I had memories of an old *I Love Lucy* episode in which Lucy missed the U.S.S *Constitution* leaving New York City and is brought onboard with a helicopter. This was not going to happen for John.

We reached the entrance to the lagoon. The pilot got off onto the pilot boat. John was not there. The pilot boat sped away. So there I was, at sea, John on the shore with no clothes, no money, and no passport! The ship kept the passports in the manifest office so they could clear customs in each country. Had the next destination been in another country, John would have been in a terrible bind. Fortunately, the next stop was Naples. So I settled in for three days at sea and assumed John would meet up with the ship once we rounded the boot of Italy.

John has his own stories of his time in Italy. The ship's agent in Venice was unwilling to do anything to help him board from the pilot boat. He had his credit card so he went to the railway station and bought a ticket to Naples. The train was jammed and he had to stand most of the way. The agent in Venice made arrangements to have John met at Naples and taken to a hotel. The way John tells the story, after he got off of the train at eleven o'clock at night, a taxi driver was waiting holding a sign with his name on it. He got in the cab and the driver drove and drove and drove. Finally, he pulled up in front of a dump of a hotel and told John he owed him something like sixty Euros. John paid and went into the hotel. He paid for the room and rode the rickety elevator up to his floor. He walked into the room, opened the drapes, and looked out—at the railway station. He could have walked across the street. Instead he was literally "taken for a ride" by a Naples taxi driver. There was no heat in the hotel, it was November 10th, and he was freezing. The front desk clerk told him the heat was not turned on until November 30th. The following morning John left the hotel and checked into a Holiday Inn. Sometimes the creature comforts of an American hotel can be soothing and welcome.

John decided to make the best of his mishap. He hired a driver to take him to the ruins at Pompeii. He bought a new wardrobe, black suit, shoes, shirt and tie, and headed off to the opera to see *Lucia di Lammermoor* at the Teatro di San Carlo. I give him credit. It was an awful thing to miss the ship, but rather than moping about it, he figured out how, to use a cliché, to turn lemons into lemonade.

The following day, the *Norwegian Sun* arrived and John came back to the ship convinced I was going to be furious. I was not. I was rather impressed with his ability to deal with a complex problem and make the best of a bad situation. We then sailed on to Cannes. Cannes was cold, rainy, and since it was November, deserted. We made our way to the bar at the Carlton Hotel and after chatting with a few locals made our way back to the ship. Next: Barcelona.

Barcelona is an impressive city, filled with great Gaudí architecture, Joan Miró sculptures, and Roy Lichtenstein pieces scattered all over town. I was busy filming things and John went off to a museums. That night we went to see *The Cunning Little Vixen* at the Liceu Opera House and after we had dinner at Els Quatre Gats, The Four Cats, Pablo Picasso's old Barcelona hangout.

From Barcelona we flew back to Heathrow and returned to Los Angeles. It had been our first trip abroad. There were some problems (like John missing the boat), but in general we traveled well together. John was always willing to do anything. He was not a foot dragger. Nothing spoils travel as much as a traveling companion who isn't willing to try something new. John always had one answer to any suggestion: "Yes." That's a great trait in both a traveling partner and a life partner.

Back in Los Angeles, John returned to work at l.a.Eyeworks. I started transferring the film at Fotokem and logging the shots for my stock footage library. I had some travelogue lectures in the winter/spring season, but my speaking tour was pretty light that year.

John decided that Pearls, his old pug, needed a friend. We talked about it and mutually agreed to adopt another pug. John called up Pug Rescue and a particularly crazy woman named Sherry showed up at his office with a dog named Dexter, a handsome three-year-old pug. I was twenty minutes late. The bond was built in those twenty minutes, and for the next fourteen years, Dexter was John's dog. In spite of my feeding him, playing with him, walking him, and caring for him like a spoiled child, he was always John's dog. The rescue person gave us a long sad story how the dog got into rescue. What she failed to mention was the dog was a terrible "marker." From the moment he arrived home we battled his "marking" issues. He peed on everything just to show you that it was *his* territory. Ultimately, he stopped, but he was a lot to handle in the beginning. And as for giving Pearls a friend—well, Pearls was just as nice to Dexter as she could be—for three days. On the fourth day, she realized he was there to stay and she turned on him. She terrorized him until the day she died, which for Dexter was none too soon.

Christmas was approaching. John was more or less living at my house in Hancock Park. We decided to put up a Christmas tree. *That* was an experience. John had very definite ideas about a Christmas tree and, of course, so did I. There is nothing quite as tense as two overly controlling homosexuals putting up a Christmas tree together for the first time. John strung out his Christmas lights and I commented, "I think twinkle lights are tacky." Well that got me in a boatload of trouble. I spent years apologizing for that remark. We did put up the twinkle lights but it seemed that every ornament that went onto the tree elicited some negotiation. Our first Christmas tree was stressful. "Peace on earth" it was not, but we got through it. It was, of course, a fabulous looking tree. We had a big holiday party and we learned that we made a great party-throwing team. We knew how to stage-manage large events and people loved coming to Rossmore Avenue for our holiday events.

When I was shooting in Russia in August, I did not feel particularly well, but I put off dealing with it because I had the Mediterranean shoot coming up in November. I was losing weight. I have always fought to keep my weight down so I wasn't bothered by what I regarded as an unexpected blessing. But after the Mediterranean trip, John thought I looked too thin and he insisted that I see a doctor. I am not sure why I went to his doctor instead of my own but I did.

But I'm getting ahead of myself. First, there was Russia.

John Sanger and me on our first trip abroad onboard the *Norwegian Sun* sailing out of Istanbul. Notice how thin I was. That was not intentional. 2001.

CHAPTER THIRTY-FIVE

MOTHER RUSSIA

To any opera fan, the late Anna Russell was a comic legend. She traveled the world with her one-woman show skewering serious music with her "lectures" on opera. In one of her most famous routines, she describes the entire story of the Wagner Ring Cycle (which lasts close to fifteen hours) in about twenty minutes. After some preposterous explanation of a Wagnerian plot line, with the audience in gales of laughter, she stops, turns to the crowd and says, "You know I'm *not* making this up!" I mention this as prelude because, like Anna Russell, I'm *not* making this up.

In all my years of travel, I had never been to Russia. Many experienced travelers have never been to Russia. Yes, you want to go, you feel obligated to go, but on some level it seems like a trip to the dentist; the travel equivalent of a root canal. I finally decided the time had come to visit Mother Russia, to see the Kremlin, the gold onion domes, St. Petersburg, the Volga, and Lenin himself. I was shooting for my stock footage library. A shortage of Russian footage existed at the time.

I made the trip in August 2001. My travels to the former Soviet Union were fraught with problems. Customer service was a concept unknown to the Russians. Seventy years of Communism will do that to you. And it all started at LAX.

The Cunard Line use to have an advertising slogan, "Getting there is half the fun!" This is not a motto that Aeroflot, the Russian Airline, was using in 2001. To fly from Los Angeles, to Moscow, Aeroflot seemed the logical choice. It was the only carrier with non-stop service. You left LAX at 6:40 p.m. in the evening and arrived twelve hours later at 5:30 p.m., Moscow time, the following day.

Things got off to a bad start when, shortly after takeoff, the flight attendant announced, that, "due to an electrical failure," there would be no cabin lights and no in-flight movies. For seven hours, we simply sat in the dark. I couldn't help but wonder whether the "electrical failure" extended to other parts of the plane, like the landing gear.

The passengers were almost all Russian, lots of babies, and lots of crying. One of the four flight attendants in coach spoke some English, the rest almost none. The attitude of the flight attendants was surly. They had all the charm of prison guards.

Two hours into the flight dinner was served—in the dark. I squinted at the meal and wondered which catering service at LAX had prepared this. Was it possible they brought it with them from Moscow? Was it airline food that had already traveled halfway around the world?

In an attempt to discourage the Russian tendencies toward overindulgence in liquor, Aeroflot had no bar service in economy class in 2001. However, back in the day, they made up for the lack of one vice by encouraging another—smoking. And everyone smoked—*a lot*. The air in the cabin was blue.

As the night droned on, babies cried, muscles cramped, the plane bounced around, and then the first rays of light appeared and out of the window was the Arctic, icebergs and all. We were now on the other side of the world.

Breakfast was a two-inch square of chocolate cake and one cup of coffee. About this time the lavatories ran out of toilet paper. They soon resembled a third world train station. Finally, two hours late, we arrived at Sheremetyevo Airport in Moscow.

Passport control at Moscow was legendary. Everyone from flights arriving from all over the world were herded into a round, dank, low-ceiling room with no windows. The air was stale, tempers were short, and everyone was exhausted—and smoking. There were literally hundreds of people pushing and shoving toward two Passport Control officers who moved with the same "customer service" speed as a disgruntled toll taker on the Triborough Bridge in New York. Two hours and fifteen minutes later, I passed through Passport Control. There was not a "Welcome to Russia" offered by the agent.

I hauled everything out of baggage claim by hand and emerged into the chaos of the arrivals hall. Since we were two hours late, the driver who had been paid in advance to pick me up had long since gone home, so now I had to face the Taksi Mafia. The Taksi Mafia is the plague of the Moscow Airport. Hundreds of unlicensed taxi drivers (theoretically, anyone in Moscow with a car is a taxi driver) mumbled in hushed tones under their breath, "Taksi?" It had the feeling of a drug deal going down. I had been warned: Do not take these taxis unless you speak Russian. I opted for an "official" taxi, which charged $60. A Muscovite would have paid about $5.00.

I followed a man who had, what appeared to be, an official looking taxi badge hanging from his jersey. He took me to a booth where I handed over $60. I was given a receipt then taken upstairs and taken to a parking lot and put in an unmarked car. The tout mumbled something to the driver and off we went—except it took an hour to get out of the parking lot. The parking lot fee attendants were clearly in training to become Passport Control officers. Eventually, we were on our way.

Moscow is beautiful at night. Advertising, which had not been allowed under the communists, now filled the streets with color and bright neon lights. Everything, at least on the main thoroughfares was floodlit, spruced up, freshly painted or in the process of restoration. The ride was actually rather exciting. I was finally in Moscow, the heart of Russia. The Kremlin loomed ahead as the taxi turned down Tverskaya Street. The red glow of the rotating glass stars atop the Kremlin towers created a scene that felt like a John le Carré novel. I could, in my mind, almost hear the sounds of the boots of the Russian Army marching across Red Square.

I had reserved a room at the Intourist Hotel. In spite of all the warnings that it was a dump, I booked it because it was central. It was only a block from the Kremlin and Red Square and it was cheap, $85 a night. Certainly more affordable than the National Hotel next door where a room was $400, or the Metropol down the street where the rate was even higher.

The taxi pulled up in front of the dingy entrance on Tverskaya Street. There was no bellman. I hauled my own bags, suitcases filled with clothes, cameras, and 16mm film. The man at reception handed me a key and I offered a credit card for payment. He refused it—how odd. I was told to come down in the morning and settle my bill. (I was there for four nights and I was expected to settle my bill each day.)

As I walked toward the elevators, I noticed one of the new guest services Moscow hotels were providing: prostitutes. They roamed the hotel lobby freely. They didn't harass; they were there for convenience. But if you made the slightest eye contact they would respond in a flash. I passed on this option and went directly to my room. I opened the door to a tiny room decorated in 1970s Soviet style. A brown tattered velveteen bedspread, worn carpets, a scarred nightstand, and two wall sconces in fake gilt hanging five feet above the bed and connected to electrical outlets with dangling cords. The bath was small; the shower was covered in mildew.

The following morning after a meager breakfast, I was out of the hotel and on my way to see the sights. In spite of the hassles, the sights of Russia are remarkable. Red Square, the Kremlin, St. Basil's Cathedral, the onion domes, all freshly restored, the jewels of the Czars, Russian Orthodox art. It's hard to absorb it all. And in the middle of Red Square, is Vladimir Lenin himself, embalmed in a glass-spotlighted coffin. It was eerie: The father of modern Russia right there in front of your eyes.

The guards in Red Square were suspicious and there are lots of rules about photography. A plainclothes policeman in front of St. Basil's Cathedral stopped me while I was filming. He demanded loudly, "Passport!" He and three other policemen examined my passport and visa and after several minutes of mumbled conversation decided I was harmless and moved on. Nothing happened, but these encounters were very disconcerting.

I moved around on the Metro. The Metro is the pride of Moscow and one of Stalin's grandest projects. It was built with what was essentially slave labor. It's unlike any other subway system in the world. Grand chandeliers, elaborate plaster ornamentation, marble, mosaics, huge bronzes, stainless steel art; each station is unique. During my time in Moscow, it was a bit shabby, dark, and seedy, but you could see that in its heyday it was a wonder to behold. The trains themselves are worn and dark—but they're fast and frequent—every fifty seconds during rush hour. A twenty-ride card costs seventy rubles, about two dollars and twenty cents—eleven cents a ride.

But it was confusing beyond belief. Many rides involved changing trains at transfer points and there were no English signs anywhere. Few Russians spoke English so asking for help was pointless. Finally, I found a map at a kiosk that showed the stations on a street map with both Cyrillic and Roman spellings. The map was invaluable.

Meanwhile, back at the ranch…

I needed to make a local phone call from my hotel room. First I was sent to the cashier in the lobby to pay for the call, then to the telephone office to submit the receipt. Then they turned the phone on in my room, I went back, dialed nine, and, voila!—a local call went through. But the next day I needed to call St. Petersburg. So, back to the cashier and back to the telephone office. This time the phone was passed to me from the telephone office window. A four-minute call to St. Petersburg was twenty-five dollars.

Finally, four days later, it was time to check out. I expected this to be a simple matter. It was not. I was sent to a mystery guestroom on the fifth floor that had been converted into a small, messy office. A young woman had been assigned to my "account." I already knew her because she had been pounding on my door at 7:00 a.m. for the past three days insisting I come down and pay the bill.

The checkout procedure was Byzantine. It took a half-hour. She wrote out the entire bill by hand. I looked around the office and realized there were no computers. Everything was still being done manually.

Once I was done with checkout, I hauled my bags out of the hotel, got into a taxi and off I went to the M.S. *Mayakovskaya* docked at the North River Station. To make the trip affordable, I booked a cabin on one of the Russian riverboats that traveled between Moscow and St. Petersburg. The boats traveled down the Moscow Canal, the Volga, across several lakes, and down the Neva River before arriving in St. Petersburg.

The boat was one of about a dozen that were built in the late 1970s in East Germany to ply the St. Petersburg-Moscow route. My boat had three hundred passengers on board; about a quarter were American, a quarter French, a quarter German, and a quarter Russian, with a few Swedes and Finns thrown in for good measure. It was like the Tower of Babel.

My cabin was situated next to the entrance to the dining room and in front of my cabin door was a group of sofas, one of the few places on the boat to sit and talk—and smoke. It was unbelievably noisy: Every language and accent imaginable, from French and German to Southern drawls and New York accents like nails on a blackboard.

One of Joseph Stalin's many massive projects was the building of the Moscow Canal to link Moscow with St. Petersburg and the sea. The boat proceeded through the canal passing through a series of locks. As we approached each lock, the decoration was different. Bronze statues honoring the glory of the Soviet workers stood atop locks in the middle of nowhere; elaborate designs seen only by ship captains and lockkeepers. Stalin's projects were all oversized and grandiose. His achievements, from the Seven Sisters, the giant gothic-spired Moscow skyscrapers mostly built as grand apartment houses for the party elite, to the monuments and fountains, were easy to build. He had cheap labor. Anyone who questioned the party line was made part of a national unpaid labor pool.

When Stalin took power in 1924, there were 38,000 political prisoners in the gulags. At the height of his rule, eight million political prisoners filled the camps and were literally worked to death on projects ranging from power plants to dams, the Moscow Canal, and the Metro. I mention this only to remind travelers that all this grandness came at a price. It was accomplished using prisoners whose only crime was disagreement with the Communist Party chiefs.

The first morning of the river cruise, I got up for breakfast, which was announced for 8:00 a.m.. I arrived late at 8:30 to empty trays, a few slices of cheese and apple juice. The woman overseeing the buffet said, "Finished. All gone." I learned to be early, get in line fast, and grab what I could.

In the afternoon, we arrived at our first Volga port, Uglich, a hardscrabble, impoverished village. Here you saw the downside of the Soviet collapse. Poor elderly people selling bouquets of wildflowers for a few rubles. There were no restored, floodlit monuments; only the stark reality of the economic morass Russia faced after the collapse of the U.S.S.R.

From Uglich, we sailed on to Kostroma where the Romanoff dynasty was founded. I filmed more Russian Orthodox Churches and more monasteries. The next day we docked in Yaroslavl and I filmed more churches and monasteries. For a nation that espoused an official policy of atheism for seventy-four years, there were an awful lot of churches. And it's a good thing they weren't torn down because after the fall of the Soviets, the Church came roaring back stronger than ever. The Russian Orthodox Church today has considerable political power. From Yaroslavl, the boat continued down the Volga River. We soon left the river and began passing over a series of large lakes.

Life on board the M.S. *Mayakovskaya* was pretty basic. Get up, run to eat, watch the river, get off at the port for a few hours, eat dinner, and then take in the evening's entertainment. The entertainers tried very hard. I did like the vocal quartet that sang African-American spirituals with Russian accents in the style of the Modernaires; "Lit maw pipple go!"

By this point I had adjusted to life on the boat. I expected this kind of journey would attract an adventuresome group but it did not. It attracted older people, some infirmed, and in a few cases extremely boorish. One guide, telling the story in Kostroma of the accession of the first Romanoff Czar and the subsequent support the Romanoff's gave the local monastery, elicited a loud interruption by one of the men in our group who asked, "Who the hell did the Romanoffs steal the money from?" The guide looked flummoxed. Noël Coward addressed this problem in his musical *Sail Away* with a song "Why do the wrong people travel and the right people stay at home?"

The following morning we docked in Goritsy, a peasant village on the River Sheksna. I wandered around the village. It was all wooden houses, little plots with flowers and vegetables, somewhat messy, certainly not spruced up for tourists. The people who lived here were old. The young had left long ago. One woman opened her home to travelers for tea. It was tiny, with a very low ceiling, neat, and very basic. The guide suggested a one-dollar contribution. It seemed exploitive but this probably made the woman the most successful entrepreneur in the village.

The next day we passed through a set of six locks and into Lake Onega en route to Kizh, an island in the lake, known for the Church of the Transfiguration. The church is made completely of wood, it has twenty-two wooden onion domes, and there is not a single nail in the entire structure. It was built in 1714 and is the crown jewel of Russian wooden architecture. When it was proposed that it should be demolished, the Bolsheviks responded that it would stand as a testament to the labor, skill, and hard work of the proletariat—a fortunate decision.

We left Kizhi and proceeded toward St. Petersburg with one more stop to make. A tacky, pseudo, Disney-like village called Mandrogi. It's a newly constructed "typical" Russian village of nothing but souvenir shops in cute, brightly painted houses, and is about as far from a real Russian village as Beverly Hills is from the South Bronx.

In the morning we approached St. Petersburg on the Neva River in a pea-soup fog. St. Petersburg was a project of Peter the Great. He moved the capital from Moscow to St. Petersburg and turned Russia's eye toward the West. The palaces, the stately buildings, the churches, the Hermitage Museum, the art—the feeling is more like Paris than Moscow.

The greatest art of the Hermitage, the Impressionist and post-Impressionist paintings, were not bought by the Czars, but rather by private collectors. Russian collectors saw value in the Impressionists' work at a time when the European collectors regarded it as worthless. By the time it was considered important, private Russian collectors owned the very best pieces. After the Bolshevik Revolution, the private art was confiscated and sent to the Hermitage where it remains to this day.

The palaces of St. Petersburg are impressive. Catherine summer palace is an eye-popping gargantuan mass of gold leaf, marble, amber, and malachite.

A glance at these places gives you some idea why the Bolsheviks came to power. Yet, oddly enough, the Soviets treasured these ostentatious piles of wealth. They took care of them after the revolution and restored them after the siege of Leningrad during World War II (as Saint Petersburg was then known). When I asked a guide why the Bolsheviks didn't demolish these Czarist homes, she said it was because Russian workers had built them and that was reason enough to save them.

After having been aboard the boat for ten days, I couldn't take another M.S. *Mayakovskaya* meal. So I took the St. Petersburg Metro to the Grand European Hotel. I had dinner in the Russ Restaurant. It was elegant, impeccably served, the ambience unrushed and it cost $78 plus tip—about what you would have expected to pay for a meal in a first class restaurant in New York in 2001.

This was the conundrum of Russia. Everything was so extreme. The service was either awful or exquisite, the food terrible or gourmet, the hotels fleabags or palaces. And the people reflected this as well. They were rich or poor; no discernable middle class. I did return to St. Petersburg in 2010 and there seemed to be more of a middle class, but the income gap between the super-rich and the very poor is massive. And this dichotomy developed in less than a decade. Under Communism, a modicum of equality existed, though the party elite hardly lived like common Soviet citizens. Still, there wasn't this huge gap between rich and poor.

If you can overlook the problems, Russia provides some of the greatest sights of the world and experiences you will never forget. St. Petersburg was an impressive conclusion to a trip that had been filled with frustration and awe—each delivered in heaping amounts.

But wait. It's not over yet. I had to get home.

At 8:00 a.m. the following morning, a driver arrived to take me to Puklovo Airport in St. Petersburg. The check-in procedure for my flight to Moscow was slow and maddening. The personnel of this airline, one of the "Babyflots," were totally unhelpful.

My baggage was overweight. I was given a tag and sent to the baggage office on the other side of the terminal. I found the *kassa* (cashier) where I was to pay. It took ten minutes of hand calculations to determine that I owed 1,075 rubles (about thirty-five dollars).

I asked if US dollars were accepted (I had whittled down my rubles to a minimum since they can't be exchanged in the United States). The answer was no.

I was sent to the exchange office in another building where I changed $100 into rubles, assuming I might have more of the same in Moscow. Back to the *kassa* to pay, then with a receipt, back to the ticket agent to check my bags and secure a boarding pass.

Now it was time for security. I had twelve thousand feet of unprocessed motion picture film in carry-on cases. I can't begin to describe the terror these security checks held for professional photographers in the days of film. In 2001 I was still shooting film and one bad X-ray machine could, in a fraction of a second, destroy all of my work. I asked for hand inspection of my film. The security guard took me aside and rummaged through the film, and then he rummaged some more, all the while muttering something. I couldn't understand what he was saying but he kept repeating, in a rather hushed tone, one particular word. Finally, it dawned on me; he wanted money, a bribe. I peeled off three twenty-dollar bills and he indicated with two fingers raised that I needed two more. I was then allowed to proceed through security and my film was passed around the X-ray machine.

The plane was a scary looking Tupolev from the old Soviet fleet. I knew the maintenance standards were probably minimal and nothing got fixed until it broke or fell off. We took off and an hour later landed in Moscow at Sheremetyevo Terminal I, the domestic terminal. The international flights leave from Sheremetyevo Terminal II. No one bothers to tell you that Terminal II is fifteen miles away. It's like landing at LaGuardia in New York and leaving from Kennedy. You have to claim your luggage and deal with the Taksi Mafia or one of the overcrowded minibuses. My flight from St. Petersburg arrived at 11:25 a.m. My Aeroflot flight to Los Angeles was to leave at 2:50 p.m. It seemed like more than enough time. I was wrong.

Let me, for once, spare you the details and just say that at 2:45 p.m., five minutes before departure, there were eleven policemen, security officers, a bomb squad officer, the Aeroflot manager, and the airport manager standing over me, looking at my bags of film and conversing heatedly in Russian. Not one person spoke English except for a young boy who was loading bags onto the X-ray conveyer belt. He came over to me, seeing I was confused and nervous, and said in a thick accent, "They are not going to let you board the plane." I had been trying to avoid sending my film through the X-ray machine by requesting a hand inspection. What had started as a simple request was turning into an international incident. At this point, I put the film on the conveyor belt, watched it glow on the screen and thought, I'd rather take my chances with the film than not board this plane. With this done, I was allowed to board just as the door was being closed.

In forty years of making travelogues people have asked me countless times, "What is your favorite place?" There is, of course, no real answer. I love many places for different reasons. But what I do tell people is the travel experiences that remain the most memorable were never the easy trips. It was the difficult journeys, Russia, Egypt, India; places where there were countless challenges and cultural adjustments. Those were the trips that left lasting impressions and changed me as a person, in the way I thought and the way I looked at the world. For all the problems I dealt with on my 2001 journey to Russia, it remains vividly in my mind as one of the greatest travel experiences of my life.

And thankfully, the Moscow airport X-ray machine did not damage the film. It is some of the best footage I ever shot.

The Summer Palace outside of Saint Petersburg, built by Catherine I in 1717. It was heavily damaged during World War II during the siege of Leningrad.

CHAPTER THIRTY-SIX

THE OTHER SHOE DROPS

"Into each life some rain must fall..."
Henry Wadsworth Longfellow

I wonder if someone mentioned that to Noah.

For me the first signs of rain were in 1998. I was in Los Angeles, living alone, and starting to feel lousy—really lousy. I was getting ready to leave on a speaking tour and decided I should see my doctor first. I went into his office; he examined me, drew blood, and called the next day and said, "You have hepatitis."

I said that was impossible because I had hepatitis in 1974. After you have it you develop antibodies and you can't get it again. Wrong. Somewhere along the way my system had lost the hepatitis B antibody. I told the doctor I had to leave the next day for a three-week lecture tour. He said I couldn't travel, I needed rest, and that I would have to cancel my speaking dates.

In those days, you just didn't do that. I was working big auditoriums. I had shows at the Bushnell Memorial Auditorium in Hartford, the Kodak Auditorium in Rochester, the Carnegie Institute in Pittsburgh, and Constitution Hall in Washington D.C. for the National Geographic Society. Canceling a lecture tour was (I thought) not an option. There were too many tickets sold and my lecture fees added up to a significant amount of money, which I would lose.

And I thought I was invincible. So the next morning, sick as a dog, I went to LAX and boarded a TWA flight for New York. I slipped into my seat, went to sleep, and never woke up once during the entire flight. I was wiped out. (It was the last time I flew on TWA before the merger with American Airlines and the dissolution of the Trans World Airlines brand; a sad day for travel and for me personally because of my connection to TWA.)

I got off the plane and went to my apartment in Manhattan. The next day I took the train to Hartford to start the Bushnell shows. I made all the dates over the next three weeks. I was as sick as I had ever been. But like most people who get hepatitis, I slowly recovered. Within a few weeks I felt more or less like my old self and frankly I never gave it another thought.

But by late 2001, when I was in Russia, I was not feeling well again. I should have gone to my doctor after I returned from Moscow, but I had the Mediterranean shoot ahead and I didn't want anything to interfere with that. So John and I went on the Mediterranean cruise and when we returned to Los Angeles in December of 2001, he insisted I go to the doctor. I balked. I didn't want to go to my doctor. So he made me goes to his. I don't know why I went; I had my own internist. I did it partly to appease John and to shut him up. Labs were drawn beforehand and a couple of days later I went in to meet John's doctor, Dale Prokupek. Dr. Prokupek looked at my labs, flipped the pages and then looked me straight in the face and the first words out of his mouth were, "You need a liver transplant."

What!? This isn't possible. I'm a little tired but otherwise I feel OK. Dale Prokupek showed me my labs. All the liver enzyme numbers were drastically elevated and my albumin was 1.9. He said, "The albumin is the last thing to go. Once it is that low, your liver is probably beyond hope of recovery. You need to start looking for a transplant."

Normally, a liver biopsy would be performed to determine the severity of the cirrhosis but my INR (an indicator of the ability of the blood to clot) was so bad that a biopsy could have caused me to "bleed out." Besides, the lab numbers told it all. My liver was toast, and this to someone who never drank anything stronger than red wine.

What are the five stages of grief? The first is what? Oh, yes, denial. I stormed out of Dale Prokupek's office huffing and puffing. He couldn't be right, how outrageous to say something like that to a patient on the first meeting. I proceeded to find another doctor, Dr. Soraya Ross, who was willing to say I didn't need a liver transplant—yet. I believe she was trying to let me settle into the reality of the truth slowly. She knew the first day she saw me that my liver was going fast, but she humored me for a time into believing I could recover.

Filming in Rome. I may have been smiling but my health was failing fast. 2001.

My path downward was like a runaway freight train. I went from excellent health to near death in a matter of months. I started losing weight dramatically. The symptoms of liver failure started arriving on my doorstep. The first occurred while I was in Palm Springs with John. I couldn't remember where I had left my car keys, nothing to be concerned about, but when John picked them up off the coffee table and gave them to me, I couldn't remember how to unlock the door, or start the car, or—and thank God John stopped me—put it into gear and back out of the garage. I had encephalopathy, a common condition of liver failure. It is a type of dementia caused by too much ammonia in your system. It turns your brain to mush, and it happens fast. I had all the major symptoms of liver failure but the encephalopathy was the worst. It stopped my life like a puncture in a balloon. I eventually forgot how to sign my name.

As I began to write my memoirs some time ago, I was amazed at how good my memory was. I can recall minute details about events from decades ago; where I sat in a theater to see a show, what I wore to a party in college. But much of my memory of what happened between December 2001 and November 2002 is a blur. What follows is sketchy. Some of this is due to self-imposed amnesia, a desire to forget a terrifying episode of my life; the other part is simply the fact that my brain was temporarily checked out.

In my quest for a transplant, I went to Cedars-Sinai in Los Angeles and spoke with Dr. Paul Martin. He said, yes, I needed a liver transplant, but no, they did not do liver transplants for HIV positive patients. He offered a vague comment that San Francisco General Hospital was considering these surgeries but he offered no help in contacting them. And then he got up and walked out of the room. His bedside manner was like that of a robot.

I drove home in shock but I remembered my first meeting with John. John had told me of his medical problems and that he had been considered for a liver transplant by a doctor in Pittsburgh. In 2000, when I met John, liver transplants were not done on HIV positive people. It was assumed that the anti-rejection drugs that transplants required were incompatible with a compromised immune system and the patient would die following transplantation. Dr. John Fung disagreed with that theory. Larry Kramer, the celebrated author and playwright, was one of Dr. Fung's first HIV positive liver transplants and he thrived. The surgeries were considered revolutionary, and they were successful in spite of the naysayers who said the patients wouldn't survive. I contacted Dr. Fung and he was willing to give me an evaluation in July in Pittsburgh. It was now April.

My first hospitalization occurred in May 2002. I went out to dinner with my best friend at the time, Scott Anderson. We walked to Larchmont Village, had dinner in an Italian trattoria, and walked back home. I opened the door to my house and proceeded to throw everything up. I had a fever of a hundred and four. Scott took me to the ER at Cedars-Sinai. I remember sitting in the waiting room. And the next thing I remember was waking up in a hospital bed with John sitting beside me. Five days had passed. Five days that are a complete blank in my mind. I had been in a coma because of extremely low sodium. Too much salt is bad, not enough salt can kill you. Who knew?

When John saw my eyes open he called the nurse. She came in and asked me a few questions. Did I know where I was? No. Did I know what day of the week it was? No. Did I know what year it was? Hesitate… hesitate… 2001? 2002? Did I know who the president of the United States was? George Bush! Bingo! One right! I had come out of the coma with no apparent brain damage. John had my medical power of attorney. He told me much later that the night before I finally came out of the coma the doctors were asking him to consider signing a Do Not Resuscitate order in case my heart just stopped. He did not sign it.

There were three more hospitalizations at Cedars-Sinai before my transplant evaluation in Pittsburgh. By the time I left for Pittsburgh, my weight had dropped from 175 to 120 (it would eventually go down to 106).

I could no longer work so, for the first time in my career, I canceled the shows I had scheduled for the coming season. I had a new job: saving my life. The complexities of the organ transplant system are daunting. I spent every waking hour on the computer trying to learn and advance my case. Getting an organ transplant is one of the hardest and most draining experiences a person can face.

John did not go with me to Pittsburgh. I was determined to do the transplant evaluation by myself. John had taken so much time off of work to help me already that he trusted my belief that I would be OK. I was stubborn, and I was also delusional.

Two close friends from Manhattan, Jerry Douglas and John Stellar, did not believe I should go through this alone and they drove out to be with me. The transplant evaluation process is grueling; many tests, lots of doctors, lots of blood draws. I arrived at the Pittsburgh airport alone and took a cab to a Holiday Inn in the neighborhood where the hospital was located (oddly enough, walking distance from the Carnegie Music Hall where I had shown my travelogues countless times). John and Jerry arrived that evening and we all went out to dinner at a nice restaurant and had a pleasant time. After dinner that night Jerry, John, and I agreed that we would meet in the lobby at eight o'clock, have breakfast, and then go to the hospital for my first appointment at nine.

I only know what happened from what I was told later. John and Jerry were in the lobby the following morning waiting for me at eight o'clock.

I was not there. By 8:30 they were concerned and called my room. No answer. They got hotel security to open the door and I was lying face down on the bathroom floor, unconscious in a pool of my own vomit. 911 was called. So rather than walking in the door of the University of Pittsburgh Medical Center, I arrived for my transplant evaluation through the E.R. A couple of days later, I came to and John Sanger was again sitting beside my bed. John and Jerry had called him and he took the next flight to Pittsburgh.

John and I had been together less than two years. Most people would have walked away. No one should be saddled with this much bad health from a partner this early into a relationship. But John was committed to the relationship "in sickness and in health." This philosophy would be tested repeatedly in the coming years, but for the moment it was just the two of us in Pittsburgh desperately trying to get me approved for a transplant.

The doctors evaluated me. I was so sick there was serious concern about whether or not the hospital would consider me a viable candidate. The waiting list for transplantation is not based on the length of time you have been on the list, but rather a complex algorithm called the MELD score (Model for End Stage Liver Disease). The higher the score, the sicker you are, and the closer you are to death, which means the closer you are to the "front of the line." My MELD score was almost off the chart.

I completed the evaluation. I was discharged from the hospital and I returned to Los Angeles. This was not something that was going to happen immediately even though I was incredibly sick. Finally, two weeks later, I got a call from the hospital in Pittsburgh and I was told I did not meet the criteria for transplant and that I would *not* be put on the list. I needed to have an undetectable HIV viral count and my hepatitis had to be completely resolved. These were impossibilities given the state of my health.

My primary care physician, Dr. Philip Musikanth, went directly to Dr. John Fung and said, "Why did you put this man through all of this if these were your criteria? Why did you ever bring him to Pittsburgh?" Dr. Fung, who is a remarkable individual, listened. John wrote him directly and pleaded my case. I do not know this for a fact, but I believe Dr. Fung overruled the transplant committee and put me on the list—and not a moment too soon.

The hospital called me in Los Angeles. I was told to return to Pittsburgh. John quickly went about tying up loose ends, getting Katie and Amy, two dear friends to take our pugs, covering things at his office, closing up the Rossmore house. And on October 30, 2002, we went to LAX to board a red-eye for Pittsburgh. As we started to board (I was in a wheelchair by this time, my skin was yellow; I was obviously a very sick man), the gate attendant called the chief flight attendant out. They both looked at me with concern. They asked John if there was anything they should know. For a moment, US Airways was not going to allow me to board the plane because I was too sick to fly. John said, no I was just weak but I would be fine. Reluctantly, they let me on the plane.

We arrived in Pittsburgh at dawn the following morning. John was busy trying to rent a car, gather our bags, and deal with me in my helpless condition. We had rented a small apartment, but it was not going to be available until the beginning of the week so we went back to the Holiday Inn. The next morning we went into the restaurant for breakfast. The meal was brought, I ate it, became violently ill and passed out right in the restaurant. Another call to 911 and another ambulance ride to the hospital. I suspect that Holiday Inn never wants to see me again.

I was admitted through the E.R. and I never left the hospital from that point on. I was on the waiting list but the right organ had to be found; the right blood type, even the right size. Dr. John Fung and Dr. Bijan Eghtesad, the two surgeons who would do the transplant, told John I had only about a week or so to live. On November 8th, John was told there might be an organ match. A man was being removed from life support. We knew nothing about the person (anonymity is a given regarding organ donors). The wheels were set into motion for my transplant to take place that night. Twenty-nine tubes of blood were drawn, a CAT scan was ordered, and a flurry of activity was underway. My mind was addled from the encephalopathy and a variety of drugs that I was on to keep me alive. My hospital room was beside the roof deck heliport and all night long, as I waited for the transplant to begin, helicopters kept arriving and taking off, bringing organs and patients. Snow was swirling, lights were flashing, and the sound of the rotor blades droned on. It was the most surreal night of my life.

Transplants, for a variety of reasons, almost always take place in the middle of the night. I was wheeled into a pre-op room at 2:00 a.m. The anesthesiologist was late. Once he arrived, everything went into motion; a dozen medical people surrounded me. John leaned over and squeezed my hand as they wheeled me away, and for some reason I shouted, "Let's rock and roll!" In a few moments I was transferred to the operating table. The anesthesiologist said, "I'm going to give you something that is going to make you sleepy..." And the next thing I knew I was coming to. The surgery had been eleven hours.

My recovery was slow. I was in the ICU for days. I was in the hospital a total of twelve weeks. I had been so sick and so close to death that the climb back with the new liver was difficult. Much of the recovery is just a blur. I have no memory of the first week at all. John tells me that I vacillated between being nearly comatose and aggressively agitated. At one point, the nurses had to tie me to the bed. I was determined to get up and walk out. They gave me Haldol and then I crashed. It was a chaotic nightmare, but slowly I got better.

I had many hallucinations because of the narcotics. One night I was starting the French Revolution. I can remember the nurses hovering over me saying, "Yeah, right... to the battlements..." Another night, John was sitting in a chair beside me reading a book. There was the steady hum of machines and the blips of vital signs on the monitor overhead. Somehow, as I looked out at the hall lights, I saw Broadway. In my slurred speech I said, "Oh John, look over there—the lights of the Barrymore Theater! I've seen so many wonderful shows at the Barrymore Theater." John rolled his eyes and said, "Yeah, the Barrymore Theater, sure Doug..." and went back to his book. Just another night in the ICU.

After three weeks in intensive care, I was transferred to "the floor," a regular hospital room. Then I had to learn how to walk again. I had been bedridden for so long my muscles had atrophied. The physical therapy that was required to get me back on my feet was torturous. Eventually, I got out of the hospital and returned to our small Pittsburgh apartment. We remained in Pittsburgh for another month. I was itching to get back to L.A. I was going into the post-transplant program at Cedars-Sinai (the very institution that had refused to help me). But I was ready for California. It had been a long winter in Pittsburgh.

After begging, pleading, and cajoling, I finally got the doctors to release me. John paid our final bill at the apartment, drove us back to the airport, turned in the rental car, put me in a wheelchair, and pushed me to the gate. We flew home and when I got out of the taxi and walked into the backyard of our Rossmore house on that warm February night in 2003, I felt I had made it through. I had come back from the brink of death to live another day, another year, and the rest of my life.

I wrote a letter to my donor family. I got a response. All of it was kept confidential and handled through UNOS, the United Network of Organ Sharing. In my letter I thanked the family for making the decision to "donate life" by allowing their loved one, who had passed away, to give life to me. I received a handwritten reply. The woman spoke of her father as a kind and good man. I never knew any more than that but I am forever grateful to that family that made that decision on what had to be the hardest night of their lives.

Three years later, during Christmas of 2006, John and I were in New York and went to see Raul Esparza in a revival of *Company*, the Stephen Sondheim musical—at the Barrymore Theater. At the end of the show, Bobby, the lead character, sings "Being Alive." I listened to the lyrics, looked around the theater, and choked up at the irony of it all. "Being Alive" in the Barrymore Theater with John Sanger was as good as it could ever be.

If you have gotten this far into this book, stop for a moment. Check your driver's license. Are you an organ donor? If you are not, go to DonateLife.com and register. Your decision today could save someone's life in the future.

And to Dr. John Fung, Dr. Bijan Eghtesad, the University of Pittsburgh Medical Center, and John Sanger, my deepest thanks. I am alive today because of all of you.

With my best friend, Steve Sharp at the INTRAFILM convention in Las Vegas in May of 2003. I was six-months post-transplant. I still looked pretty beat up but I was on the mend.

CHAPTER THIRTY-SEVEN

SAILING DOWN TO RIO

After returning to Los Angeles from Pittsburgh it took time to regain my strength, but I slowly recovered and I was pretty much back to my old self by June. John and I left in the Cessna and set out on a cross-country trip to New York. We stopped in Santa Fe, Kansas City, Chicago, Traverse City, and Pittsburgh; finally landing at Teterboro. We spent four weeks in Manhattan seeing shows and friends. We then made our way back to California, stopping in Lancaster, Indianapolis, Saint Louis, and Colorado Springs before flying back over the Rockies. The trip lasted seven weeks. It was a personal accomplishment to have come so far and be back in the left seat of my plane.

When you are threatened with death and you beat it, you swear your life is going to change. You're not going to get upset about the small things. You're going to appreciate every day and discard all your bad habits. Were it only that easy. Within a couple of months, I was arguing with people over the same small things that had aggravated me before. I realized that, in spite of staring death in the face, not much had really changed. My sister made a blunt but realistic observation. "Doug, you had a liver transplant, not a personality transplant." I was just me—as I had always been.

Once I was back on my feet: the nagging question—what now? What am I going to do with the rest of my life? In the hospital I had great plans to change the world, but those plans faded as time went on. I realized I was likely to carry on much as before. I had made my living shooting travel movies and that was what I was likely to continue doing.

Anyone who survives anything remotely as serious as I did will usually have a motivating reason—a reason to live. For many people, it's their children; they want to see a daughter graduate from college, or a son get married, or a grandchild start school. I had no children so I didn't have that motivation, but I did have one thing I wanted to live for. I wanted to sail on the *Queen Mary 2*.

The *Queen Mary 2*, launched in 2004, is not a big deal today, but in 2002 when Cunard announced she was being built, it *was* a big deal. Cunard had been sailing the *Queen Elizabeth 2* on transatlantic crossings and long world cruises since 1967. I had spent over 400 days on the *QE2* and made three films onboard. I loved the ship but she was getting old. Cunard was faced with a decision: retire the *QE2* and stop the transatlantic service, which they had maintained continuously since 1840, or build a new ship. Cunard opted for the latter and announced they were building a new flagship, the biggest ship in the world, the *Queen Mary 2*.

The laying of the keel of the new ship occurred when I was extremely sick. The likelihood of me sailing on the new Cunard flagship seemed remote. I was on a downward trajectory and didn't expect to live to see the ship launched. By the time I was in the hospital waiting for my transplant, the building of the new Cunarder was underway. I wondered; would it be possible? Could I actually, someday, recover enough to sail on the *Queen Mary 2*? This was the dream that kept me fighting to live.

As I slowly recovered, I started getting fidgety. I kept trying to find something new and challenging to do, but nothing presented itself. I wanted to sail on the *Queen Mary 2*, but I assumed I would do that as a passenger. My days of making travelogues were over. But were they? I still had contacts at Cunard. The Carnival Corporation had bought the company some years before. A woman named Julie Davis, who I had worked with when I made my film *Cruising the Orient on the QE2*, was still with Cunard. She didn't know that I had a liver transplant and had nearly died. As far as she knew, I was still traipsing around the country showing travelogues.

The *Queen Mary 2* was to be launched in January, 2004 in Southampton. After a short cruise around the British Isles, she would head out on her first transatlantic crossing, arriving in Fort Lauderdale, Florida on February 11th. Then she was going to sail to Rio de Janeiro for Carnaval, a twenty-four day round-trip journey.

I wrote Julie Davis at Cunard. I reminded her who I was and the films I had done on the *Queen Elizabeth 2*. I proposed a new film titled *Sailing Down to Rio on the Queen Mary 2*. I was still thin, weak, and my face was gaunt. I had some ways to go to become my old self. But I sent the letter off and frankly I never expected to ever hear from anyone at Cunard.

A couple of weeks later, Julie Davis called. She did indeed remember me, and yes, they were interested in having me make the film. I fumbled for words because I didn't expected this response. If there had been Skype in 2003 and Julie Davis could have seen what I looked like that morning in my tattered bathrobe, there is no way on earth they would have let me onboard their new ship. But I had enthusiasm in my voice and the deal was made. They would comp John and me to Rio and would offer assistance onboard so I could get the sequences I needed. I hung up the phone and called out, "John, you will never believe who that was…"

Planning got underway immediately. This shoot would be challenging because I was finally making the shift from film to digital cinematography. I purchased a state-of-the-art (at the time) digital camera, a Panasonic DVX100 and set out trying to learn how to use it. For an old film cameraman, this was a challenge. On the 16mm camera there were really only two things you had to set, the focus and the f-stop. That was it. Hold it up and shoot. On the digital camera, there must have been a hundred settings, things I had never had to deal with before; white balance, audio settings, external microphone patches, variable shutter speeds, 60 frames interlaces, 24 frames progressive… yikes, I felt like an old man booting up his first computer.

It took me time to learn how to use the camera and even longer to learn how to edit the material. Editing film was physical. You ran the film (or a work print copy of the film) through a viewer, cut it with scissors, and glued it to the next scene using a splicer. With non-linear digital editing, everything is different. The images exist electronically on a hard drive, you can cut, change, go back; nothing was irreversible. There were a thousand things to learn and it nearly drove me insane. Ultimately, I learned digital editing with books on my lap, reading, experimenting, and occasionally making horrible mistakes. I had an out; Rick Ray, a long-time travelogue colleague, much younger, and a man very savvy with Final Cut Pro editing software. Whenever I got into a really difficult bind—like somehow deleting the entire program and having no idea where it went—I would call Rick and he would talk me through it. The single hardest thing was to shift my thinking from film as a physical medium to digital elements that do not physically exist. They are just billions of zeros and ones on hard drives. You can't reach out and touch them.

After weeks of study and a few practice shoots (I shot the Hollywood Christmas Parade as practice before facing the Rio Carnaval parades), I felt comfortable enough to head to Fort Lauderdale to board the *Queen Mary 2*. John was coming along to help. It was the blind leading the blind, but he gave me emotional support on a shoot where I was none too sure of what I was doing. We checked into the Bahia Mar Hotel. I was both nervous and excited as the new project began.

On February 11th, we got up at 3:00 a.m. to film the predawn arrival of the *Queen Mary 2* at Port Everglades. I related the story at the very beginning of this book. The ship appeared as a light on the dark horizon, and we watched the point of light get bigger as the ship neared, finally passing right in front of us. It was a moment to remember.

We boarded the *Queen Mary 2* that afternoon. The ship was scheduled to sail at three o'clock, but the twenty-six hundred passengers had brought more luggage than Cunard dreamed possible and it took an additional three hours for the longshoremen to load everything. Finally, at six o'clock with dusk falling, we left the port and sailed out to sea. I was once again working on a ship, producing a new film, and only a year after my life-saving transplant. Life can send you some surprises if you stick around long enough to enjoy them.

John and I made our way to our stateroom on the boat deck in the bow of the ship. It was a perfect location for shooting. The stateroom was stylish, reasonably large, and had a nice balcony; however the dining room was in the aft of the ship and it was quite a schlep to dinner each night.

Of all the features of the *Queen Mary 2,* the most stunning is the Britannia Dining Room. It is two stories high and seats twelve hundred and fifty people. There are two sittings each evening, the first at six o'clock and the second at eight thirty. The ceiling is simulated stained glass like a giant Tiffany window; the end of the room is covered in a huge tapestry of the *Queen Mary 2*. In the center of the room is the Captain's table where invited guests join the master of the ship each night, and connecting the first and second floors was a wide, sweeping staircase. When I first saw this grand entryway, I thought back to Thayer Soule's comments about Burton Holmes and his many transatlantic crossings. Holmes told Thayer that when sailing on an ocean liner, you should always be fifteen minutes late to dinner. By doing this you would be the last person to enter the dining room, and therefore all eyes would be on you. This advice probably said a lot about Burton

Holmes' ego, but Thayer passed it on to me. It became known between John and myself as "The Lore." Burton Holmes, father of the travelogue business, had passed it on to his protégé Thayer Soule, and Thayer had passed it on to his protégé, namely me. I felt honor-bound to continue the tradition, so each night, John and I would walk down the sweeping staircase in our tuxedos at 8:45 p.m. Was anyone really watching? Did it matter? I have no idea, but I was continuing "The Lore" of how to enter an ocean liner dining room. And of course, wouldn't you know it, the first night out I tripped and went tumbling half way down the stairs—and yes, all eyes were on me!

The *Queen Mary 2*, the largest ship in the world at the time of her launch, 150,000 tons. She gave me the will to survive so I could sail on her. 2004. Photo courtesy of the Cunard Line.

Cunard still had fixed seating. They maintain this policy even today while most other shipping lines have dropped it. I always requested the biggest table possible to improve our chances of having copacetic tablemates. We were assigned an officer's table with the ship's doctor. The doctor, however, never showed up. The act of engaging in conversation with strangers at a ship's table, people you are going to dine with for a long time, is an art. Once everyone was seated, people introduced themselves, and small talk ensued. You ask questions that are non-threatening and you very slowly move into more substantial topics like current affairs. You never know what people think when you first sit down, and I can tell you from countless conversations at sea, that it's often a surprise. The people you would expect to be the most conservative are often very liberal, and the couple you were certain would be liberal, are surprisingly conservative. If people tend to be of the same mind, table conversation can be very lively and engaging. If everyone is in different corners, conversation tends to be shallow and superficial.

We had four women from Spain who spoke no English but were very pleasant, the doctor who was never there, a man from Phoenix who was traveling alone and seemed quite hard of hearing, and "Andy and Rose Marie." I have no memory what their names actually were. They were not married, they were friends, but he looked just like Andy Rooney of CBS's *60 Minutes* and she looked like Rose Marie, the television actress from the old *Dick Van Dyke Show*. And they were simply awful. He was a doofus and said little, but "Rose Marie" was a loud-mouthed, opinionated boor who had to let you know immediately her opinion on *everything*. She started off with a tirade on how Muslim terrorists had targeted the ship; that the Queen's Royal Hussars were onboard in plainclothes to protect us, and we would likely find out that there were bombs onboard and we should all know how to get to our life stations quickly since the ship was probably going to sink. Well, how's that for a conversation opener! I tried to be polite and suggest that I thought that was not going to happen, then she immediately shifted to politics. The Iraq War was raging at the time and people had differing opinions about the wisdom of that military intervention. I would normally have kept my opinions to myself, but she had a way of baiting you. She was looking for a fight. I like lively conversation and I actually enjoy talking to people who have different opinions as long as the conversation is civil, but this woman just insulted us faster than any person I have ever met at sea. She said something that, for the life of me, I can't recall, but it was the straw that broke the camel's back. John and I looked at each other and nodded. We got up from the table and left the dining room. On the way out, I told the maître d', David, who was someone I knew from the *QE2*, that he *had* to get us another table. We could not spend twenty-four days with this woman.

The next evening we went into the dining room and David said, "I have wonderful table for you." He took us up to the upper level and seated us at a large table with eight other gay men. Well, how great can this be? Wrong. We had gone from the frying pan into the fire. They were insufferable and shallow beyond words. John and I had nothing in common with them. They were frighteningly right wing. We were left out of most conversation and it was one of the most uncomfortable dining experiences I have ever had. We had changed tables once so we couldn't really change again until we got to Rio. In Rio we did change to another table for the return trip and that group, while not unpleasant, was dull. The only other man at the table owned a lawn mower business in Texas and I learned more about lawn mowers than I ever wanted to know.

The second day out, my Cunard onboard handler slipped a note under our cabin door and told us that we were going to be taken to the bridge to meet the Captain at two o'clock. I was to film the bridge and to interview Commodore Ronald Warwick. I knew Ron Warwick from 1985 when I made *Queen Elizabeth 2 Sails New Zealand and Australia*. He was the staff captain and I was seated at his table for thirty-seven days. When I walked onto the bridge, I introduced myself and mentioned that I had been with him and his wife on the *QE2* back in 1985. He mumbled, "Well, if it was 1985, that *wasn't* my wife." Not a good way to start things off. The Commodore had been barraged with interviews ever since the ship launched. People far bigger than me, anchors of national news shows, reporters from *The New York Times*, had all interviewed him. I looked small by comparison and he had no memory of me at all. We did the interview, and filmed around the bridge, which is all computer screens and keyboards, no big brass wheels anymore.

The next day we went to the engine controller room; again a maze of computer screens, immaculately clean like an operating room. The chief engineer, Brian Wattling, was more pleasant to us and gave a good interview in which he talked about the unique design features and propulsion system of the ship. The *Queen Mary 2* has rotating pod propellers that steer the ship and are positioned by computer programs using GPS. The ship has no rudder.

The fourth day out was our visit to the galley. The executive chef was Jean-Marie Zimmerman, the first French executive chef Cunard had ever hired. It used to be a joke about Cunard and French Line ships that the Cunarders had great service, beautiful cabins, wonderful entertainment, and terrible food. Before the 1990s, Cunard ships had full British crews, and their way with food was not renowned. Today, crews come from all over the world and they turn out a staggering number of meals. Twenty-six hundred passengers as well as fourteen hundred crewmembers: four thousand people, twelve thousand meals a day, three hundred and sixty-five days of the year. It's quite an operation. I filmed during the evening dinner rush and it was fascinating to see how choreographed all of it was.

The first port was St. Thomas, the Virgin Islands. John and I rented a car and drove around looking for things to film. There really isn't much there, but I got enough to create a brief sequence. It's not a particularly favorite island of mine. From St. Thomas the ship sailed for five days to Salvador de Bahia. The city had changed little since 1982 when I was shooting the world cruise film, but I had to shoot new footage because I was now working with a digital camera. The city has the largest collection of baroque architecture in the Western Hemisphere. It is also poor and largely black, the most African city in Brazil, a result of the slave trade and the early Portuguese plantation owners.

From Salvador we sailed on to Rio, arriving in an early morning mist, the lights of Copacabana could be seen in the distance, and the Christ Statue was barely visible in the clouds. After docking, we left the ship and set out to film. I hired a guide and driver but they were terrible. Eventually, I let them go and used taxis to move around. To make things more difficult, it rained almost the entire four days we were there. The weather was so bad that when I went to cut the final film, I had to use film footage I had shot in 1998 under clear skies. Rio in gray, rainy weather is not photogenic. The footage wouldn't work. I was fortunate that I had my own stock footage to draw from; great shots of Copacabana, Sugar Loaf Mountain and the cable car ride to the top, the Christ the Redeemer Statue and the cog train up Corcovado Mountain. But it was a challenge in post-production editing to get the film and digital elements to closely match.

The highlight of the trip was the Carnaval parades. I had purchased box seats right in the center of the Sambadrome parade route. As we arrived we moved through throngs of people; the noise level, the crowds, it was all crazy. Then we walked through an archway and there it was; the Carnaval Samba Parades right in front of us, and they were dazzling. It is the single most colorful event I have ever filmed in my life. The parades begin at nine o'clock and run until seven o'clock in the morning for four nights in a row.

Carnaval in Rio, the biggest party on earth. I was filming *Sailing Down to Rio on the Queen Mary 2*. 2004. Photo by John Sanger.

Each samba school has 5,000 samba dancers and eight floats. The schools (and they aren't really schools, they're loosely organized social groups) compete for prizes. One of the oddest things about the judging is how much emphasis is placed on timing. Each group has exactly one hour and fifteen minutes to move their dancers and floats down the route. Starting and ending exactly on time is critical to be eligible for prizes. This is ironic since Brazilians are the least punctual people on earth. If the parades didn't have these rules, the group that was to start at nine wouldn't have their act together until eleven—or later.

85,000 people watch from the grandstands and 35,000 people participate in the parades each night. A half a million people pass through the Sambadrome during the four nights of the Carnaval parades. For me, the most significant aspectsof the parades is their social relevance to Rio. The people in the parades are the poor from the favelas, the shantytown slums that cover the hillsides of Rio de Janeiro. They work throughout the year making the costumes, building the floats, and practicing the dances, and once a year the world comes to see them. Poor people rarely get any recognition, but in Rio, once a year, the poor are celebrated for their creativity and energy. Carnaval in Rio is, in many respects, a celebration of collective self-esteem.

Four days later, at 5:30 a.m., *Queen Mary 2* sailed out of Rio, Carnaval was over for another year. On the return trip I relaxed. Most of the shipboard material had been filmed on the southbound journey. The return allowed some time to lie on the decks and enjoy shipboard life. The *Queen Mary 2* is no longer the largest ship in the world, others have taken that title, but she is still my favorite ocean liner. I cross on her regularly to visit London and go to the theater.

Back in Los Angeles, I set to work cutting the film using new digital editing skills that I was still trying to master. The film was finished on time for the first show in January of 2005 at El Camino College in Southern California. I was still at it, making films, giving lectures, and traveling the world; all because of the miracles of modern medicine.

A new liver, a new lease on life, and a new headshot to go with it all. 2004.

CHAPTER THIRTY-EIGHT

A SETTLED LIFE, MARRIAGE, AND A FEW BUMPS ALONG THE WAY

Once *Sailing Down to Rio on the Queen Mary 2* was finished, my life returned to a normal routine. I would leave in the autumn on my lecture tour, come home for Christmas, and go back out on the road again in the late winter and spring. I had expected the new film to be a big success. I thought the title was reminiscent of the old Fred Astaire, Ginger Rodgers movie, *Flying Down to Rio*. But nobody saw the connection. The film did lousy business. Crowds were small and the whole industry was dying for all the obvious reasons; videotape, DVD, cable television, and the Internet made the idea of watching a film narrated in person by the producer seem quaint at best. I stuck with it because it was really the only thing I knew how to do, but I could see the handwriting on the wall. This was a business in its final days. Still, I managed to eke out a living and I enjoyed traveling around the country and getting up on stage.

Continuing the lecture tour also gave me an excuse to keep flying my airplane. It was starting to become a financial drain because my lecture fees were stagnant and the number of shows was decreasing. The only thing going up was the cost of fuel. When I started flying, aviation fuel was about $1.75 a gallon. By the mid-2000s it was anywhere from $6.00 to $8.00 a gallon. My plane held 163 gallons of fuel and burned 26 gallons an hour. I started saying, only half-jokingly, that I took my lecture fee after every show and handed it to the fuel truck driver the next day to gas up the plane. My love of flying was becoming expensive, but it would take almost another decade before I finally let go of the airplane.

John and I were traveling more and more for pleasure. I still took my camera and shot footage for my stock footage library, but I wasn't making feature-films any longer. It didn't seem like a good long-term investment. The days of cruise lines comping me or governments hosting me were going away. People had figured out better ways to get travelers on planes and ships and into hotels than by partnering with live-lecture travelogue makers.

I did release another film called *Cruising the Orient on the QE2*, but I made it out of the material I had shot in 1999 during my long stock footage shoot in Asia. I didn't originally shoot the material with a feature-length film in mind but when I looked closer at the shots, I realized I had enough footage. I got another season out of the lecture market by releasing the film.

In 2003, after my transplant, John and I went on a Panama Canal cruise from Los Angeles to Fort Lauderdale on Celebrity's *Summit*, next was a Bermuda cruise on Holland America's *Veendam*, a Baltic Cruise on Cunard's new *Queen Elizabeth*, a Caribbean cruise on Holland America's *Noordam*, several crossing on the *Queen Mary 2*, and a Princess Cruise to the Mexican Riviera on the *Star Princess*. I've probably forgotten a few, but we were at sea a lot.

The three of us, John, Dexter, and I flew across the country. We stopped in Grayling, Michigan to visit Fran and Brooke Reidelberger. 2009.

In 2005 we made a two-month trip to Europe starting in London and ending in Nice. We took the Eurostar through the Chunnel to Paris and drove for several weeks through France and Switzerland, stopping to see John's friends at the l.a.Eyeworks offices outside of Geneva.

We flew the Cessna back and forth across the country with Dexter, our pug, in the cockpit. I sold my New York apartment when I got sick in 2002. I didn't expect to survive, and I was trying to get my affairs in order. Of course, I didn't die and wished I hadn't sold it. In 2006 we purchased another apartment in the same building. The building was called the Fontaine but John called the building "Tara." When we moved back in he said, "With God as my witness, I'll never live without a doorman again!"

"When are the two of them going to stop talking so we can get in the air?" 2009.

We went to Broadway—a lot. For years we saw every Tony nominated show. We would typically make four trips a year and stay for a month at a time. We would see between fifteen and twenty shows each time we went. Before we would leave New York, we would take our piles of *Playbills* (we both collected our own and were oddly protective of our personal—not shared—collections) and stack them in order of worst to best, and would then flip them over to reveal our choices. We almost always agreed on the worst, not always on the best. It was a ritual that ended every theater binge in New York. We were big fans of Marilyn Maye, the legendary jazz singer, and we went every New Year's Eve to hear her at the Metropolitan Room. Traditions; they are the scrapbooks of your life.

The phrase: "Oh, I don't want to do that..." was never uttered between us. We had subscription tickets to the Los Angeles Opera, and when we were in New York we would go see the Yankees play and the next night go to a Broadway show. Two friends were aghast when they asked us what we had done that weekend and we said we had gone to a Coney Island sideshow to see a sword swallower, a fire eater, and a Fatman. And we loved a good topless show in Las Vegas. When John and I first met, it was serendipitous that we had both seen *Jubilee!* in Las Vegas *twice*.

Our love of Las Vegas was amped up when we became friends with Mike Widman and Nick Crincoli, who were "whales"—high rollers in the Vegas casinos. They would invite us to go with them for three-day weekends. We got the most amazing hotel suites, ate in the best restaurants, and had great seats to everything from Madonna, to Justin Timberlake, to Ricky Martin, to Pink—all because Mike and Nick loved to gamble. I'm not much of a gambler, but John loved to play craps and would often be up half the night throwing dice. I have great memories of Las Vegas and the four of us. We were like the Ricardo's and the Mertz's.

One of life's experiences that everyone must eventually face is the death of one's parents. My father died in June of 2005. He was 86. I rushed to Kansas City to make it home before he passed. He died five minutes before I walked into our family home. If only I had taken an earlier plane, if only I had gone one day before. You replay those decisions over and over in your mind. My mother was nearly inconsolable. They had been married 66 years. The grief over the loss of a long time spouse is one of the most difficult emotional challenges of life and no one knows the depth of it until you go through it yourself.

John flew to Kansas City for my father's funeral. My parents were very fond of John. My Dad was well regarded; a hundred and fifty people from ten different states came to his funeral. John and I, and four other relatives, carried his casket to his grave. It was a powerful moment. My father had lived a long and rich life and he gave me two of the greatest gifts anyone could ever ask for; the ability to travel the world and his unconditional support for everything I did.

My mother died four years later. She was 89. I was in Kansas City this time. My sister Roxanna and brother-in-law Art had come from Tucson. They had gone out of their way to take care of both of my parents in the last months of their lives. I arrived in time to do a few things, but my sister assumed most of the responsibility. Again, John came for the funeral and again John and I, with four others, carried my mother's casket to the grave. John was with me to bury both of my parents. I was not able to help him in that regard because his parents died long before we met. My mother's funeral was on a cold bleak rainy day; there were not so many people. John sat in the pew and held my hand and I remembered how much he cared for my mother.

My parents were both dyed-in-the-wool Democrats. My father was a union man and both of them had political and social values that were very liberal for their time. I always considered myself a progressive, but John was more to the left than me. We would get up in the morning, sit down over coffee, and start reading the newspaper and comment on events of the day. John considered me to be mildly conservative. I didn't see myself that way, but sometimes we would get into an argument about some current events issue and after I had said something John deemed not liberal enough, he would throw the paper down and say, "I'm going to go call your mother!" And he would. He would call Kansas City and say, "Maxine, you will not believe what you son just said..." And the two of them would go on. They were practically communists.

* * *

I fully recuperated from my liver transplant and my health continued to improve. John's unfortunately did not. I knew when we meet in 2000 that he had a failing liver (I did not know mine was failing at the same time and more quickly). I entered the relationship aware this was an issue that was looming on the horizon.

In April 2003, after I had returned home to Los Angeles from Pittsburgh, we booked a cruise to Mexico on a Princess ship as a celebration of my renewed health. The day before we left, John became ill. He was determined to make the trip and managed to get onboard, but he never left the cabin during the journey. He had a respiratory condition; a violent cough and a fever. It was at the time of the SARS epidemic and while I was fairly certain his illness was not SARS, many of the symptoms were the same and we were afraid he would be quarantined and removed from the ship if he went to the sick bay. So he just toughed it out and I brought him food from the buffet. He never got off the ship. It was a disappointment for him but it was also the beginning of his own downward health spiral.

Soon it was apparent that his time was coming. He enrolled in the liver transplant program at Cedars-Sinai, hoping he could get a transplant closer to home and not have to travel so far. When I was seeking a transplant, Cedars-Sinai would not consider me because I did not meet their criteria. By the time John needed his transplant, they had changed their criteria and John met the requirements. He enrolled in the program, but I don't think Cedars-Sinai ever thought they would give him a new liver. What I believe they did get was a significant amount of money per patient from the National Institutes of Health for their HIV positive transplant program *study*. John would become a part of the study—and a part of Cedars cash flow, something that would continue for years.

John complied with everything. He was optimistic and wanted to be in Los Angeles for his surgery. After two years in their transplant program, he fell out of the criteria by a small change in his lab numbers and they dropped him. He went in for a regular clinic visit and was asked what he was doing there. It was so cold, so callous, and, I felt, so related to the money they were getting from the NIH. Cedars would no longer get the reimbursement for John because, by the rigid standards of the NIH, he no longer qualified for the study. His HIV viral load was not undetectable. It was miniscule, but the NIH study required it to be undetectable. John was apoplectic. He had invested two years of his life waiting. He did everything they asked and they just unceremoniously dumped him.

I called Cedars-Sinai and spoke to the head of the transplant department, Dr. Fred Poordad. I explained how upset John was. Dr. Poordad said, very calmly, "Why don't you two come in for a meeting." Two days later, we were escorted into a conference room. Dr. Poordad came in with Kristen Baker, one of the transplant coordinators (I later realized this was to have a witness for legal protection). John presented his case; that he had been compliant, followed every request and that, after all, his HIV viral load was incredibly low. Poordad then went into a song and dance that they couldn't take the risk and waste an organ on someone who still had a detectable viral load. At that point I spoke up and said that I had been transplanted in Pittsburgh five years earlier with a very high viral load. Dr. Fred Poordad, chief of the liver transplant department turned, looked at me, his eyes like steel, and said—and this is an exact quote—"So what, Doug, God loves you." There is nothing like the ego of a transplant surgeon. No one challenges them, and if you do, expect no mercy.

Ultimately it was a blessing in disguise. If John had held on for a liver transplant from Cedars-Sinai, he would have died waiting. Instead he went to the Cleveland Clinic. The two surgeons who had done my transplant at the University of Pittsburgh Medical Center had both moved to the Cleveland Clinic. It was still not easy and it took another year and a half and many trips to Cleveland, but ultimately John got his transplant on Valentine's Day, 2008 performed by the same surgeons who had done mine in 2002.

John's moment for accepting an organ occurred at a particularly inopportune time. I had been with him in Cleveland for several weeks. He had been hospitalized. His condition was declining. He was too sick to be transplanted. That is the catch-22 of transplants; if you're not sick enough you can't get a transplant but if you're too sick you can't get one either. John had a fever and it ruled out an immediate operation.

Meanwhile, I was still trying to meet as many of my travelogue lecture dates as I could. I had to cancel a lot, but I had an important series of shows in Seattle and Portland. I asked the doctor if John was likely to die in the next four days and he said, "No." I asked if he was likely to get an organ and be well enough to be transplanted in the next four days and again he said, "No." So I went to the airport and flew off to Seattle to do three shows, then drove to Portland to do the final show. I got up the next morning to drive back to Seattle and catch a flight back to Cleveland. On the way my cellphone rang. It was John. He was very anxious. They had found an organ and he had to accept it or reject it in the next hour. The surgery would take place that night. I said, "Take it" and sped ahead to ninety miles an hour (it's amazing I didn't get a ticket). I ran into the Seattle airport, shoved myself to the front of the ticket line, and pleaded my case. "Get me on the next flight to Cleveland." The airline people were great, they told me to hurry to a gate; a flight to Minneapolis was leaving in twenty minutes.

I grabbed the ticket and rushed to security. Again, long lines, I went to the front and I don't remember what I said but I was allowed through and I made the flight as they were closing the door. I changed planes in Minneapolis and arrived in Cleveland at 11:15 p.m. It was snowing hard, I grabbed the first cab I could see and said, "The Cleveland Clinic… fast." We arrived in about twenty minutes; I paid the driver and went running into the building. It was nearly midnight. I came flying out of the elevator, out of breath, and there was John, on a gurney, ready to be taken into the O.R. I held his hand, looked into his eyes, and told him everything would be all right. They wheeled him off and I went to a waiting room to sit up all night. Finally, about 11:30 a.m. Dr. John Fung and Dr. Bijan Eghtesad came out. They told me the surgery was successful and I could see John in the ICU in twenty minutes. I went in, he was still heavily sedated but he managed a smile and I thought: How many couples can claim the same organ transplant and the same team of surgeons? Not many.

John's recovery in Cleveland was fairly rapid because he had not been as sick as me when his transplant occurred. I spent twelve weeks in the hospital in Pittsburgh. John was discharged after fourteen days. I thought it was too early, but John wanted to leave the hospital and who could blame him. We had rented a small apartment in Cleveland Heights, so I took him to his new Cleveland home—and then it started to snow—one of the biggest blizzards Cleveland had seen in years. We were trapped but John continued to improve (in spite of the fact that I was doing the cooking and I am the worst cook in the world).

We stayed in Cleveland another six weeks. John made many trips back to the clinic for checkups. On a Thursday, a month after his surgery, I took him in to see Dr. Eghtesad. John was not scheduled back to see the doctor again until the following Tuesday. I asked, in passing, if, given how well John was doing, I could maybe take him on a short out of town trip for the weekend. The doctor looked surprised but said he saw no reason why not.

John and I left the clinic, our bags were already packed, we didn't even return to the Cleveland apartment. We got in our rented Volvo and sped off to the Ohio Turnpike—our destination was New York City—700 miles away. We fled Cleveland like two prisoners on a jailbreak. We spent the night in Pennsylvania at some cheap motel, and the next morning drove on, finally crossing the George Washington Bridge. I looked over and John had a smile on his face. I pulled up to our apartment building on east 72nd Street, our doorman Tony was shocked to see John but helped him into the lobby while I parked the car.

Of course, we came all this way to see Broadway shows. As curtain time approached, our doorman hailed us a cab and off we went into the heart of Times Square. John was using a cane. We got into the mass of traffic at 7:45 as people are coming out of the subway, getting out of cabs, walking, all heading to theaters with eight o'clock curtain times. We were stuck at

John leaving the Cleveland Clinic on February 28, 2008 after undergoing his own liver transplant with the same team of surgeons I had.

47th and Seventh Avenue. John said, "Doug, pay the driver," and proceeded to get out of the cab. We were going to the Belasco Theater on 44th Street east of Seventh Avenue. John pushed ahead waving his cane, determined to make it to the theater on time. We were seeing a play called *Passing Strange*, written by the musician and performance artist Stew (quite good, I might add). We got to the theater just as the curtain was going up; John forged ahead down the aisle and took his seat. At that moment, I knew John was back. I knew he was going to recover, I knew our life ahead would be great and filled with excitement and fun.

And it was.

* * *

John had always been politically active. He was one of the original members of ACT-UP (Aids Coalition To Unleash Power), a rowdy group of rabble-rousers who sometimes did outrageous things, but a group that finally got the attention of the public and the drug companies and even the government. ACT-UP was instrumental in getting promising drugs to market and changing the face of the AIDS epidemic. John did every gay rights march for every cause—ever. I was in agreement with him on most things, but I was less proactive.

After the fight to get medical attention for the epidemic that had decimated our community, the next issue that came to the top was legal rights, meaning, among other things, marriage. Many people don't understand why marriage meant so much to the LGBT community. *It's about the money*. Marriage is a legal contract and it comes with many legal benefits. Gay people had to fight for everything from visiting someone in a hospital to rightfully inheriting property.

In 2004, California introduced domestic partnership. It was "marriage-lite." It conferred state legal rights but no federal rights. In reality, all the rights that were most important were federal. When domestic partnership became an option, John and I agreed it was the right thing to do. All it involved was filling out a form, having it notarized, and returning it the state. We got our domestic partnership notarized at a UPS Box Store. John was driving and I kept singing in the car, "I'm getting married in the morning, ding dong the bells are gonna chime... get me to the box store on time!" We had a celebratory lunch. California is a community property state so what was mine was now his and vice versa—and the debts and obligations became joint as well.

Our wedding day, September 20, 2008.

In 2008, the California Supreme Court ruled that it was unconstitutional to deny same sex couples the right to marry. In June, marriage was opened to LGBT people in California. I don't recall asking John to marry me, nor him asking me, I just remember him running around the house, calling his friends, and announcing we were going to have a September wedding. We decided on Saturday, September 20th and started planning the affair. If we were going to do it, we were going to do it right: a big garden wedding in our backyard in Hancock Park.

For anyone who has ever planned a wedding, you know there are a thousand things to do. In most weddings, the bride and her mother will do the bulk of the planning. But like decorating our first Christmas tree, I can't tell you how much tension a wedding between two men can produce. It started over the typeface for the invitation. It took a week to resolve that matter alone. By the time the wedding approached, there had been nothing that hadn't been negotiated to death. Two days before the wedding, we spent an hour at a paper supply house negotiating the paper stock we were going to use for the program. It was that kind of craziness. And to make it even more complicated, I was loosely an Episcopalian and John was a Nichiren Buddhist, so the whole service had to be woven into something that covered everything and everybody.

But the day of the wedding came, the guests arrived, our friends Neil Tadken, an Episcopal priest, and Nicole Angileri, a Nichiren Buddhist, were ready to perform the inter-faith wedding. We walked down the garden aisle to Marilyn Maye singing "Good Morning my Dear, I Love You Today," vows were said, rings were exchanged, tears were shed, cheers went up, and we were married. John always said it was the happiest day of his life.

Our honeymoon was a trip to London on the final crossing of the *Queen Elizabeth 2*. The *QE2* was finally being taken out of service after forty years of continuous sailing. She sailed for Cunard longer than any other ship they ever owned and now Cunard was selling her to the government of Dubai where she would end up as a museum and hotel (a plan which remains on hold to this day). For me, it was bittersweet. It would be the final time I sailed on this ship that had taken me around the world.

John and I had a nice cabin booked by our travel agent Suzie Fisch. We were in the Britannia Grill at a table for eight. We walked in the first night and there were four women, two were friends from the U.K. on holiday whose husbands were at home, the other two were a mother and daughter from Augusta, Georgia. John and I sat down. Two seats remained empty. Conversation started and was slightly awkward, as it often is the first night out. The presidential election between Barrack Obama and John McCain was approaching in a few weeks. The mother from Georgia decided to speak up and say that she had sent in her ballot and she had voted for Obama.

The *Queen Mary 2* and the *Queen Elizabeth 2* depart New York in tandem for the final crossing of the *QE2*. John and I were onboard the *QE2*. October 2008. Photo courtesy of the Cunard Line.

Both mother and daughter turned out to be liberals and good conversationalists. This allowed the Brits to both speak up and say how much they loved "Mr. Obama" and how they never could understand "Mr. Bush." So all was well, six like-minded people setting sail from New York. Finally, the other two seats were about to be occupied. Two men walked in, obviously gay (one was the former city manager of West Hollywood). They sat down and John and I thought how great, two other gay men. One of the British women looked at the new tablemates and said, "And are you excited about Mr. Obama?" and the younger of the two said, "Hell no! He's going to put us all into concentration camps!" (Where this came from is still baffling. What kind of reasoning goes into such a comment?) Our two gay tablemates were to the political right of Attila the Hun. I was aghast. How could these two men who had watched the last president try to pass a constitutional amendment denying us marriage rights be so hateful toward the first presidential candidate who had spoken out for us? Like most things, it was about money. They were very well heeled and were far more concerned about their bank balance than anything else. Each night, six of us would come in early and talk up a storm about politics and world affairs and then the two guys would come in late and conversation would turn to topics like weather and sports.

John and I flew back to Los Angeles from London, and we arrived home about a week before the election. Things were looking good for Obama but they were not looking good for us. After the California Supreme Court struck down the laws that prevented same sex marriage, a group, largely funded by a coalition of churches, got an initiative on the California ballot called Proposition 8. The proposition would prohibit same sex marriage in California through a popular vote of the people. The LGBT community was blindsided by the proposition and disorganized in how to fight it. They chose the wrong approach. They should have argued it as an issue of love and family. Instead they argued it as a civil rights issue.

On the night of the election, John and I watched the returns. At eleven o'clock Obama was declared the winner, at 11:02 it was announced that Proposition 8 had passed. I don't ever recall a time in my life going from elation to depression so fast. The first African-American president had just been elected, and the citizens of our state had just declared our marriage void.

Ultimately, the issue would go back to the courts. The California Supreme Court, which had initially said the denial of the right was unconstitutional, said the issue had been presented to the voters and the voters had passed it. The Court allowed it to stand—but—and it was a big "but"—the sixteen thousand couples (which included John and me) who had married would remain legally married.

Numerous books have been written on the subject as it wound back through the legal system. Finally, in 2013, Proposition 8 was declared dead in California and same sex marriages resumed. More importantly, in the Windsor case, the Supreme Court overturned the Defense of Marriage Act (passed under President Clinton) as unconstitutional. DOMA, as it was called, denied all federal rights and benefits to same sex couples. The ruling against DOMA finally ended the federal policy of not recognizing couples like us. John and I had remained legally married through it all and now we had all state and federal rights. And then, in June of 2015, the Supreme Court ruled that all laws banning same sex marriage were unconstitutional and the long fought struggle was over once and for all.

After the passage of Prop 8 in California there was hurt, bewilderment, and anger. One of the many rallies that took place which we participated in. 2008.

CHAPTER THIRTY-NINE

THE UNEXPECTED TURNS OF LIFE

So I was married. John's health was good, as was mine. We were enjoying our lives, but John felt a lack of purpose. He didn't feel like returning to his demanding job, but he couldn't quite figure out what he wanted to do. After my own transplant, it was making the film on the *Queen Mary 2* that motivated me back to living a full life. For John, it would be college.

John had not completed a university degree. Growing up on a farm in Lancaster County, Pennsylvania, he wanted to go to college. He was accepted to Penn State but he needed money, so he made a deal with his father to milk the cows morning and night for the whole summer, freeing his seven siblings to do other things, and in exchange his father would give him one thousand dollars to pay his first year tuition. John would get up at five in the morning and milk forty cows. They had milking machines but it was still a lot of work. He would then herd the cows out to the pasture and at five o'clock in the afternoon, he would herd them all back to the barn and repeat the process. He did this from the end of May in 1970 until Labor Day. He was ready to leave for school the next week. He went to his father, proud that he had fulfilled his commitment and earned his first year tuition, and his father looked at him and said, "I'm not going to give you the money; college is a waste of time."

John was dumbfounded. Though looking back, his father had gotten all of his other sons to drop out of high school to work on the farm. There was no appreciation of education in the family; there was, in fact, an open hostility toward it. John's father expected him to work on the farm for the rest of his life. Why did he need a college degree? He cheated his son.

After Paul Sanger reneged on his promise, John was unable to enroll at Penn State. So he got into his battered Gremlin and set off driving west. And he just kept driving until he reached L.A. He had a sister, Rachel, in Los Angeles and he knew California (at the time) offered free college to residents. He moved in with his sister and enrolled at Los Angeles City College. But his money for daily living expenses ran out quickly and he had to go back to work. Over the years he would take night classes and try to continue his studies, but work prevented him from ever getting a degree.

After several years in the accounting department at Capitol Records, he took a position at l.a.Eyeworks, eventually becoming their chief financial officer. John had extensive accounting experience because his father was an auctioneer and John did much of the bookkeeping for the auction sales. l.a.Eyeworks became his life. The company, started by Barbara McReynolds, Gai Gherardi, and Margo Willits was one of the leading fashion eyewear design firms in the world. The employees were treated like family. John was respected and appreciated. He found a home and a family that loved him. He stayed with them for over twenty years until his health declined.

He could have gone back to work after his transplant, but I encouraged him to go back to school and get his bachelor's degree. So he enrolled at California State University Los Angeles in the theater department and began work on his B.A. It was the happiest I had ever seen him. He flourished in the academic world. He was cast in various plays; he loved to act. He played Uncle John in *The Grapes of Wrath*, Captain Brice in *Arcadia*, Le Grue in *Red Noses*, the Trader in *American Pilot*, and his favorite role, Mr. Maraczek in *She Loves Me*.

At times I felt ignored because he was so involved in university life. Our travel had to be planned around the academic calendar, and when he wasn't rehearsing he was reading and writing papers. I would go to bed night after night while he stayed up until dawn working on class projects. But watching him blossom late in life (he was fifty-nine when he went back to school) was worth it. In 2012 he graduated Magna Cum Laude with a Bachelor's Degree in Theater.

But I had little to do. Since John was so preoccupied with school, I decided to start work on a project I had long considered but kept putting off: a retrospective film of my forty years of filmmaking. It would be a look back on my life of travel and how the world had changed. I shot no new footage for the picture, but it ended up being the most complex film project I ever did. I looked back through forty years of film, much of which I had not seen in decades. Reels of film were brought out of the Pacific Title Archive film vault. I oversaw film-to-digital transfers of early footage from the 1960s and 1970s. Some of the film needed restoration work. It was a big undertaking and an unexpected review of my life. As I looked at footage I hadn't seen in decades, I remembered events that surrounded each film shoot, both good and bad. When the film was finally completed (the rough cut was five hours long and had to be trimmed down to 95 minutes), I had to choose a title. I settled on *Around the World–One Man's Journey*.

I had cut back on my travelogue lecture tours largely because I had no new films to offer, but my memoir film gave one final boost to my lecture career. As John was starting his senior year at Cal State L.A., I went back out on the road with my "new" film and again stood on stage night after night. The audiences were smaller and the auditoriums were not the grand theaters I had once worked in, but there were still enough shows to do one final tour.

And of course I flew the Cessna. As I made each landing and takeoff in cities across America, I realized I was probably doing it for the last time. It was going to be difficult to justify the cost of the plane once my lecture tour was over.

I had some intense flying experiences during that final tour. I left Burbank one day heading to Rochester, Minnesota. Out over the Arizona desert, weather started building in front of me. I kept diverting to the south trying to steer around it, but finally I had to cross the Rockies at Albuquerque and I had to enter the clouds. They were icy so I asked Air Traffic Control for "higher" and went up another 2,000 feet and I was on top again at 15,000, but the cloud layer was rising ahead. I finally got to 18,000 feet and my plane, which was not turbo-charged, could go no higher. The clouds were coming in under me and I was soon in a solid layer. I looked out at the wings and ice was staring to form on the leading edge. I had already crossed the Rockies so the decision at this point was to go down to a lower altitude where I would lose the ice. ATC stayed with me as I managed a fairly rapid decent at 2,000 feet a minute. The ice continued to build and every minute or so I would hit the toggle switch that inflated the rubber de-icing boots. I finally came out of the clouds but I was far off course and ended up landing in Liberal, Kansas to fuel. Not wanting to spend the night there, I continued on. I was flying into a rare northeast headwind, which slowed me down and I didn't have enough fuel to make Rochester so I landed in Sioux Falls, South Dakota. I was tired so I checked into a hotel and figured I would fly the final short leg to Rochester the next morning. At the time I left the airplane on the ground in Sioux Falls, there wasn't even the rustle of a breeze. I had dinner and slept soundly.

The following morning, I got up and the windows in the hotel were rattling. Outside were gale force winds out of the west at 35 knots gusting to 45. If I had only gone on the night before... But it was too late to consider that lost option. I had to get to my show that night and I didn't want to abandon the plane and drive because I was continuing on to Milwaukee. Takeoff was manageable because the winds were coming pretty much straight down the runway, but landing was going to be dicey. Rochester had only one north-south runway and the expected winds at Rochester were going to be 40 knots gusting to 45 out of the west-northwest, a serious crosswind condition. The flight was bumpy but I had a massive tailwind and I was approaching Rochester in no time. The winds had shifted slightly but it was still going to be a major crosswind landing. I opted to head the plane straight in on final approach with one wing down and the rudder pedal hard to the right. It's a delicate move with little room for error. As the runway got close, I held the rudder, flared, then put the nose down and quickly got control of the plane on the landing roll. Intense as the experience was, as a pilot it is satisfying to do a complex landing.

I made my way on to Portland, Maine over the course of two months, landing and doing shows along the way. By early May I had done my last travelogue lecture and it was time to head back to L.A. I was going to stop in Kansas City for a few days to visit my alma mater UMKC and attend commencement. At takeoff in Portland, the ceiling was only 300 feet. Heavy fog and rain made landing conditions at the field poor, but it's fairly easy to takeoff in a low ceiling and just fly into the clouds. I knew I would break out into clear skies at about 4,000 feet. Once I was on top of the clouds, I headed toward Buffalo. Another weather front was ahead and I had to get through that as well. I finally got on top at 12,000 feet and I was in the clear from there to Ohio. It was now late in the afternoon, and it was spring; and that means thunderstorms. I flew parallel to a line of developing thunderstorms about ten miles to the north. I was flying parallel to the line and it was one of the most amazing shows of nature I have ever seen as thunderheads built up off my right wing, towering to 40,000 feet. The thunderheads were blazing white, and under the anvils the sky was black and I could see the pouring rain. It was nature at its most dramatic and it was moments like this that made being a pilot so cool.

Finally, with the sun having set and nightfall upon me, I circled from the south to land at downtown Kansas City; the giant TV antenna of the CBS affiliate, one of the tallest in the country, was clearly visible as I skirted around the tower and headed toward the junction of the Kansas and Missouri Rivers and set the airplane down on Runway 1. I had made it halfway across the country that day. I checked in to the Aladdin Hotel ready for a good night's sleep.

The following day, I was escorted around the University of Missouri-Kansas City. The University hosted me for commencement and I was shown the changes that had occurred in the forty years since I graduated. I am proud of my alma mater and feel that UMKC was, and remains, a great Midwestern university.

From Kansas City I flew on to Los Angeles by way of Colorado Springs and the Grand Canyon. Landing at Burbank completed my 58th coast-to-coast flight in N9924F, my Cessna 310. It was quite an accomplishment for someone who didn't learn to fly until he was forty.

But finances were closing in. My lecture fees had plummeted, the stock footage business had changed, and now shots sold for a fraction of what they once did. Videotape was gone and DVD's were being replaced by online streaming, which pays only pennies to the intellectual property owner. In other words, I was living way beyond my means. It was time to make some serious changes.

The first was to sell the Rossmore house in Hancock Park. I loved that home. It had been the scene of countless parties and many happy occasions, but maintaining it was costly. I put it up for sale. The house had increased in value since I bought it, but I was trying to sell during the serious real estate slump that followed the 2008 financial crash. It took almost a year. The day I handed over the keys was tough. The house represented so much of my life. John and I moved from Rossmore to a home in the hills of Los Feliz east of Hollywood. The house was smaller but it had a great view of the mountains and the city.

But the biggest decision was yet to come—selling the airplane. The plane was getting old. It was a 1974 model. The engines were 300-horsepower Continentals and they had 1,881 flying hours each. The engine manufacturer issues a TBO: "Time Between Overhaul." The TBO on these engines was 1,700 hours; they were almost two hundred hours past overhaul time. Overhaul is not a requirement, it is a recommendation, but high-time engines past TBO make a plane difficult to sell. Overhauls are extremely expensive. Plus the avionics needed to be upgraded and it needed a new paint job and a new interior. Overall, it needed a boatload of money spent on it and the cost of actually flying it had skyrocketed. It just didn't make financial sense to keep it.

So I put it on the market—and I overpriced it. Looking back, I overpriced it because I didn't want to sell it. Various people came and looked at it. I loved talking "airplane" with potential buyers and thoroughly enjoyed the *selling process*—as long as I didn't have to actually face *selling* it. Then someone came along and wanted it. He offered me less, I refused, and then he said he would pay the full price. I was stuck—or at least I felt I was stuck. The day of the sale I was to meet the buyer at a bank in Encino and oversee a wire transfer of the funds. Driving out on the Ventura Freeway, I got off at Laurel Canyon and started to head back home. I wanted to back out of the deal. I knew on some level it was a mistake to sell the plane. I waited in a parking lot for a few minutes but then changed my mind and continued on to the bank. The wire transfer was made and it was now time to deliver the plane. The buyer was not rated to fly a multi-engine plane so I took him to Burbank Airport and flew him to Ryan Field in Hemet, California where he was going to base the plane. Once on the ground, a Certified Flight Instructor (who was going to train the buyer to fly the plane) got onboard in the co-pilot seat, the buyer moved to a back, and I flew us back to Burbank; all the while explaining the various features of the plane. At Burbank I got out of the plane, the instructor moved into the pilot seat, and the buyer moved from the back to the front co-pilot seat. And *that* is when I made my fatal mistake. I should have just walked to my car and driven off—but I didn't. I sat down on a bench and watched my cherished Cessna 310 taxi to the end of Runway 8. Tower cleared them for takeoff and down the runway she rolled, lifting off and soaring into the sky. In 58 coast-to-coast trips and 2,975 hours of piloting, I had never seen her fly. I was always in the pilot seat. This was the first, final, and only chance I would have to see my flying machine in the air. And I will admit; I broke down and cried. In some ways it was more emotional than the death of my parents. I wasn't aware until I watched my Cessna 310 fly away how much of my self-identity was tied up in that plane and the fact that I was a licensed, instrument rated, multi-engine pilot who, for twenty-five years, who saw America from a front row seat at 12,000 feet.

Finally, with the Rossmore house sold and the airplane draining someone else's bank account, I felt that John and I could relax, and of course the first thing we did was take a big trip to Spain and Portugal. We stayed in Madrid a week and then took the high-speed train to Seville and rented a car, which we drove throughout southern Spain and on to Lisbon before returning to Madrid four weeks later. It was probably the best trip John and I ever took. I was not shooting film so I didn't have to worry about things like the weather. We loved Spain and Portugal and both of us were in great health and really enjoying our lives.

It would be the last overseas trip we would ever make.

Back in Los Angeles, John entered the master's program at Cal State L.A. The master's program (as anyone who has completed an MA will attest) was much harder than undergraduate work. John was a perfectionist and researched everything to death. He pushed himself beyond what I felt was wise. At one point I commented that he had had a liver transplant and he had been HIV positive for thirty years now and maybe he should take things a little easier.

It was normally a two-year program but he was trying to complete it in eighteen months. He had finished all of his coursework and the only thing that remained was his thesis. He was writing a thesis comparing *The Boys in the Band*, a play written by Mart Crowley in the 1960s, and *Love, Valor, Compassion*, written twenty-five years later by Terrance McNally. The thesis was to examine the cultural shift in gay identify between Stonewall and the beginning of gay liberation and the "end of the party" when AIDS began to take people down in the prime of life. *Love, Valor, Compassion* shows a community of people who have changed and matured and learned to care for each other, a major step forward from the self-loathing, closeted community of men depicted in *The Boys in the Band*. But it was a thesis that would never be completed.

On Thanksgiving Day in 2013, John and I were in Palm Springs to have dinner with our friends Tom Stonehouse and Jim Edwards. John had just finished his term papers and was deep into writing his thesis. He was in great spirits, the life of the party, his usual social self. We had arrived at three o'clock and left about seven . John said goodnight to the hosts, we both thanked them and got in the car. I said, "What a great Thanksgiving dinner." He agreed but added, "I'm not feeling well." I can still see his face as he uttered those words.

We went back to our weekend place in Palm Springs. He laid down on the bed and I felt his forehead. He had a fever—102 degrees. I gave him an icepack, some Tylenol, and I assumed it was just some twenty-four hour bug he had picked up. But the fevers continued through the night. There wasn't much to do until Monday morning other than go to an emergency room. The fevers worsened through the weekend. By Sunday night we decided to return early to Los Angeles. In L.A. the fevers would spike, lessen, then spike even higher. I took him to his doctor, Dale Prokupek, on Monday morning. Dale drew blood and sent us home, but I didn't think things looked good. We returned the following day and he said that John's was pancytopenic, which means all his blood counts had crashed. John was admitted to Cedars-Sinai, the same place that had tossed him off the transplant list in 2006. The doctors thought it was leukemia or lymphoma. A bone marrow biopsy was ordered but the bone marrow appeared to be fine. Blood cultures were drawn, every imaging test imaginable was done, test after test after test—and no conclusion. The doctors were unable to figure out what was causing the low blood counts. Units of whole blood and platelets were poured into him but nothing helped. He entered the hospital on December 2nd; he was discharged on Christmas Eve at 9:00 p.m. with no diagnosis and no answers. He remained home through the holidays. On January 2nd his fevers started going back up and I took him back to Cedars-Sinai for a second admission. All of the tests were repeated and still there were no answers. On January 17th he was discharged to in-home hospice care. The hospital had done all they could but there were still no answers as to what was wrong. The hospice people came, papers were signed, the nurse would stop by three times a week, and the rest of his care was in my hands.

And then to everyone's surprise, he started getting better—a lot better. The fevers went away, he started getting more energy, his mood improved, and I thought, once again, he was going to beat whatever was tormenting his body. We both agreed he might as well go off of hospice because he was clearly getting better. Hospice was stopped and he immediately started doing things, driving, cooking, shopping; he was on the mend. We went down to Palm Springs for ten days. Back in L.A. we saw two operas, *Lucia de Lammermoor* and *Billy Budd*, and the Barry Manilow musical *Harmony* all in the same week. He was back. Or so I hoped.

John had about six great weeks. Then on March 17th he went to his doctor. Dale Prokupek was astounded at how well he looked. John said he felt good, had more energy, and was even considering going back to the gym. He only had one small complaint, a little nodule between his teeth on his lower gum and he was going to see the dentist the next day. The doctor said, "Let me take a look." John pulled his lip down, the doctor looked at it and I watched the blood drain out of his face. He said, "It's Kaposi sarcoma."

No two words ever brought as much dread to gay men in the early days of the AIDS epidemic as "Kaposi sarcoma." KS is a disfiguring disease of purple lesions. It was originally called the "gay cancer" and, in fact, is a type of cancer of the blood vessels. KS was thought to have been vanquished with the new HIV drugs in the mid-1990s. Most doctors today have never seen it. John's HIV viral load was undetectable, and his T-cell counts were actually higher than usual. Why did he have this horrible, awful, opportunistic disease that once terrorized the gay community?

Because his blood counts were so low, chemotherapy was not an option. It was decided to do radiation. He had ten treatments and he was healthy enough to drive himself to the first seven. But then the illness took over. In just a few weeks' time, the Kaposi sarcoma had spread.

There was no answer. He never left the house again except to see doctors. His breathing worsened. On April 29th I took him back to the hospital because he was in respiratory distress. It was clear that he was not going to recover. He was started on morphine and plans were made to discharge him back to in-home hospice care. He returned home by ambulance. He was too weak for me to be able to drive him. He was carried into our home, the hospice nurse was there; he was nearing the end.

The next afternoon at 3:30 p.m. the house was empty. It was just the two of us, and our pug Dexter. I held his hand; I got close to his face and said, "I love you." For five seconds he opened his eyes—and then they closed and he was gone.

We all want to think that AIDS is really over in America; that HIV is a chronic treatable condition that is more of a nuisance than anything else.

I watched my husband, John Sanger, die of AIDS related complications, Kaposi sarcoma—and the date was May 6, 2014. AIDS is not gone. It really never went away.

John Dennis Sanger, December 19, 1951–May 6, 2014.

EPILOGUE

Following John's death I was numb with grief. But death requires a lot of attention and I was thrown in a whirlwind of phone calls, faxes, emails, letters, and legal forms that would consume me for months.

I planned his memorial service, which was held at Saint James in Los Angeles on June 7, 2014. He was well liked, about a hundred and forty people attended, including a lot of students and faculty from Cal State L.A. Individuals from the various spheres of John's life spoke, Neil Tadken, our Episcopal priest friend who married us, delivered the homily. To honor John's Buddhist traditions, an incense ceremony was incorporated into the service. People walked forward, took a pinch of incense from a bowl and dropped it into the burner beside a large portrait of John, and as the smoke climbed up into the rafters of the nave, each person said a silent prayer, remembered, smiled, cried, the emotions were all over the place. I had only expected John's Buddhist friends to participate but everyone went forward, making the service far longer than I had planned (one friend said it was the only memorial service he had ever been to that needed an intermission). It was touching to watch all these people of John's life, my life, and our life, come up and pay a final tribute.

After the various remembrances, and Neil's homily, I got up to deliver my eulogy. I had, over a career of forty years, given over 6,000 live-lectures, almost 12,000 hours of public speaking. But this was the hardest public speaking assignment of my life. I had rehearsed the eulogy until I knew it by heart. I didn't want to break down. I wanted to be strong for John. As I began, a peace settled over me, and the words flowed out with ease.

It may seem like an odd way to conclude my memoir and some of these stories have already been covered earlier in the book, but this is what I said.

TRAVELOGUE

Hello, I'm Doug Jones, John's husband.

John Sanger and I met, December the 15th 2000. We met through a dating service. Before computer dating became popular, John and I used a service called Romeo 2, I have no idea what the 2 stood for but they claimed to have a software program that could produce the perfect date. John and I later believed their complex algorithm consisted of writing our names on darts and giving them to monkeys to throw at a wall. I was going to cancel the last date, which was with John, but it was just dinner and I was on my way to the Burbank airport to fly to Palm Springs, so why not?

I walked into a restaurant in Silverlake. Seated in the back was a handsome brooding man with a stylish goatee, two earrings, and hair color that—even though I am colorblind—I suspected was not God-given.

We discovered that we had a lot in common; travel, opera, theater, even flying; John had taking flying lessons as a kid. It was not love at first sight but it was good enough to warrant a second date. I left the restaurant and walked to my car.

A couple of years ago I asked John what he thought as I walked away that night. I expected him to say something to the effect of, "I was impressed you were flying your plane to Palm Springs," but no, John paused and said, "Well I thought... a little bowlegged."

On our second date we went to a movie. As the film started John reached over and took my hand. And from that moment on our second date, to the very last breath of his life—holding hands, would define who we were. We held hands in the movies, at the theater, at the opera, on airplanes. We didn't do it in an obvious way, we did it surreptitiously, but we always did it.

John and I had an incredible first year together, truly magical. But then I became sick—and then John became sick. Illness became a constant companion.

Through all these years of bad health we lived each day as though it were our last. We traveled in spite of sickness, we went to theater and opera at times when we should have gone to the E.R., but we pushed ahead and tried to make every moment count.

In September 2008 we were married. John said it was the happiest day of his life. And shortly after he returned to the university to complete his studies. He was an academic at heart. He flourished in the university environment. He got his Bachelor's degree in theater and entered the master's program. He would have completed it this winter were it not for his illness.

EPILOGUE

John became sick on Thanksgiving Day. He had a rebound in February and March and I thought he was going to pull through again. Countless people, many sitting here today, helped. You brought food, visited John in the hospital, and stayed with him at home for a couple of hours so I could get a short break. As I look out I see friends and family who went out of their way—and to each of you I say a deep and heartfelt thanks.

John died from complications of AIDS on Tuesday, May the 6th at home. It was just John, me, and Dexter our pug. The Sunday before John died he was still in Cedars-Sinai. I felt it was all right to slip away and come here to church. Father Tom delivered the sermon. It was based on a gospel reading about Jesus revealing himself to the living on Easter morning. Frankly, with all due respect to Tom, I didn't really pay much attention to the sermon. I had a million things churning through my mind. But at the very end of the sermon, Tom looked out at the congregation and said, "Where will you see the face of Christ today?"

This brought to mind a story. The story does not reflect well on me, but it says a lot about John.

John had returned from visiting some people that, frankly I didn't care for very much. He was sitting in the kitchen reading the paper, I was puttering around and turned to him and said, "I just don't understand why you hang out with those losers."

John looked at me, paused, and said, "Well, didn't Jesus hang out with losers?" And of course he was right. Jesus did hang out with losers, the poor, the sick, Samaritans, and shepherds. Jesus hung out with a lot of losers.

And it was in that moment that I realized that John Sanger, true to his Buddhist practices and principles to the end of his life, was, in point of fact, the most Christ-like man I ever knew.

I left the church that morning and went to Cedars-Sinai, those final words of Tom's sermon ringing in the back of my mind. I walked into John's room, sat down beside him, took his hand, and looked into his face—and I saw the face of Christ, the face of the Buddha, the face of God—for after all, what is God, if not the power of love.

And as I look out over all of you who have come here today to honor John, I see in each of you the face of God, for what I see are faces filled with love.

Rest in peace John. I will join you in a future day and together we will once again hold hands and walk The Great White Way.

TRAVELOGUE

As I finish this book I am onboard a ship sailing off the North Cape of Norway. What lies ahead? I have no idea. But if the rest of my life is anything like the first 68 years, I will have more stories to tell.

Doug Jones
Onboard the M.S. *Rotterdam* in the Arctic Ocean

POSTSCRIPT:

Two things:
First: It will come as no surprise that I bought another airplane. Another twin Cessna 310, an R model, N168ED, which I continue to fly between New York and L.A. I just couldn't keep my head of out the clouds. Second: In late May of 2016, two years after John's death, I got a note from Shiz Herrera. Shiz had been John's faculty advisor at Cal State LA. She was the first person John met on the campus and the two of them hit it off immediately.

Unbeknownst to me, Shiz and several of John's professors joined together and petitioned the provost of the university to grant John his Master's in Theater degree posthumously. They felt he had done the work and was so close to finishing his thesis that he deserved it. In early June, the president of Cal State LA, William Covino, signed the papers approving the posthumous awarding of the degree. And Shiz continued: "Would you like to come to commencement and receive it on his behalf?"

On Saturday, June 11, 2016, as Cal State LA graduated 8,000 students, I was taken to the commencement dais and an announcement was made that The California State University Los Angeles was presenting to John Dennis Sanger, posthumously, the degree Master's in Theater and that it would be accepted by his husband Doug Jones. There was a cheer that went up in the stadium, President Covino handed me the diploma, Dean Peter McAllister and four of John's professors shook my hand.

To use a Yiddish phrase, I was a bit verklempt.

So John, you got your Master's, and most importantly, the people whose lives you touched remember you at Cal State LA.

Commencement, Cal State L.A. Receiving John's posthumously awarded Master of Theater diploma. 2016.

My new wings. N168ED, a Cessna 310R. 2015.

Still flying high. 2016. Photo by Roxanna Harvey.

TRAVELOGUE MAKERS AND PRESENTERS OF ANOTHER TIME

One of the purposes of writing this book is to preserve some of the history of this form of entertainment that is in its final days. There are still about a hundred travelogue series scattered across America. By the time you read this book that number will have dwindled. The travelogue business is a shadow of what it was at its peak in the 1970s and 1980s when there were over ten thousand individual travelogue shows across North American. The reasons for its decline are obvious. It is no longer necessary to go to a lecture hall, listen to a speaker, and watch a film to learn about places. But for decades it was an important source of information about travel and world culture for American audiences. Like any business, it had its stars and lesser-known personalities. What follows covers a patchwork of different people.

BURTON HOLMES

No discussion of the history of this business would be complete without acknowledging the father of the live-lecture travelogue, Burton Holmes.

Burton Holmes was born in Chicago in 1870. Booth Tarkington once said of his fellow Hoosier, Cole Porter that, "He was not born with a silver spoon in his mouth but rather service for twelve." The same could be said of Holmes. He was born into wealth. He had wanderlust and family money made it possible to fulfill those dreams. He traveled all over the world when such travel was rare, even for the affluent. He would go for extended periods of time, living in places like Japan and Ethiopia, cultures that were only seen by true adventurers in the 19th century.

He had an interest in the relatively new art form of photography and he would shoot pictures of his adventures using a bulky box camera. He returned to Chicago and had the idea of showing his photographs and speaking about his travels. His first performances as an illustrated travel lecturer were for carefully selected women from his mother's social circle. He was charming, the women loved him, and what started out as a novel avocation for a wealthy scion of Chicago society gradually grew into a thriving business.

Holmes was not the first travel lecturer. John Stoddard had a large following throughout America. Stoddard would hold audiences in rapt attention with tales of travel using photographic illustrations on the stage. Holmes, by chance, ran into Stoddard while traveling in Europe and latched onto him. Stoddard liked the dapper young Holmes and one day announced, with no warning, that he was quitting the lecture business. Holmes was waiting in the wings (not unlike Ruby Keeler in *42nd Street*) and picked up John Stoddard's business overnight. In those days, the programs were held in large city auditoriums and involved showing glass slides using the "magic lantern." The glass slides were painstakingly hand tinted. Burton Holmes had several artists who worked like minions using tiny brushes to add color to the black and white glass images that he would bring back from his travels. Early in his career, he was giving a program for the Chicago Camera Club when he came up with the name "Travelogue". He coined the term and it has stuck for over a century.

Eventually motion picture technology arrived and Holmes hired a cameraman and they would return with rolls of 35mm film. These images were cut into new programs and Holmes would head out onto the lecture circuit with new tales of adventure from the far corners of the globe. He started his annual lecture tour with a one-week engagement at Carnegie Hall.

No one else ever really achieved his level of fame. He was a true personality, an American household name. People wanted to see the films, but mostly they wanted to see and hear the man. Holmes had a dynamic way of capturing an audience's attention and holding it for a full evening of entertainment.

Holmes had his own organization, Burton Holmes International. They would "four-wall" the shows. The advance men would go out and rent the halls, place the advertising, arrange for publicity, and get the ticket agencies geared up to sell the tickets. It was not unlike a concert promoter today. Holmes also published his lectures in sets of books that were illustrated with his still photographs. Over 150,000 sets were sold and the books were his most profitable venture.

Holmes was perceived to be a great success, but his privileged background made him a poor money manager and he relied on others to handle his financial affairs. He made and lost several fortunes in his years of presenting travelogues.

He owned a stunning duplex apartment in Manhattan on Central Park West. He had a passion for collecting Buddhas and the apartment was filled with them. His maid called the place "Buddha-pest." There are photos of Holmes lounging in a kimono in his apartment that looked like it had been transported from the Great Far East.

He lost the apartment in a bankruptcy sale. Robert Ripley of *Ripley's Believe it or Not* newspaper fame bought it, and Holmes headed to Hollywood where he would remain for the rest of his life. He bought a house at the top of Whitley Heights, he was accepted into Hollywood circles, and he seemed content to make California his final home.

On Hollywood Boulevard he has a star on the Hollywood Walk of Fame. He was the only travelogue lecturer to achieve that honor.

THAYER SOULE

Thayer Soule was Burton Holmes protégé. Thayer was also my mentor and the travelogue maker who helped me the most in establishing my own career.

Thayer grew up in Rochester, New York and was surrounded by photography in the hometown of Kodak. He went to Harvard, spoke fluent French, and like Holmes, had wanderlust. Thayer met Burton Holmes on a trip to Europe and Holmes took a fancy to him, much like John Stoddard had done with Holmes himself. In time, Thayer became Burton Holmes' right hand man. While on a filming trip with Holmes to the Mountains of the Moon in Uganda, he met Nancy, who would become his wife and mother of their two children, Cindy and Robin.

Thayer was interwoven into the whole Burton Holmes operation. He did much of the shooting using a Kodak Cine Special. By the time Thayer arrived, the Holmes operation was shooting 16mm color film. The bulky 35mm cameras were put into storage and the new 16mm cameras were considered a wonder—not unlike modern digital cameras are today. Thayer would work in the editing room getting the new show ready for the fall lecture tour, and in time Thayer was sent out to do the shows himself.

Thayer wanted more recognition and as the Holmes operation wound down in the mid-1950s, Thayer went out on his own. He established a solid career making over forty films and spending over fifty years on the travelogue circuit. His films documented many places that had not been filmed before but he also liked filming the known, popular destinations of the world.

One year, I was president of the travelogue trade association, INTRAFILM, and I was in charge of overseeing the annual convention. I asked Thayer to deliver the keynote speech. The day of the general meeting, Thayer got up and proceeded to tell a story of being at the Sundome outside of Phoenix watching a travelogue. At the intermission the two women next to him said, "Let's leave, this is boring." And Thayer, in his speech, said they were right. It was boring. The speaker had no life to his presentation. Thayer went on to talk about how, as travelogue makers, we often didn't deliver the dynamic shows the audience deserved. I kept thinking to myself that Thayer had seen me at the Sundome just a few weeks before. Was he talking about me? Afterward I asked him. Thayer being rigidly honest said, "I'm sorry, Doug, but yes."

Well that hurt! It was like a knife in my side. But it did wake me up. I had been in the business for about twenty years and I was starting to take the audience for granted and not putting out 110%. I hated that reprimand, but I took it to heart and think my shows improved because of it.

Thayer's wife Nancy died in a tragic car accident. It took a lot out of him. He remarried. Ruth, his second wife, eventually became completely overwhelmed by Alzheimer's. Thayer had retired and he took care of Ruth in their Sun City, Arizona home. Then Thayer got sick with something that could have been treated with antibiotics—and he refused care. He went into a hospice and died a few weeks later. I spoke to him a few days before he died and had a chance to thank him for everything he had done for me. I still think about Thayer often. He helped me, he befriended me, and he made me a better person and a better travelogue maker.

CURTIS NAGEL

Curt Nagel was the first travelogue maker I ever saw present a film. Curt was Bostonian by background and he had a thick baronial voice that, even in the 1960s, put him back several decades in stage style. He, more than Thayer, really carried on Burton Holmes' style of presentation.

Curt was involved in the development of the original Technicolor process in Boston. Curt and his partner William Moore shot travelogue shorts for 20th Century Fox. At the time, commercial movie theaters would show a feature, a second feature, a newsreel, a cartoon, and a travelogue—and the biggest theaters had a stage show as well. Going to the movies meant five or six hours outside of your home. This was, of course, long before television.

The studios had travelogue production teams that would produce twenty minute, one-reel travelogues. The best known was James Fitzpatrick who made *Travel Talks* for MGM. He shot in Technicolor. That might not sound impressive until you saw the camera. The original Technicolor camera was a monstrosity running three separate strips of film. Using the camera in a controlled studio setting was fairly easy. Taking it out into the field, overseas, and to the far corners of the globe was a huge undertaking.

James Fitzpatrick had a flat, nasal voice. He narrated these travelogues and always finished each twenty-minute film with the phrase, "And now as the sun slowly sets in the west we bid fond farewell to…" There was always a cheesy sunset shot at the end. Looking at them today, they are quaint, but the Fitzpatrick travelogues became a source of ridicule that followed the word "travelogue" for decades. I, and many other travelogue producers, spent our careers trying to buck against this negative image that was so ingrained in people's minds.

While Fitzpatrick was making the *Travel Talks* for MGM, Curt and Bill were shooting the *Magic Carpet of Movietone* shorts for Fox. This came to an end by the 1950s. Television was emptying the commercial movie theaters and the studios were cutting back on the extras that went with feature presentations. Curt and Bill jumped ship and headed to the live-lecture travelogue business competing with Burton Homes, Thayer Soule, and a handful of other well-known personalities of the time. They also had a local television show in Los Angeles where they would show their films, have guests, and parade out exotic souvenirs from their travels.

Curt and Bill were "business partners." The travelogue business actually had a lot of LGBT people. But, of course, no one was out. Everything was wrapped around the concept that these people were business associates. There were about ten gay couples, both men and women, who made travelogues and appeared on the travelogue lecture circuit. Curt and Bill were one of those couples. They were an odd pair. Curt was short and dumpy, he had an egg shaped head and his pants were always pulled up to his chest. Bill was dapper, tall and classically handsome in a 1950s sort of way. He always had a big smile, striking horn rimmed glasses—and he drank too much. Their manager, Michael Koehler, always accompanied them. Michael was in charge of handling their bookings. They were all in their 60's and 70's by the time I knew them, but when they were young— they had all known one another since they were in their twenties living in Brooklyn—I suspect they were a wild group of handsome gay men prowling New York.

Bill died first in the 1970s. Curt continued on, Mike driving him around the country to show the films, always traveling in the biggest Cadillac available. They stopped by to see me in New York once. By this point Michael and Curt were two pretty elderly men. I asked them their plans for the rest of the evening expecting them to be heading off to a Broadway show. Curt, with a glint in his eye, said, "We're going to the Adonis." The Adonis was a gay porno house on Eighth Avenue in Midtown (long since gone). I was surprised but more power to them; and off they went.

KEN RICHTER

Ken Richter was the single most eccentric person I ever knew. He was a Harvard graduate who majored in astronomy. He lived on a small farm just south of Lake Champlain in New York State. He had an airplane, a Cessna tail dragger, and he had a grass landing strip in front of his house. He made travelogues all over the world and was one of the stars of the field.

He was an inventor and he developed various pieces of equipment that were used in aviation and commercial photography. He got an Academy Award for technical achievement for inventing a device for calibrating camera lenses. He was obsessed about image sharpness and the clarity you see in Hollywood films today has some of its roots in the Richter Collimator.

He wore the same Brooks Brothers charcoal suit every day of his life. He bought a new one each year and relegated the old one for everyday use while keeping the new one for his matinee lectures (we all wore tuxedos for the evening shows).

He developed some of the most highly sophisticated electronic equipment used in aviation—and yet he had no telephone. He did not believe in telephones. His wife, Shirley, did his travelogue lecture bookings and it was all done by mail. She used a Smith Corona typewriter and wrote on onionskin paper no doubt to save on postage.

If you needed to reach them in an emergency, you had to call a neighbor who would go up to the house and tell them they had a phone call. This was maddening to travelogue booking sponsors who were paying the phone bill. Long distance calls were expensive back then and people often waited ten minutes while the neighbor went to get Shirley.

Ken and Shirley made some amazing films. In 1950, the Ford Motor Company gave them a new car, which they shipped to Morocco. Ken and Shirley picked up the new Ford at Tangiers and went driving through the Sahara desert to shoot a film called *Two Tickets to Timbuktu*. The film made Ken famous in the 1950s and he showed it all across America. By the time I knew him, he was shooting more prosaic subjects. I met up with him in Grand Rapids in 1974 where he was showing a new film on Germany. The sequence before intermission was a typical Ken Richter idea—midnight in a cuckoo clock factory. This may sound lame but it was actually pretty funny, and for the people in the hall, the laughter was genuine.

It was a more simple time but Ken made good films and in his day he was one of the most popular filmmakers of the travelogue field. Thousands of people across America looked forward to Ken Richter's annual appearance.

DON COOPER

Don Cooper was the only person besides Burton Holmes to have a true public following. He could sell tickets on his name alone. The film subject was secondary. Don was a humorist. He had a Will Rogers style of wry observation. He had impeccable timing and an ability to make almost anyone laugh. He got his start in Alaska. He was a lumberjack and the story he always told was that he lent a friend $75 and took his 16mm Bolex camera as collateral. The debt was never repaid so kept the camera and started shooting film. Don learned to use the camera and his films captured the beauty of the state. Don's images were breathtaking; the snow, the ice, the glaciers, the wildlife, it was a pristine wilderness that had never been seen by most people.

Supposedly, some Hollywood film people were on a fishing trip to Alaska in 1958 and Don showed them some of his footage, along with his funny narrative observations. Word got back to Jack Douglas in Los Angeles who had a national television show called *Bold Adventure*. Don was invited down to L.A. to appear on the show and it launched his career.

During the peak years of my own career, Don was the industry star. He got the highest lecture fees, sold the most tickets, and drew the biggest audiences. He was the top showman in the field. And he was an incredibly nice person. Few people get to the top of their field with no enemies in tow. Somehow Don managed to do it. He lived by the credo, "If you don't have something nice to say, don't say anything at all." He was a genuinely caring person who had a deep love of the environment. In the midst of his humorous shows, he always left the audience with a message about ecology, long before environmentalism became a national conversation.

Don, for all his success, lived very simply in De Borgia, Montana with his wife Ruth. He had a brother Dennis (who was the endless butt of jokes in the films) who went on lecture tours as well. On Don's tenth appearance in Spokane, Washington, the *Spokesman-Review* newspaper wrote that Don had entertained over 99,000 fans in the Spokane Coliseum; quite an impressive box office feat. He was a bright, hopeful, person, loved by everyone who knew him.

LISA CHICKERING AND JEANNE PORTERFIELD

Chickering and Porterfield were a well-known travelogue team of the 1960s and the 1970s. They were cultured New Yorkers who came from rarefied backgrounds. Lisa was the heir to the Chickering Piano Company and Jeanne's family, from New Orleans, had significant wealth. They lived in a lovely rent-controlled apartment on the Upper East Side that they *never* gave up.

I first met Lisa and Jeanne in Kansas City in 1967 when they were showing *Europe's Mini Countries*, a film they had made about Andorra, Lichtenstein, Luxembourg and Monaco. The film was interesting and they were fun. I was nineteen and they would have been in their forties.

They were trailblazers. They set out on a trip to France in the 1950s. Lisa was a chanteuse and had a gig in Paris. They intended to only be gone for a few weeks. Instead they spent three years traveling around the world before they returned home. They were professional photographers, shooting both motion picture film and stills, lugging equipment and traveling into countries and places where women simply did not go alone—but they did. They were gutsy and endured patronizing men who felt they shouldn't be out there mucking around in their professional fields. Every young woman who has doors opened for her today owes something to women like Lisa and Jeanne who broke barriers and helped women move forward in male dominated professions.

That's not to say they were easy. They didn't get all their passports stamps without ruffling a few feathers along the way. They were tough, outspoken, and Lisa particularly could be demanding—but they got what they went after, both in terms of experiences and photography. In addition to their work in the travelogue business they had a thriving travel still photo business and they were regular contributors to *The New York Times* Travel Section and various national publications. I knew them more from the lecture circuit. I followed them into theaters around the country and while the booking sponsors loved them and audiences warmed to their charming stage style, the all-male theater crews did not. Many of those men, largely union IASTE stagehands and projectionists, had a chip on their shoulder about women coming into their theaters and projection booths.

I once went to see them show a film called *Winter in Mexico* in some town in New Jersey. It was not a great auditorium and the projectionist was not a professional but some dorky high school kid. Lisa went to the booth and oversaw the threading of the film and focusing of the picture. The microphone sound levels had been checked for the live narration and the show was ready to begin. Lisa and Jeanne came out onto the stage and did their introduction together. Jeanne would then narrate the first half of the film and Lisa would narrate the second half.

After the introduction, the house lights went down, and the film began. The picture was completely out of focus. The projectionist had screwed up the focus adjustments that had been carefully made during the setup. Before digital projection, focus was the single biggest aggravation travelogue lecturers endured.

The film looked awful. Jeanne was narrating, and Lisa interjected softly into the microphone, "Could the projectionist please focus the film." This was met with no response. Lisa interjected the same comment a second time, again no response. For Lisa, there would be no third time. She left the stage and went stomping up the aisle in her high heels toward the projection booth. She passed me in the side aisle. Then she paused, turned around, came back, leaned over to me and said in a not-so-stage-whisper, "There's going to be a murder in a minute!" I waited. About one minute passed and suddenly the sound of yelling was coming out of the projection booth, like coyotes attacking a possum. The film went in and out of focus wildly, finally settling on a sharp spot. Jeanne never missed a beat from the stage. Lisa pulled herself back together and made her way back down the aisle and back up onto the stage. The high school kid projectionist looked dazed at the end of the show.

They were always referred to as "the girls" in the male dominated travelogue field. In retrospect, it was patronizing, but in the 1960s and 1970s, I don't think it occurred to anyone—even Lisa and Jeanne—that there was anything wrong with the moniker.

Jeanne died in 2010. I am still close to Lisa, who only upon reaching her ninetieth birthday revealed her true age. We are neighbors in New York and the two of them provided me with some of my best memories. I knew they were gay. But I never pressed the issue. While I was openly out to them, they never came out to me. It was only after Jeanne's death that Lisa seemed willing to acknowledge the obvious. They were together for sixty-six years. They were happy, but the times and the culture did not allow them the freedoms that I would know.

MAGGIE POTTER

Maggie Potter was the private impresario of the World Geographic Society in Los Angeles. She presented her shows at the Wilshire Ebell, an old theater in Hancock Park. Maggie also had shows in Fresno, Burbank, and at the La Jolla Playhouse. She was married to Russ Potter (who I had waited to no-show in Philadelphia with his Belgium film). Russ was the voice of the Pageant of the Masters, a Laguna summer tradition involving actors creating tableaus on stage of famous master paintings.

Maggie was a hot head. She took a liking to me but I knew that could change on a dime. In looking back, she was clearly bi-polar, but in those days we didn't think to analyze people's behavior. She turned to fortunetellers for solutions to her problems. Southern California was full of fortunetellers. My Aunt Ruth, my Uncle Allen's fourth wife practically kept them in business going from one to the other.

Maggie would do the same, moving from one fortuneteller to the next, going to séances, trying to contact the dead. She was a part of that nutty world that was Los Angeles in the 1940s and 1950s. I met her in 1971 and her interest in the occult remained to the end of her life.

Part of her draw to all of this was an incident of many years before. Maggie was running the World Geographic Society shows in the 1930s at the gigantic Shrine Auditorium and she had booked Martin Johnson to speak. Martin and Osa Johnson were early adventurers who had traveled to far off lands, remote jungles, and exotic cultures. They returned to America and showed their films in theaters and auditoriums. They actually got their start showing and narrating short clips from exotic places on the B.F. Keith vaudeville circuit. Their first film was made in 1912, *Cannibals of the South Seas*—how's that for an enticing title! Martin and Osa Johnson were big celebrities and Maggie had nearly sold out the Shrine for his appearance. It was January 13, 1937.

As she told the story to me, she got a premonition, a vision, the evening before the show that Martin Johnson's plane was going to go down. She called his agent trying to reach him. The agent was dismissive. She tried to find out the hotel he was staying in the night before in Salt Lake City but she was unsuccessful. She said she did everything in her power to contact him and tell him not to get on the plane. And when she was unable, she simply sat back and waited.

The following morning, on the radio, was the news—A Western Air Express passenger plane had crashed into the mountains coming through the Newhall Pass trying to land at Burbank. Martin and Osa Johnson were onboard. Martin was dead. Osa was severely injured but survived. The show was canceled and Maggie was never quite the same.

GEORGE LOURBIS

George Lourbis was the P.T. Barnum of travelogues in California in the 1970s and 1980s. He lived in San Francisco and had figured out he could put these shows on in big prestigious auditoriums and make money. He called his travelogue series Explorama and he ultimately had shows up and down the state, twenty-four in all. He presented at the Ahmanson Theater in Los Angeles, the Paramount in Oakland, the Masonic Auditorium in San Francisco, the San Diego Civic Theater, and a dozen other smaller venues. He was young, handsome, clever, and he was gay.

We had a love/hate professional relationship, probably because we were so much alike. When I first met George, it was to preview *Paris of the Parisians*. He did not book programs unless he had seen them and knew that they were up to his standards.

George showed up for the preview, which was held in the office of Gertrude Purple Gorham—yes that was her name. Gertrude Purple Gorham was a Los Angeles talent agent for the western United States. They did travelogues but also music, dance, straight lectures, and other sundry shows. George watched the program in their offices in the heart of Hollywood. He had various suggestions to make on editing changes he wanted. I agreed and I got a contract to do his shows.

George had a production manager named Jimmy Hawk who went to all of the performances and oversaw everything from the setup of sound and picture to counting the box office receipts. Jimmy would drive me to the shows and spend much of the commute bitching about what craziness George had put him through that day.

Jimmy was from Oklahoma and had family back in the Sooner State. One day he picked me up in front of the place where I was staying. He looked at me with the widest grin I have ever seen and said, "The well came in." They had struck oil on his family's Oklahoma property and he knew his fortunes were about to change. He no longer needed the paycheck, but he stayed with George long after the oil royalties started flowing in.

George had a not-too-hidden secret. He loved hustlers. George was very handsome but some part of his controlling personality preferred to pay for sex than sleep with someone who might actually like him. Jimmy told me that George single handedly kept the hustler population of San Francisco in business for years.

I was showing *The Magic of Venice* for Explorama in 1979 at the Paramount. It was the last show of the run. The film had done well at the box office and George was pleased with the ticket sales. He showed his gratitude in a way that only George could. It was Saturday night and Jimmy drove me back to the apartment where I was staying after the show. Twenty minutes after I walked in, the buzzer rang. I thought, "Who on earth could that be?" I went to the intercom and said, "Yes?" The reply was, "I have a delivery from George Lourbis." I buzzed this unknown person into the building at 11:30 at night. I opened the door and there stood a six-foot tall blond hunk who was simply breathtakingly handsome—with an ear-to-ear grin on his face. He was wearing a pair of tight jeans, a cowboy hat (!) and no shirt. Around his waist was tied a giant red bow and a card. I took the card, opened it and it read, "Thanks for the great shows. Enjoy!" It was signed, "George and the Explorama staff."

I should report that I said, "Thanks but no thanks" and quietly closed the door. But come on… I was thirty-one, unattached, alone and on the road. And the bow was so *big*. I let him in and while I will spare you any graphic details, after he left, I decided it was the single best closing night gift I had gotten in my life. George did know how to say "Thank You" with style.

George was absolutely terrible with money. He spent way too much and he was always robbing Peter to pay Paul. I often had to wait months after my appearances to get paid. By 1986 he had backed himself into a corner. I had the very last show of the 1985-1986 Explorama season. I was showing *The Great World Cruise of the Queen Elizabeth 2*. It was a popular film and we had big audiences. But it was obvious from Jimmy's demeanor that the house of cards was falling.

George had collected all the subscription series revenues for the 1986-1987 season from his 18,000 subscribers in those final weeks of the 1985-86 season. And Jimmy knew there was not going to be a 1986-1987 season. The robbing Peter to pay Paul had finally hit the wall. The creditors were lined up. The series was going to go down, leaving all those season tickets subscribers holding the bag, the money gone, and no future shows.

Jimmy drove me to the Paramount Theater in Oakland. It was the largest show of the series. Jimmy looked at me in the car as we parked at the stage door and said, "Protect yourself." I knew what he meant. There was not going to be enough money to pay all the creditors. I mulled over the idea of demanding that I be paid for the shows I had done over the previous two weeks before I walked on stage. I was owed about $17,000. I knew it would place George in a terrible bind. But I thought he would somehow get the money together if he thought his flagship show was not going to go on.

In the end I did not demand the money. I did the Paramount show, and within days he declared bankruptcy and I never saw a cent of my twenty-four show run.

GENEVIEVE HATT

Genevieve Hatt was simply one of the nicest people you could have ever wanted to know. She was the executive secretary for the Chicago Geographic Society. She oversaw the programs, which were presented at Orchestra Hall.

Gen was supportive early in my career and took me under her wing like a mother hen. She once found paper clips and secured the French cuffs of my tuxedo shirt backstage when I had forgotten my cufflinks. It was like having mom around.

Gen had to deal with the management of the hall, which was no easy task. The Chicago Symphony Orchestra operated the hall and it was as unionized a hall as I have ever worked. Believe me, you touched nothing yourself. You need to plug in something? The union electrician did it for you. You wanted the microphone stand moved to the center of the stage? The union stagehand did it for you. If you so much as touched something you were entering someone's turf and you would be in trouble.

The worst thing about the hall was its policy on recorded music. We all had background soundtracks for our films with music, effects, and ambient sound. While sound on film was not a new idea, for decades we played music tracks by running a tape deck from a lectern on the stage. Most halls had no way to get the sound from the projection booth to the sound system or the stage and even if they did, the speaker had to control the volume. You had to be able to ride the music up and down, over and under your voice as you narrated the film. It sounds primitive, and in some ways it was, but it was the way we did things for decades until wireless sound systems came along.

Orchestra Hall, being run by the orchestra, had a policy that if recorded music was used, ten union musicians had to be paid—and they did not work cheap. This effectively killed the use of any music with the travelogue films. So whenever I would go to Orchestra Hall, I had to reconfigure my narration and deliver the show without any music. This was nerve-racking because I often had sequences that were built around the mood the music created. But I did it and in some ways it was good because it made me think on my feet and speak extemporaneously.

The shows were held on Saturday afternoons and Tuesday evenings. One Saturday I was backstage in my dressing room talking to the projectionist before giving him my film and a nervous man came up, peered in the open door, and wanted to know what time the show would be over. I told him about four o'clock. He acted anxious and wanted to know if I could get the program over earlier. I was puzzled and said it would depend on the length of the intermission; we might be able to shorten it by five minutes. He disappeared but returned and kept poking his head into everyone's space—very odd.

At 2:00 p.m. the president of the Chicago Geographic Society introduced me and I went onstage and did the program. We shortened the intermission by five minutes and I went back for the second half. I wrapped up the show at 3:55 p.m. and went center stage to take my bow. As I came offstage into the wing, there stood an elderly man, a woman I presumed to be his wife, and the nervous assistant. The older man looked at me, and said, "Very nice, young man, very nice."

It was Vladimir Horowitz.

Vladimir Horowitz was the most famous concert pianist in the world at the time. He had this peculiar policy that he would only perform his piano recitals at 4:00 p.m. on Sundays and his auditorium rehearsals had to be at 4:00 p.m. on Saturdays. It was his only Chicago appearance for the year and the nervous young man's job was to see that Vladimir Horowitz was on stage for his rehearsal at exactly 4:00 p.m. I have no idea how the concert went, but I did meet one of the legends of classical music in the wings of Orchestra Hall. Meanwhile, Gen Hatt stood in the background smiling through this brief encounter with a living legend.

DOUG JONES TRAVELOGUE FILMOGRAPHY

Belgian Panorama 1968
Paris of the Parisians 1970
New York City–Broadway U.S.A. 1971
The Hawaiian Adventure 1973
The Magic of Venice 1974
Royal London 1976
Egypt–Gift of the Nile 1977
Portraits of America–The National Parks 1979
San Francisco–The City at the End of the Rainbow 1981
The Great World Cruise of the Queen Elizabeth 2 1982
Queen Elizabeth 2 Sails New Zealand and Australia 1985
Portraits of the Great Far East 1986
Great Cities of Europe 1988
The Great Alaska Cruise 1989
The Great Canadian Train Ride 1990
Cruising to Bermuda 1994
The Great Trans-American Train Ride 1995
Sailing Down to Rio on the Queen Mary 2 2004
Cruising the Orient on the QE2 2005
Around the World–One Man's Journey 2011
Non-Feature Stock Footage Shoots
Brazil, Argentina, Chile, Peru 1998
Australia, Bali, Brunei, The Philippines, Hong Kong, China 1999
Japan, Vietnam, Thailand, Singapore 1999
Thirty destinations across the United States 2000
Hawaii 2001
Russia 2001
Turkey, Croatia, Italy, France, Spain 2001

Doug Jones Travelogues are available on DVD from:
InternationalTravelFilms.com

ACKNOWLEDGEMENTS

I would like to thank New York drama critic Michael Sommers for his interest in this project and his willingness to read the first draft of my manuscript. It takes a great friend to wade through your life in its most over-written form.

I would like to thank Cynthia Lang for her very perceptive comments regarding style, structure, and word usage. The reader can thank Cynthia for the removal of about a thousand unnecessary usages of the word "that."

I would like to thank my editor Robben Barquist for his perceptive comments, suggestions, and help in shaping the final manuscript.

And most of all I want to thank everyone that I have written about in this book. Your lives have enriched my own more than I can ever express. I hope I have done you justice in telling your stories.

www.ingramcontent.com/pod-product-compliance
Lightning Source LLC
Chambersburg PA
CBHW031249230426
43670CB00005B/101